COVID-19 "Humanitarianism"

Geopolitics and International Relations

Series Editor

David Criekemans (*University of Antwerp*)

VOLUME 4

The titles published in this series are listed at *brill.com/geop*

COVID-19 "Humanitarianism"

*Geopolitical Logics of Chinese, American,
and Russian Assistance*

By

Mariya Y. Omelicheva
Brittnee Carter

BRILL | NIJHOFF

LEIDEN | BOSTON

Originally published in hardback in 2024.

The Library of Congress has cataloged the hardcover edition as follows:

Names: Omelicheva, Mariya Y., author. | Carter, Brittnee, author.
Title: Covid-19 "humanitarianism" : geopolitical logics of Chinese,
American, and Russian assistance / by Mariya Omelicheva, Brittnee
Carter.
Description: Leiden ; Boston : Brill/Nijhoff, 2024. | Series: Geopolitics
and international relations, 2666-6669 ; volume 4 | Includes
bibliographical references and index.
Identifiers: LCCN 2024008561 (print) | LCCN 2024008562 (ebook) | ISBN
9789004692664 (hardback) | ISBN 9789004692671 (ebook)
Subjects: LCSH: COVID-19 (Disease)–Law and legislation–China. | COVID-19
(Disease)–Law and legislation–Russia (Federation) | COVID-19
(Disease)–Law and legislation–United States. | COVID-19 Pandemic,
2020–Political aspects–China. | COVID-19 Pandemic, 2020–Political
aspects–Russia (Federation) | COVID-19 Pandemic, 2020–Political
aspects–United States. | Humanitarian law–China. | Humanitarian
law–Russia (Federation) | Humanitarian law–United States.
Classification: LCC K3575.C68 O44 2024 (print) | LCC K3575.C68 (ebook) |
DDC 362.1962/4144–dc23/eng/20240224
LC record available at https://lccn.loc.gov/2024008561
LC ebook record available at https://lccn.loc.gov/2024008562

Typeface for the Latin, Greek, and Cyrillic scripts: "Brill". See and download: brill.com/brill-typeface.

ISSN 2666-6669
ISBN 978-90-04-73837-9 (paperback, 2025)
ISBN 978-90-04-69266-4 (hardback)
ISBN 978-90-04-69267-1 (e-book)
DOI 10.1163/9789004692671

Contents

Acknowledgements

Our story with COVID-19 began as it did for many others. We barely paid heed to the early news of the novel coronavirus discovered in the remote Hubei province of central China indulging in the wishful thinking that our lives on the other side of the globe would be spared of the infectious disease. Not a month passed when the first case of coronavirus was registered in the United States and a few weeks later the World Health Organization declared a global pandemic caused by the SARS-CoV-2 virus. One-by-one, countries around the world issued national emergencies followed by stay-at-home orders, curfews, quarantines, and other restrictions on people's movements and gatherings with the goal of reducing the spread of COVID-19. The US government shut down non-essential businesses and travel prompting cancellations of in-person classes in public schools and universities.

Few could fathom the challenges that laid ahead: days turned into weeks, and weeks turned into months as we watched a skyrocketing death toll caused by the novel coronavirus and the heroic efforts of doctors, nurses, first respondents, community volunteers, and other public servants to stem the tide of human suffering. Uncertainty and fears about the future were compounded by the lack of scientific understanding of the deadly pathogen and the glut of false, misleading, and rumor-laden information that undermined the efficacy of prophylactic and preventive measures. As we struggled to adapt to the new reality of mask wearing, shortages of disinfecting materials, online meetings, and schooling the kids while teaching fulltime ourselves, we quickly realized that, while COVID-19 turned lives upside down, ruined national economies, and amplified the preexisting social divisions, it had little effect on the fabric of international relations. Geopolitics appeared to be impervious to coronavirus. COVID was a flashpoint reminding of the dangers of eroding international cooperation. Yet, instead of strengthening collaborative resolve in coping with the deadly disease, many countries, including the most powerful states, like the US, chose to react individually rather than collectively to the health crisis, by putting their national interests above the individuals who bore the brunt of the pandemic. As scholars of international relations, we watched with analytical curiosity how global health and medical humanitarianism, and global health security and geopolitics coalesced in front of our eyes. We were concerned with the mounting geopolitical tensions between the US and China and their consequences for a range of issues that require international collaboration.

With everything that COVID-19 took away from us, it also offered an opportunity to extend our intellectual pursuits in a new (for us) direction of the geopolitics of humanitarian aid. Based in Washington, D.C., Mariya has born witness to US policymakers' and analysts' obsession with great power competition that stifled meaningful consideration of the US–China rivalry for the global commons. Working for an institution of professional military education, whose curriculum reflects US government concerns, she felt a strong demand signal for a book that comparatively and critically examines the sources of US, Chinese, and Russian competition, and illuminates the role of ideas and discourses through which these countries define their place in the world as drivers of international discord. Mariya is immensely grateful to the leadership and colleagues at the National War College, National Defense University, for affording her space and time to write this book, and offering a receptive audience for presentations, in which she tested some of the book's arguments.

The research for this monograph was generously supported by the University of Kansas (KU) General Research Fund, and the KU Department of Political Science Walter Thomson Scholarship, Allan J. Cigler Award, and the Departmental General Funds. We would like to thank KU's hardworking student assistants, Cora Caton and Faelan Jacobson-Davies, for collecting data for this project, and Daniel Smith for producing maps for the book. Brittnee would like to thank Thomas Ringenberg for his support during the book's research and writing process.

We would also like to thank Brill's editorial team and staff: Jason Prevost – for seeing the merit in our monograph; Dr. David Criekemans – for invaluable comments on the early drafts of the manuscript; and Katie Short – for making sure the book has come through.

Figures, Tables, and Maps

Figures

Tables

Maps

Introduction

On 11 March 2020, the World Health Organization (WHO) declared COVID-19, the disease caused by the SARS-CoV-2 virus, a global pandemic marking the beginning of the COVID era. By then, the novel coronavirus had appeared in 114 countries and was rapidly spreading around the world overwhelming hospitals and morgues and revealing shortfalls in medical supplies and personal protective equipment (PPE). A week after the WHO announcement, Italy became the first country reporting more COVID-related deaths than China, an original hotbed of the crisis. The news signaled a shift in the epicenter of the health crisis to Europe.[1] Desperate for doctors, nurses, ventilators, and PPE, health and public officials from Lombardy, one of the worst-hit regions of Italy, issued pleas for help. The Italian government led by Prime Minister Giuseppe Conte sent a distress message to the European Commission asking for assistance.

The European Union met Italy's distress call with silence,[2] but China responded promptly airlifting medical experts from the Chinese Red Cross and a large shipment of medical supplies marked with signs "The friendship road knows no borders."[3] Additional doctors, medical equipment, and gear arrived in several tranches over the following weeks. After China, Cuba sent a medical brigade to Rome and, just days later, several Russian IL-76 military planes delivered medical equipment, pharmaceuticals, virologists, and epidemiologists to the COVID-19-striken regions of Italy in a humanitarian operation dubbed "From Russia with Love."[4]

---

1 Erin Schumaker, "Timeline: How Coronavirus Got Started," *ABC News*, September 22, 2020, https://abcnews.go.com/Health/timeline-coronavirus-started/story?id=69435165.

2 Daniel Boffey, "Revealed: Italy's Call for Urgent Help was Ignored as Coronavirus Swept Through Europe." *The Guardian*, July 15, 2020, https://www.theguardian.com/world/2020/jul/15/revealed-the-inside-story-of-europes-divided-coronavirus-response. The European Commission later apologized to Italy for lack of help in coronavirus crisis ("European Commission Apologises to Italy for Lack of Help in Coronavirus Crisis," *France24*, March 4, 2020, https://www.france24.com/en/20200403-european-commission-italy-ursula-van-der-leyen-apology-coronavirus-covid19-giuseppe-conte).

3 Sylvia Poggioli, "For Help on Coronavirus, Italy Turns to China, Russia and Cuba," *NPR*, March 25, 2020, https://www.npr.org/sections/coronavirus-live-updates/2020/03/25/821345465/for-help-on-coronavirus-italy-turns-to-china-russia-and-cuba.

4 Robin Emmott and Andrew Osborn, "Russia Aid to Italy Leaves EU Exposed," *Reuters*, March 26, 2020, https://www.reuters.com/article/us-health-coronavirus-russia-eu/russian-aid-to-italy-leaves-eu-exposed-idUSKBN21D28K. See also Mariya Y. Omelicheva, "'Good' Samaritan? The Geopolitics of Russia's COVID-19 Assistance," *Canadian Journal of European and Russian Studies* 16, no. 1 (2020): 1–25.

Italy's democratic allies also furnished humanitarian aid. France donated surgical masks and protective suits, and Germany delivered medical equipment and protective gear to Rome. The United States deployed a makeshift hospital in a low-key operation invisible to the public and promised to send $100 million in medical supplies to Italy.[5] Rome welcomed assistance from its neighbors and friends. Yet, at the time, these responses appeared too late to correct a perception of Moscow and Beijing as more responsive and reliable partners for countries in need than Washington and Brussels.

The Chinese and Russian COVID-19 aid to Rome became an opening salvo in the debate over Beijing's and Moscow's motives for humanitarian aid.[6] Significant differences in the volume and types of COVID-19 assistance provided to countries experiencing acute crises and "vaccine nationalism" of the United States and other Western donors revived a broader discussion over the role of ethics and politics in the administration of humanitarian assistance. Beijing's effort to promote an alternative approach to foreign assistance and global health linked to its development model raised concerns about the future of humanitarian governance in the post-COVID-19 world.

The example of Chinese, Russian, and American COVID-19 aid to Italy and surrounding debates over donors' motives for humanitarian assistance represent the principal questions and main analytical themes of the book. When resources are scarce and demand is high, how do donors resolve which countries will receive humanitarian aid? Are US motives for humanitarian assistance different from those of Moscow and Beijing? What is the potential impact of alternative reasonings for and approaches to emergency relief assistance on the future of global humanitarianism? Focusing on COVID-19 aid, including the transfers of vaccines, this book engages with these questions.

---

5   Alessandra Pinna, "International Medical Aid to Italy: Solidarity or Propaganda?" *Freedom House*, April 20, 2020, https://freedomhouse.org/article/international-medical-aid-italy-solidarity-or-propaganda. Following a direct appeal by the Italian government to US Defense Secretary Mark Esper, the latter authorized the provision of humanitarian support to Rome through the Department of Defense (US Department of Defense, "DOD Humanitarian Assistance to the Italian Republic in Response to COVID-19," April 20, 2020, https://www.defense.gov/News/Releases/Release/Article/2157126/dod-humanitarian-assistance-to-the-italian-republic-in-response-to-covid-19/).

6   The debate about the Russian and Chinese motives for COVID-19 aid resurfaced in the wake of Russia's invasion of Ukraine in February 2022, when Russia's former diplomat in Milan accused the Italian defense minister of being a "hawk" in anti-Russian campaign despite purportedly appealing to Moscow's assistance in the early months of the COVID-19 pandemic (Angela Giuffrida, "Italian Former PM Faces Renewed Questions over Covid Aid from Russia," *The Guardian*, March 23, 2022, https://www.theguardian.com/world/2022/mar/23/italian-former-pm-conte-faces-renewed-questions-over-covid-aid-from-russia).

Using the theoretical insights of a critical geopolitics perspective, it puts forth contextualized and historically-grounded explanations of Chinese, Russian, and American motives for foreign aid linked to their distinctive geopolitical visions of the world, their place in international relations, and state identity.

In doing so, the book seeks to add analytical rigor, coherence, and discipline to the nomenclature of terms used to describe contemporary international relations, in general, and states' foreign policies in the humanitarian realm, in particular. "Geostrategic" competition or great power competition have become buzzwords in foreign policy circles in Washington, and many world capitals. As the vernacular of "global war on terror" elevated humanitarian issues from the realm of "low politics" to the agendas of the UN Security Council and debates about the nexus of crises, health, and security,[7] so has the framework of "great power competition" contributed to the reframing of humanitarian efforts as part of great powers' geopolitical projects aimed at accruing global power. As the example at the outset of this book demonstrates, China, Russia, and the United States have recriminated each other in using COVID-19 aid and other tools of "health diplomacy" in a continued effort to expand their regional and global influence.

Our project is set to interrogate the nexus between humanitarian crises (including the spread of infectious diseases), geography, and power by extending the conversation about COVID-19 humanitarianism to include the role that identity, history, and political discourse have had in shaping perceptions of competition among China, Russia, and the US. Our understanding of geopolitics is not limited to the analysis of the interaction between countries' geographical settings and ways in which they inform their foreign policy choices. Our conception of geopolitics foregrounds ideas, concepts, and knowledge that map specific mental images on physical spaces. We define "geostrategic" broadly as a discursive practice that justifies a certain geographic direction of a state's foreign policy requiring it to concentrate its limited military, economic, and diplomatic resources on this geopolitical space. COVID-19 aid is geostrategic and geopolitical in a sense that it is directed toward and justified by the discursive renderings of spaces for political action that become the medium for their decisions about humanitarian aid. It is from this critical foundation that we derive hypotheses about how state actions regarding COVID-19 aid

---

7 Implicit to this argument was the idea that humanitarian crises in fragile environments could adversely affect stable states through the spillover of conflict, diseases, and refuges. This concern, in turn, justified interventions in the form of counterterrorism and stabilization operations. See Alan Ingram, "The New Geopolitics of Disease: Between Global Health and Global Security," *Geopolitics* 10, no. 3 (2005): 522–545.

distribution line up with their conceptual mappings of aid, and statistically test these hypotheses using an original dataset of COVID-19 humanitarian aid and vaccine allocations.

COVID-19 aid included multi-faceted medical and other health-related initiatives designed to save lives and alleviate human suffering in crisis situations. Although, donors around the world understood that they would be unable to manage the spread of the infectious disease independently and needed to coordinate resources, adapt each other's best practices and policies, and share scientific knowledge, COVID-19 assistance often flouted these calls for solidarity, resource redistribution, information sharing, and collective action. Eerily resembling the Cold War-era contestation over alternative visions for the global health care system that the two superpowers – the United States and the Soviet Union – advanced through their medical aid,[8] the Chinese, Russian, and American approaches to COVID-19 assistance were also marked by divergent political beliefs and visions of social order. As the United States and Soviet Union raced to develop life-saving vaccines and, in the process, competed for global leadership and influence over other nations,[9] so have China and Russia rushed to develop and share their state-backed vaccines, positioning themselves as scientific and manufacturing leaders, and contrasting their policies with vaccine nationalism of the United States and Europe. A study of COVID-19 assistance, therefore, affords an exploration of complex intersections between global health and medical humanitarianism, and global health security and geopolitics. While the initiatives by China, Russia, and the United States do not exhaust the expansive field of humanitarian responses to COVID-19, the juxtaposition of Chinese, Russian, and American rationales for providing certain types and levels of medical assistance alone or in combination with security and development assistance illuminates differences in the visions for social orders and the relations of medical care and global health embedded in them. As the contemporary historical accounts of smallpox eradication have enriched our understanding of the Cold War politics, so can the analysis of COVID-19 aid be used to reframe the global health crisis into a complex project

---

8 Andrew Lakoff, "Two Regimes of Global Health," *Humanity: An International Journal of Human Rights, Humanitarianism, and Development*, 1, no. 1 (2010): 59–79.

9 Jonathan D. Moreno, Judit Sándor and Ulf Schmidt, "The Vaccination Cold War," *Hastings Center Report*, 51, no. 5 (September 2021): 2–59, https://onlinelibrary.wiley.com/doi/epdf/10.1002/hast.1282.

embedded in wider geopolitical discourses accompanying the effort to redefine or resist changes in international politics.[10]

The empirical case of COVID-19 aid provides a unique window into states'
motives for humanitarian assistance. First, the outbreak of novel coronavirus can be conceptualized as a "geopolitical event" that has left no country
unscathed and which posed an unprecedented disaster on a global scale.
International donors, including the US, China, and Russia, had to respond to a
health crisis at home while entertaining decisions about the levels of humanitarian assistance abroad. The scarcity of medical supplies, PPE, and vaccines
coupled with high demand for life-saving assistance brought questions about
donors' reasoning regarding aid allocations into sharp relief. Second, in the
years leading up to the COVID-19 pandemic, neither China nor Russia had fully
disclosed their levels of humanitarian aid. A very public display of COVID-19
aid allocations by the Chinese and Russian governments and media allow for a
systematic tracking of Moscow's and Beijing's coronavirus assistance supplied
to the countries around the world. Third, during the first year of the pandemic,
China delivered coronavirus aid to several dozen countries in a very public
show of Chinese soft power. Meanwhile, the US government was mired in an
ugly debate over its membership in the WHO and other forms of international
cooperation. China and Russia have used their COVID-19 donations and, later,
vaccine distributions, to shore up their global image and to denigrate global
leadership of the United States. The US, on the other hand, has engaged in
relentless censorship of China's handling of coronavirus outbreak and pushed
back on Moscow's and Beijing's information blitz with loud warnings about
the true motives of Russian and Chinese "humanitarian" assistance.[11] A comprehensive study of Chinese, Russian, and American COVID-19 aid transcending their mutual accusations and biased public relations campaign will add
clarity to public knowledge of the ways that these countries view the world,
make sense of their rights and obligations in the humanitarian realm, and how
they reason about foreign assistance.

10   Erez Manela, "A Pox on Your Narrative: Writing Disease Control into Cold War History,"
      Diplomatic History 34, no. 2 (April 2010), pp. 299–323.
11   Conor Finnegan, "Despite Calls for Global Cooperation, US and China Fight over Leading
      Coronavirus Response," ABC *News*, March 31, 2020, https://abcnews.go.com/Politics/calls
      -global-cooperation-us-china-fight-leading-coronavirus/story?id=69898820. *La Stampa*,
      one of the oldest Italian newspapers, published a report questioning Russia's motives,
      impugning the utility of aid, and warning of security breaches due to the involvement of
      the Russian military. *La Stampa*'s assessments were cited widely in the online and print
      media around the world.

1   Why Is Understanding States' Motives for Humanitarian Assistance
     Important

There are many reasons for a book on states' motives for humanitarian assistance. First, there is a growing demand for humanitarian aid driven by the rise
in climate change-induced natural disasters as well as conflicts. The heightened demand for aid will place upward pressure on international donors
responsible for aid allocations. Second, while states remain the most reliable
donors, their motives for aid remain uncertain. Third, the appearance of the
so-called "new" or "emerging" state donors operating largely outside of the
Organization for Economic Co-operation and Development's (OECD) Development Assistance Committee (DAC), which serves as the major agency for
setting aid agendas, has elevated the question of states' motives for providing
aid. While some humanitarian stakeholders have welcomed and encouraged
"new" donors' contributions to humanitarian causes, others have warned that
their interests and practices are often contrary to humanitarian principles
and, therefore, are threatening to the integrity of the humanitarian system
itself. Finally, China's global rise and its competition with the US over leadership across all facets of the global governance, including the international
humanitarian regime, has turned Chinese motivations for aid into an issue
of enormous significance for practitioners and scholars of not only humanitarian assistance but also foreign policy and international relations. From the
standpoint of an approach adopted in this book, the geopolitics of humanitarian assistance involve competing sets of ideas about who and why deserve
medical and other types of aid, and these ideas provide powerful rationales
for foreign policy actions that are directed at managing the disease on a global
scale. The approaches to aid used by China, Russia, and the US rest on very different visions of the social order undermined by threats to global health, and
the most appropriate means to cope with health crises. When applied to foreign aid, these visions transcend the national governance and work to create
new discursive spaces that may complement, contradict, or seek to replace the
established positions and rationales for assistance. If successful, the efforts to
change or replace the established principles and norms will produce new sites
of normative and soft power, leadership, and knowledge claims, leading to the
restructuring of international relations. Therefore, China's rise to prominence
in the humanitarian realm has been viewed as part and parcel of its broader
challenge to displace the US from the global leadership and remake the US-led
global order in its image.

1.1 State Aid Is Critical to Meeting the Growing Demand for Humanitarian Assistance

Humanitarian aid, which refers to a specific kind of charitable assistance to save lives, alleviate suffering and maintain human dignity during and in the aftermath of disasters and crises,[12] has always been funded by donations from private individuals, corporations, and governments. Individual and corporate funding is more ad hoc and tethered to media's broadcasting of disasters and crises. It, therefore, cannot substitute for bi-lateral and multilateral humanitarian aid by state governments. States can commit resources to assistance more reliably, especially in periods when other flows of income – trade, direct investments, and remittances – drop due to a pandemic or economic crisis.

Prior to the onset of COVID-19, unmet humanitarian needs already presented a major challenge for the humanitarian system. Humanitarian crises have been flaring up more frequently and become more impactful due to climate change. International assistance increased by almost one-third between 2014 and 2018, yet the pace of growth had slowed by 2019 with state donations driving the overall increase.[13] The COVID-19 pandemic intensified needs for aid by aggravating existing humanitarian emergencies and disrupting livelihoods in countries previously unaffected by humanitarian disasters.[14] According to UN Under-Secretary-General for Humanitarian Affairs and Emergency Relief Mark Lowcock, in 2020 the COVID-19 pandemic increased the number of people needing humanitarian assistance by 40 percent compared to 2019.[15]

As the world continued dealing with the combination of new coronavirus variants and their secondary effects, such as falling incomes, rising food prices, and interrupted vaccination programs, Russia's invasion of Ukraine in February 2022 caused Europe's largest humanitarian crisis in the 21st century. Hostilities in Ukraine and displacement of millions of Ukrainians across

---

12   According to the World Health Organization, complex emergencies are situations of disrupted livelihoods and threats to life produced by warfare, civil disturbance, natural disasters, and large-scale movement of people, in which any emergency response must be conducted in a difficult political and security environment (B. Wisner and J. Adams, *Environmental Health in Emergencies and Disasters: A Practical Guide,* World Health Organization, 2002, https://www.who.int/publications/i/item/9241545410).

13   Development Initiatives, "Global Humanitarian Assistance Report 2019," http://devinit.org/wp-content/uploads/2019/09/GHA-report-2019.pdf.

14   Wisner and Adams, *Environmental Health in Emergencies and Disasters.*

15   United Nations Office for the Coordination of Humanitarian Affairs, "Global Humanitarian Review," OCHA, 2022, https://gho.unocha.org.

borders compounded ongoing humanitarian crises in other parts of the world. The war has threatened future global food security by reducing supply of grains and rising prices on food commodities. International donors have always been challenged to come up with additional funding for critical response efforts to new crises. In 2020, for example, donor states funded just 35.7 percent of the $9.5 billion required by the United Nations' COVID-19 Global Humanitarian Response Plan.[16] In 2021, donors funded 48 percent, or $18.2 billion, of the total requirements for global humanitarian assistance. The global humanitarian requirement for 2022 was set at a record number of $41 billion,[17] which was increased by additional $4.1 billion for delivering humanitarian aid to people across Ukraine and those seeking refuge in neighboring countries.[18] However, the donors' ability to meet these heightened demands for assistance have been in question.

1.2 *Motivations for Humanitarian Aid by States Are Still Unclear*

In contrast to development and security assistance, which has always been pre-planned, conditional, and designed to tackle underlying structural issues in the recipient countries' economies and defense, humanitarian aid offers short-term, rapid, and unconditional relief following an event threatening human lives.[19] Grounded in the Western enlightenment ideas that ascribe each person with inherent and equal moral value, humanitarian aid calls for the protection of human life and health, regardless of ethnicity, religion, citizenship, or other identity markers. It is, therefore, supposed to be delivered without prejudice of place or politics as reflected in the principles of humanity, neutrality, universality, and impartiality of humanitarian aid. These principles have been institutionalized in the United Nations Resolution A/RES/46/182 and in a series of agreements by the OECD's DAC, considered to be the main "venue and voice" for international donors. [20]

---

16   Jacob Kurtzer, "China's Humanitarian Aid: Cooperation amid Competition," Center for Strategic and International Studies, 2020, https://www.csis.org/analysis/chinas-human itarian-aid-cooperation-amidst-competition.

17   United Nations Office for the Coordination of Humanitarian Affairs, "Global Humanitarian Overview," OHCA, 2021, https://www.unocha.org/global-humanitarian-overview-2021.

18   United Nations Office for the Coordination of Humanitarian Affairs, "Global Humanitarian Review."

19   Günther Fink and Silvia Redaelli, "Determinants of International Emergency Aid - Humanitarian Need Only?" *World Development* 39, no. 5 (2011): 741–757.

20   OECD, *Paris Declaration on Aid Effectiveness*, Paris: OECD Publishing, 2005; United Nations General Assembly, "Resolution A/RES/46/182 'Strengthening of the Coordination of Humanitarian Emergency Assistance of the United Nations'," December 19, 1991. https://documents-dds-ny.un.org/doc/RESOLUTION/GEN/NR0/582/70/IMG/NR058270

While altruism, compassion, and considerations of need continue playing an important role in decisions about humanitarian aid allocations,[21] significant differences in the volume and types of aid provided to countries experiencing acute crises suggest a possibility that other motives unrelated to need also shape donors' decisions about humanitarian assistance.[22] The perceived politicization of aid and biases in states' allocations of disaster relief assistance have been named among chief reasons for the crisis in humanitarian system.[23] Donors' responses to COVID-19 crisis and humanitarian assistance to Ukraine have animated the discussion of the perceived biases permeating humanitarian aid.[24] Humanitarian ethicists, volunteers assisting refugees fleeing crises in Africa, the Middle East, and Latin America, and non-Western media consumers have pointed out striking differences in the levels of assistance channeled toward Ukraine compared to other ongoing humanitarian crises.[25] The head of the World Health Organization, Tedros Adhanom Ghebreyesus, put it in stark terms, "the world does not give equal attention to emergencies affecting black and white people."[26]

.pdf?OpenElement. See also Michael Barnett and Thomas G. Weiss, "Humanitarianism: A Brief History of the Present," in *Humanitarianism in Question*, edited by Michael Barnett and Thomas G. Weiss (Ithaca: Cornell University Press, 2008), p. 12; The International Committee of the Red Cross, "The Fundamental Principles of the International Red Cross and Red Crescent Movement," October 31, 1986, https://www.icrc.org/en/doc/resources/documents/red-cross-crescent-movement/fundamental-principles-movement-1986-10-31.htm.

21   As the humanitarian agencies have proliferated in number and size, humanitarianism has become to resemble business with multiple organizations competing for public attention and funds. According to critics, non-state donors have become dependent on state funds acting as subcontractors for national governments (Jonannes Paulmann, "The Dilemmas of Humanitarian Aid: Historical Perspectives," in *Dilemmas of Humanitarian Aid in the Twentieth Century*, edited by Jonannes Paulmann (Oxford, Oxford University Press, 2016).

22   Devon Curtis, "Politics and Humanitarian Aid: Debates, Dilemmas and Dissension," Report of a conference organized by ODI, POLIS at the University of Leeds and CAFOD, London. February 1, 2001.

23   Paulmann, "The Dilemmas of Humanitarian Aid."

24   Constantine Boussalis and Caryn Peiffer, "Health, Need and Politics: the Determinants of Bilateral HIV/AIDS Assistance," *Journal of Development Studies* 47, no. 12 (2011): 1798–1825; David Dollar and Victoria Levin, "The Increasing Selectivity of Foreign Aid, 1984–2003," *World Development* 34, no. 12 (2006): 2034–2046.

25   Josie Rozzelle, "Whose Suffering Counts? A Discussion Looking at Crisis Coverage Beyond Ukraine," *The New Humanitarian*, April 8, 2022, https://www.thenewhumanitarian.org/opinion/2022/04/08/event-crisis-coverage-beyond-Ukraine.

26   BBC News, "Ukraine Attention Shows Bias Against Black Lives, WHO Chief Says" *BBC News*, April 13, 2022, https://www.bbc.com/news/world-61101732#.

1.3   *The Future of Humanitarian Regime and Global Governance*

Since the end of World War II, the United States has been at the forefront of humanitarian and development assistance, both in terms of the total amounts of foreign aid and in a sense of profound influence over the content of humanitarian principles and institutional makeup of the system of humanitarian assistance. The various programs and institutions, through which the aid initiatives were implemented, the discourses providing justification for humanitarian aid, and the modes of governance that grew out of these experiences constituted collectively humanitarian regime[27] that grew more global over years. In the post-Cold War period, many of the norms, principles, and practices approbated by the US during the Cold War era were institutionalized in the DAC system.[28] Although, the scholars and practitioners of humanitarian assistance have long advocated against using emergency relief funds in pursuit of donors' national interests, both the United States and Soviet Union deployed foreign assistance projects to export their systems of values and institutions, institutionalize a global order that reflected their domestic beliefs, and counter each other's foreign influence. In the end, some analysts contend that foreign aid successfully deployed in pursuit of America's national interests helped the United States win Cold War[29] turning humanitarianism into a critical facet of global governance centered in the US-led liberal international order.[30]

The experience of a divided world and the contest between the United States and Soviet Union during the Cold War era has cast a long shadow over the modern competition between Beijing and Washington. While the US has retained its status as the world's largest humanitarian donor and largest supplier of the COVID-19 aid, China has considerably increased its emergency relief spending. Beijing's humanitarian donations peaked several times in the 2010s. The People's Republic of China (PRC) set a record at $128.5 million in humanitarian aid in 2017[31] and has provided its highest ever amount of humanitarian assistance in 2020 to refurbish its international image and position itself as a

---

27   Young-sun Hong, *Cold War Germany, the Third World, and the Global Humanitarian Regime* (Cambridge University Press, 2015), p. 3.

28   William Hynes and Simon Scott, "The Evolution of Official Development Assistance: Achievements, Criticisms and a Way Forward," OECD Development Co-Operation Working Paper No. 12 (OECD Publishing, 2013), http://dx.doi.org/10.1787/5k3v1dv3f024-en.

29   Andrew S. Natsios, "The Politics of United States Disaster Response," *Mediterranean Quarterly* 6, no. 2 (Spring 1995): 46–59.

30   Noora Kotilainen, "Resilience of the Humanitarian Narrative in US Foreign Policy," in *Contestations of Liberal Order*, edited by Marko Lehti, Henna-Riika Pennanen, andJukka Jouhki, (Palgrave Macmillan, 2020), p. 233.

31   In comparison, the US spent $6.89 billion on humanitarian assistance in 2017 (Jacob Kurtzer, "China's Humanitarian Aid").

leader in the global response to COVID-19. Still, China's humanitarian contributions make up less than one percent of the global total and pale in comparison to those of the US. Yet, by bundling humanitarian aid into the lucrative packages of trade, investments, and development assistance and pushing the message that, unlike the US, it seeks no changes in the recipient countries' domestic affairs, China has strategically positioned itself as the most credible challenger to the American dominance in the humanitarian realm.[32] A heated debate is underway among Western observers regarding the implications of China's rise for different regimes within the global governance system. Some contend that China's humanitarian practices and norms, which depart from the principles institutionalized in the DAC system, intensify the "legitimacy crisis" of the traditional humanitarian regime.[33] Others raise alarms over the incompatibility of China's governance model with the pillars of liberal international order supported by and beneficial to the US.[34] To paraphrase former US Secretary of State Henry Kissinger, although "the United States is sufficiently powerful to be able to insist on its view and to carry the day often enough to evoke charge of American hegemony," it runs the risk of "becoming irrelevant" in light of China's ability to reshape international regimes to better suit the interests of Beijing.[35]

Russia's use of humanitarian aid for geopolitical benefits has not played a critical disruptive role in the humanitarian system by itself. However, jointly with China's humanitarian activities, which entwine humanitarian aid with geoeconomic and strategic goals and prioritize opaque bilateral state-to-state mechanisms of funding, Russia's approaches to humanitarianism can further the fracturing of the humanitarian system centered in the principles of OECD's DAC. What is evident is that China's and Russia's emergence as donors has significant – though presently unclear – implications for the future of global

---

32   Nana De Graaff and Bastiaan Van Apeldoorn, "US-China Relations and the Liberal World Order: Contending Elites, Colliding Visions?" *International Affairs* 94, no. 1 (2018): 113–131; Salvador Santino F. Regilme and James Parisotm, *American Hegemony and the Rise of Emerging Powers* (London: Routledge, 2017).

33   Clemens Six, "The Rise of Postcolonial States as Donors: A Challenge to the Development Paradigm?" *Third World Quarterly* 30, no. 6 (2009): 1103–1121; Felix Zimmermann and Kimberly Smith, "More Actors, More Money, More Ideas for International Development Cooperation," *Journal of International Development* 23, no. 5 (2011): 722–738.

34   François Godement, *Expanded Ambitions, Shrinking Achievements: How China Sees the Global Order* (Policy Brief March 2017). London, UK: European Council on Foreign Relations, 2017, p. 1, https://ecfr.eu/publication/expanded_ambitions_shrinking_achievements_how _china_sees_the_global_order/.

35   Henry Kissinger, "Does America Need a Foreign Policy? Toward a Diplomacy for the 21st Century (Simon & Schuster, 2001), pp. 18.

humanitarianism. The characteristics and principles of the humanitarian system of the future will depend on the practices, motivations, and normative dimensions of the main traditional and emerging donors. It is these practices and underlying logics for humanitarian assistance that are the subject of this book.

2   Argument in a Nutshell

Instead of approaching states' motivations for humanitarian aid through the essentialized lens of altruism, humanity, compassion, or geostrategic interest, this study probes the meanings of these and related terms drawing on the insights of a critical geopolitics perspective. While not a neatly delimited approach, critical geopolitics furnishes us with the valuable theoretical tools for exploring how claims about humanity, impartiality, neutrality, and geostrategic interest are operationalized and performed through specific humanitarian practices and discourses. Critical geopolitics bears witness to the plurality of geopolitical spaces, which include discursively constructed spaces that imbue specific meanings to the physicality of states, politics, and world governance.[36]

Our point of departure is that states' motivations for humanitarian assistance are contingent upon the discursively constructed geopolitical imagery – ideas, concepts, and knowledge about the state and the world – that imbue specific meanings in what donors will prioritize in their aid decisions and set the ethical context within which these decisions are made. These ideas emerge in the specific historical, cultural, and international context within which the donors operate, but also continuously evolve tempered by practices of humanitarian assistance and relations with other state and non-state donors.

Furthermore, donors' perspectives on humanitarian aid are shaped by the dominant global geopolitical discourses that produce and reproduce a certain kind of geopolitical space, often referred to as a "global order" consisting of ideas, rules, practices, and institutions defining who the main global actors are and helping them to manage interactions among themselves. As discussed later in this book, the current humanitarian regime is deeply intertwined with the geopolitical construct of the liberal international order, which has had a regularizing impact on global politics by setting parameters for interactions among actors (e.g., emphasizing free trade) and seeking to shape the very identity of

---

36   Gearóid Ó. Tuathail and Simon Dalby, "Introduction: Rethinking Geopolitics: Towards a Critical Geopolitics," in *Rethinking Geopolitics* eds. Gearoid O Tuathail and Simon Dalby (London: Routledge, 1998), pp. 1–15.

actors by exalting democracy and individual freedoms. Neither the human-itarian regime nor the global order enveloping it have been independent of the underlying power relations. The spread and tenacity of neoliberal ideas in the post-Cold War context has been buoyed by the material power of the US. The dominant humanitarian principles have been buttressed by the mate-rial power of the traditional donors. Other states entering the humanitarian realm have had to operate in, work around, or confront the dominant global order and humanitarian regime. China's rise has shifted the distribution of power at the global level. Rooted in a set of different ideas about the state and its role in global politics, China's humanitarian perspective has been perceived as a challenge to the dominant humanitarian regime. Russia's humanitarian activities rooted in an alternative geopolitical logic have also been regarded as highly disruptive to traditional humanitarian mission. This contest over the boundaries of meanings on the conceptual maps of ideas and approaches to humanitarian assistance has added a layer of complexity to donors' motiva-tions for aid and a new dynamic in the humanitarian system itself.

In short, states' motives for humanitarian aid are both complex and dynamic, and can include a confluence of economic, political, and normative concerns that are held together by historically contingent conceptions of national interest, state, international environment, and the donors' place in the world. They are further affected by the shifting global power relations and accompanying this shift contestation between the dominant and alternative geopolitical imagery surrounding humanitarian aid. These unique conceptions of national interest and ethics of humanitarian assistance coupled with the contestation over the meanings and approaches to aid propel states react to humanitarian needs in ways that reproduce the many limitations of the dominant humanitarian system, including the pervasive power hierarchies that overlay normative considerations.

To understand states' decisions about humanitarian aid, our study probes the systems of meanings within China's, Russia's, and the US' humanitarian practices and discourses punctuated by their histories of accumulated expe-riences with foreign aid. These social constructions of geopolitical spaces and state identities are, then, used to derive specific motives for the analysis of these countries' aid allocations and exploration of each nation's humanitarian and vaccine assistance during the COVID-19 pandemic. By treating the critical geopolitical perspective as an analytical tool, rather than a phenomenological position on specific ways of knowing, ontology, and epistemology,[37] we can

---

37   We are taking insight from James Fearon and Alexander Wendt, "Rationalism v. Construc-tivism: A Skeptical View," in Walter Carlsnaes, Thomas Risse, and Beth Simmons, *Hand-book of International Relations* (Thousand Oaks, CA: Sage Publications, 2002), pp. 52–72.

marry its deconstructive impetus with a systematic way of tracing the practical consequences of their geopolitical considerations. The book takes a position that such a *pragmatic* combination of empirical analysis that foregrounds the discursive constructions of geopolitical spaces and identities provides a more complete and nuanced understanding of the ways that actors come to think about and define their power and interests as well as geographic assumptions that inform their decision-making in the foreign policy and humanitarian realms.

The humanitarian activities of the United States have been influenced by historically grounded liberal ideas about individuals as bearers of inherent moral value and ethical action driven by compassion toward those experiencing suffering. The moral imperative of alleviating individual suffering due to disaster or crisis has been discursively erected into an ethical foundation for US humanitarian aid. In practice, this moral imperative has also been tempered by political interests, concerns with the effectiveness of aid, and global power relations. In the post-Cold war period, American humanitarian reasoning has overgrown with new interpretations connecting complex emergencies with certain domestic conditions, such as poverty and despotism. To adapt its humanitarian response to rapidly changing conflict and development dynamics, the US government introduced important changes to its foreign aid institutions anchoring humanitarian practices in the development assistance infrastructure. US development interventions has largely taken place under the geoeconomic rubric of neoliberal globalization and geopolitical considerations linked to the global war on terrorism. Viewing underdevelopment as a source of state failure, transnational crime, and terrorism, American development agencies have rewarded the countries opened to the liberalization of their national economies and democratization reforms.[38] The integration of humanitarian assistance within the development infrastructure introduced a range of geoeconomic and geopolitical considerations into the decisions about the allocation of humanitarian aid, thus removing a degree of independence and impartiality in humanitarian aid administration. Facing the China challenge and disruptions by Russia, the US government has introduced new tools of foreign assistance to counter the global influence of nations that may threaten US interests. These changes have also contributed to the politicization of humanitarian aid.

China has distanced itself from the traditional humanitarian discourses, principles, and practices espoused by the US. It is not a DAC member, nor is it a

---

38   Jamey Essex, *Development, Security and Aid: Geopolitics and Geoeconomics at the U.S. Agency for International Development* (Athens, GA: The University of Georgia Press, 2013).

part of the Good Humanitarian Donorship (GHD) initiative that facilitates collective advancement of what the dominant humanitarian regime considers as "good practices" in the global humanitarian system.[39] China's aversion toward the established humanitarian practices and principles is somewhat surprising. In other domains, such as peacekeeping, Beijing has shown a remarkable ability to adapt to traditional and multilateral mechanisms.[40] That it has not done so in the humanitarian realm is due to significant differences between its own repertoire of descriptive and prescriptive ideas within its geopolitical vision of the state and the world and those of the Western humanitarianism.[41]

China's emergency relief aid has been premised on a belief about the state as the primary moral agent. The central role of the state in disaster relief makes politics integral to China's humanitarian project, which has also been inextricably linked to Beijing's ideas about global development and peace. An important implication of China's state-centrism is the principle of respect for political sovereignty of the recipients of China's assistance. This political non-conditionality, however, does not extend to economic conditionality resulting from the bundling of China's aid with investments, concessional loans, and trade, which have recently coalesced in Beijing's Belt and Road geopolitical infrastructure. Still, Beijing has insisted that its principle of mutually beneficial assistance creates a "win-win" situation for co-prosperity of China and the recipients of its aid: by investing in global development and assisting in humanitarian disasters, Beijing is contributing to economic growth at home. Reversely, China's own prosperity and stability is believed to be essential for global development and piece.

Despite the long history of aid-giving, Russia's intellectual foundations for its foreign aid are less developed than those of the US and China. Moscow's broad understanding of humanitarianism and its position on development and humanitarian assistance have been part and parcel of Soviet and Russian foreign policy. The key objective of Russian foreign policy since the Soviet Union's dissolution has been the restoration of its great power status. This notion that Russia's destiny is bound to be great power has shaped foreign policies consistent with this understanding. Yet, what goes into the making of the great power identity has not been constant. The meaning of "great powerness"

---

39   See Good Humanitarian Donorship's website: https://www.ghdinitiative.org/ghd/gns
      /home-page.html.

40   Richard Gowan, "China's Pragmatic Approach to UN Peacekeeping," (The Brookings
      Institution, September 14, 2020), https://www.brookings.edu/articles/chinas-pragmatic
      -approach-to-un-peacekeeping/.

41   Miwa Hirono, "Three Legacies of Humanitarianism in China," *Disasters* 37 (2013), p. 12.

has been repeatedly redefined on the backdrop of changing global and domestic circumstances. Thus, in 2007, humanitarian aid was added as a prerequisite for Russia's status as a great power nation. The broader goals of Russian foreign policy and a set of narratives designed to strengthen its influence and legitimacy in regional and global affairs have influenced Moscow's views on humanitarian aid. The latter, therefore, has been conceived as a tool for defending Russia's interests and great power ambitions believed to be threatened by the United States. This juxtaposition of identity-based considerations and the imagery of global politics that presents the West as an arch-nemesis of Moscow has shaped Russia's approach to humanitarian aid.

This book traces the differences in COVID-19 aid allocations between the US, China and Russia to these distinct geopolitical ideas and experiences with foreign aid. As a wealthier donor at the helm of the traditional humanitarian system, the United States has directed its COVID-19 allocations to low-income countries with weak capacity to combat the consequences of the pandemic. Washington has also prioritized humanitarian aid allocations to its democratic allies and those countries that have been supportive of US foreign policy in the United Nations. Since Washington has a long tradition of channeling aid through multilateral mechanisms and institutions at home, in particular, the Department of State and USAID, most of COVID-19 assistance has gone to countries, which have been the recipients of development aid from the US government before.

In contrast, both China and Russia have favored state-to-state bilateral assistance channels and provided their aid in-kind (through the transfers of medical supplies and materials). Beijing's COVID-19 aid allocations closely trailed its development assistance packages. Countries that have signed the Belt and Road Initiative (BRI) economic partnership agreements with Beijing have been the largest recipients of its COVID-19 assistance. China has relaxed its "One China" principle but the issue of Xinjiang has become more prominent in China's foreign affairs. Neither Russian nor Chinese decisions about COVID-19 aid can be understood without considering a broader context of global geopolitical competition. Both China's and Russia's foreign aid has had a counter-Western purpose in that it has closely trailed aid allocations by the US. Yet, if China's coronavirus aid has advanced a new competing model for the practices and purpose of humanitarian assistance, Russia's COVID-19 aid has had a narrower purchase of disrupting US influence.

The close consideration of Chinese, Russian, and American ideas and practices of humanitarian assistance and how those have informed their decisions about allocations of the COVID-19 aid depict important differences in these countries' reasoning about assistance. While undeniably pragmatic, the underlying logics of interest in the administration of humanitarian aid and how those interests have come about informed by the social constructions of global order, actors and their place in global policies differ across the three countries under investigation. This is not to suggest that discursive constructions of interests, need, state, and others determine states' motivations for aid and their other foreign practices. Rather, the idea is that there are multiple, often conflicting, conceptual maps of humanitarian affairs and broader global politics and this diversity of global scripts can neither be reduced to nor assessed based on the yardstick of Western (or dominant) experiences and concepts. The understanding of different geopolitical visions of aid is important as ideas and knowledge have performative power: they stage subjects and objects of humanitarian aid, thus making certain political and ethical outcomes possible.[42]

3   Methods and Evidence

Focusing on COVID-19 aid by China, Russia, and the United States, this book seeks to answer a broader question of countries' motivations for humanitarian assistance. Our inquiry relies on a combination of qualitative and quantitative data and methods that enable us to probe beliefs and assumptions held by China, Russia, and the US about humanitarian aid, and collect and analyze COVID-19 and vaccine allocations by these countries.

Our argument is that state logics for humanitarian aid are shaped by their geopolitical conceptual maps rooted in their historical and modern-day experiences with assistance that interact with and inform their ideas and reasoning about foreign aid. The tradition of critical geopolitics directs our attention to the role of history, culture, and identity in shaping beliefs, ideas, values, and actions of actors in the international space. The production and reproduction of such geopolitical knowledge can take place at different levels: *popular*, denoting the construction of images about the state and the world by people through the mediums of popular culture and traditional and social media; *formal*, referring to the production of geopolitical thought by pundits and other intellectuals; and *practical*, emphasizing the production of geopolitical knowledge by state decision-makers through day-to-day statecraft.[43]

---

42   Mariya Y. Omelicheva, "Critical Geopolitics on Russian Foreign Policy: Uncovering the Imagery of Moscow's International Relations," *International Politics* 52 (2016): 708–726.

43   Gearóid Ó. Tuathail, "Understanding Critical Geopolitics: Geopolitics and Risk Society," *Journal of Strategic Studies*, 22 No. 2–3 (1999), p. 111.

Recognizing that geopolitical imagery is non-hierarchical and complex, we focus on the construction of humanitarian narratives at the "practical" level by state decision-makers.[44]

There are many avenues that states, through their top decision-makers, use to make their ideas, values, and beliefs available and known to others. First, there are written records. The norms and principles of foreign aid are often codified in legal documents: concepts, programs, laws, and executive decisions. Second, the meanings attributed to humanitarian aid and aid practices can be identified from the actual verbal and written communications by government representatives and pundits. Third, the observable practices of states' engagement in the provision of humanitarian assistance also express their adherence to certain principles, ideas, and norms. To discern Chinese, Russian, and US beliefs and ideas about humanitarian assistance, we have systematically examined their legal documents, statements of political leaders and government representatives, publications of state agencies, and writings of scholars in addition to actual practices of humanitarian assistance.[45]

At the core of our empirical analysis is a new comprehensive dataset of COVID-19 and vaccine allocations by China, Russia, and the US that we deploy in the statistical analysis of the donors' aid motivations. The US government has systematically reported its official development assistance and humanitarian aid flows, and we used data from US government's official reports in the book. To collect data on COVID-19 donations by China and Russia, we created a search algorithm that we applied in the Nexus Uni (formerly LexisNexis Academic) featuring more than 17,000 news for extracting relevant content.[46] Supplemented with searchers on the digital government platforms, we identified all known COVID-19 aid allocations by China and Russia in the first year of the COVID-19 pandemic.

Each donation was coded as an event with the date of the aid transfer, donor (state, agency/organization within the state), recipient, type and volume of donation, and other characteristics of the event recorded. For a COVID-19 donation to be recorded in the dataset, it had to be confirmed in at least two different sources. Each record was handled by three researchers: an original coder, one of the authors, and a third researcher who transformed the volumes of in-kind assistance into their dollar value. We paid special attention

---

44   Mariya Y. Omelicheva, "Critical Geopolitics on Russian Foreign Policy."

45   While we consulted most of the primary documents in Russian and Chinese, whenever possible, we cite their English translations and other English language sources.

46   See LexisNexis webpage: https://www.lexisnexis.com/en-us/professional/academic/nexis-uni.page.

to distinguish donations from purchases, which were occasionally misrepresented in the press. To standardize donations into their dollar equivalents, we defined a reference list of values, including the lowest and the highest possible value for the product based on the known market prices. In this way, we calculated the value for over 30 different medical products. The totals for each recipient of COVID-19 aid were aggregated over the year and integrated with the available resources on various country-level co-variates for the analysis of states' motivations for the coronavirus aid distribution.

4   Overview of the Book

The book begins with a brief discussion of what humanitarian aid entails and how it relates to other types of international assistance in Chapter 1. It offers a succinct overview of the commonly held "need-," "interest-," and "merit-based" explanations for humanitarian aid to contrast its approach from those adopted in the literature on assistance. To understand states' decisions about humanitarian aid, the book utilized critical geopolitics lens, which views foreign policies as constitutive of historically contingent, culturally-specific, and dynamic geopolitical logics consisting of certain meanings and reasonings about the world, the roles played by states, and their identities. These meanings become the medium for states' decisions about humanitarian aid. The chapter discusses the historical circumstances that gave rise to the geopolitical logic informing the modern ideas of neutrality and impartiality of humanitarian assistance and their evolution in the late 20th and 21st century. These ideas are, then, juxtaposed to deeper historical and cultural roots of China's and Russia's beliefs about humanitarian aid. It also discusses how the concentration of global power in the US elevated certain geopolitical conceptualizations as dominant conceptions of global humanitarian regime and how changes in the distribution of power at the global level have spilled over into the contest over ideas and approaches to humanitarian aid. The chapter concludes with a series of theoretical expectations about the motives of Chinese, Russian, and America humanitarian aid that are further explored in Chapters 2–5 of the book.

The empirical chapters are structured in similar ways. Each begin with an overview of the donor's profile in the humanitarian field followed by the discussion of their geopolitical logics used to derive specific motives for the analysis of these countries' aid allocations and exploration of each nation's humanitarian aid. These motives are, then, tested on the novel data of COVID-19 aid. Thus, Chapter 2 on China discusses its rising humanitarian profile, which has roots in over half-century of experiences in the development assistance sector. It emphasizes a different geopolitical logic for humanitarian action and modalities of humanitarian financing deployed by Beijing. The chapter develops these ideas about humanitarianism into testable expectations for China's COVID-19 assistance analyzed next. The chapter concludes that China's COVID-19 aid is part of its broader vision of global health as a foreign policy objective driven by interests in creating an international environment that is favorable to China's internal development and its rise to global power.

Chapter 3 begins with an overview of Russia's resurgence in the global development and humanitarian fields following the development aid hiatus of the 1990s. The first section details Russia's broad understanding of humanitarianism and traces the roots of Russian beliefs and assumptions about humanitarian assistance to the Soviet experiences. This discussion illuminates the primacy of national interests in Russia's aid distribution, linkages of aid-based decisions with the great power status, and the Cold War legacy of looking at foreign aid through the lens of great power competition. The analysis of Russia's COVID-19 aid presented in the second part of the chapter reveals several motivations for Moscow's humanitarian assistance. While some of Russia's aid has been tied to the humanitarian objectives, it has also been an integral part of Moscow's strategy for projecting power on the global stage and supporting diverse political objectives.

The US has been among the largest humanitarian donors, and it has also led the humanitarian response to COVID-19 pandemic (in terms of the total volumes – in dollars - of COVID-19 aid). Yet, Washington's COVID-19 assistance has been constrained by the lack of supplies and capacity to meet many domestic demands and the official rhetoric threatening to introduce deep cuts to its foreign assistance budget. Chapter 4 illuminates the perennial tension between the universalizing logic that has linked US humanitarian decisions to the imperative of reducing human suffering regardless of the place or space affected by the crisis, on one hand, and the geostrategic and geoeconomics discourses foregrounding American security and economic interests in the administration of its foreign assistance, on the other. This tension played out during the Cold War period and became particularly prominent following the Soviet Union's dissolution. In the post-Cold war period, especially in the post-9/11 context, the US has become embroiled in numerous interventions and conflicts. As the humanitarian aid personnel found themselves working alongside the US diplomats and military in complex emergencies, the disaster relief aid has become an integral part of US strategy to transform conflicts, bring the warring parties to a negotiating table, and set the stage for political and economic reforms. Institutional changes in the structure of American aid have chipped away from humanitarian assistance independence. Because of bureaucratic transformations, humanitarian aid has become linked to development assistance leading to politicization of aid.

The last chapter of the book explores trends in vaccinations' allocations by China, Russia, and the US. It offers an overview of the rapidly evolving landscape of COVID-19 vaccine distribution involving several leading candidates, and puts forth a preliminary analysis of the determinants of vaccine distributions. We find that many of the same considerations explaining COVID-19 aid account for the patterns of vaccine allocation practices by the donors. The final chapter of the book offers the overview of fundings and charts a way forward for both traditional and "emerging" donors to operate side-by-side in the global humanitarian system facing an array of challenges.

CHAPTER 1

Critical Geopolitics Perspective on Humanitarian Assistance

What motivates state donors to provide humanitarian aid? Traditionally, states' decisions to furnish humanitarian assistance have been attributed to one of the three explanations.[1] The need-based explanations ascribe aid decisions to donors' compassion toward people in need, afflicted by the dire consequences of a crisis or natural disaster. In the "interest-based" accounts, humanitarian aid is no different from other foreign policy tools that are used toward attaining national interests. Concerns with the effectiveness of foreign assistance are at the heart of the "merit-based" models suggesting that international donors channel foreign assistance to those countries, which have the best institutional frameworks for spending foreign aid.

Instead of treating the concepts of "need," "interest," or "merit" as self-evident and distinct antecedents of states' foreign policy decisions, this book treats them as parts of geopolitical discourses through which states, represented by their elites, construct the spaces for political action that become the medium for their decisions about humanitarian aid. Using the theoretical insights of the critical geopolitics perspectives, the book maintains that the direction of a country's intent is shaped by historically contingent, donor-specific, and dynamic geopolitical logics consisting of certain meanings and reasonings about spaces (including conceptual renderings of spaces), identities, and actors. Furthermore, these meanings and experiences with foreign assistance reside in the global context featuring normative orders and power

---

1 See, for example, Jean-Claud Berthélemy, "Bilateral Donors' Interest vs. Recipients' Develop-ment Motives in Aid Allocation: Do All Donors Behave the Same?" *Review of Development Economics* 10, no. 2 (2006): 179–194; Constantine Boussalis and Caryn Peiffer, "Health, Need and Politics: the Determinants of Bilateral HIV/AIDS Assistance," *Journal of Development Studies* 47, no. 12 (2011): 1798–1825; David Dollar and Victoria Levin, "The Increasing Selec-tivity of Foreign Aid, 1984–2003," *World Development* 34, no. 12 (2006): 2034–2046. These frameworks are consistent with the explanations of state behavior offered by the major the-oretical schools of international relations. Aid as a tool for strengthening power and security or cooperation comports with the realist and liberal institutionalist thinking respectively. Aid as a reflection of new international norms and ideas that impart responsibility for the fellow human beings is consistent with assumptions of constructivism (Denghua Zhang, *A Cautious New Approach* (ANU Press, 2020)).

relations that underpin them. Global humanitarian regime has been embedded in the broader structures of liberal international governance with the US at the helm. Shifts in the distribution of global power, like those triggered by China's rise, have been perceived as threats to the dominant normative order, including ideas and principles of the global humanitarian regime. This contestation between the dominant and alternative conceptual architectures of humanitarian assistance introduces an additional dimension to states' motivations for aid.

This chapter begins with a brief overview of the state of knowledge about the determinants of humanitarian aid. We, then, articulate the critical geopolitics perspective on states' humanitarian decisions that calls for understanding humanitarianism in terms of the ways in which states actively construct the space of political action by drawing on historically contingent and culturally-specific ideas about themselves and the world around them. The chapter discusses the historical circumstances that gave rise to the geopolitical logic informing the modern ideas of neutrality and impartiality of humanitarian aid and their evolution in the late 20th and 21st century. These ideas are, then, juxtaposed to deeper historical and cultural roots of China's and Russia's beliefs about humanitarian assistance. The chapter concludes with the discussion of the ways in which the concentration of global power in the US elevated certain geopolitical conceptualizations as dominant conceptions of global humanitarian regime and how changes in the distribution of power within the international system have spilled over into the contest over ideas and approaches to humanitarian aid.

1   Taking the Stock of Knowledge on Humanitarian Aid

Humanitarian assistance falls under the broader rubric of foreign aid, which also includes development and security assistance. Development assistance involves funding or financing, usually on favorable terms, provided to developing countries with the goal of supporting their economic, environmental, social, and political development.[2] Military aid encompasses the transfer of military articles, services, and financial aid in support of sales of military equipment and training, and military education that are designed to enhance

---

2   Other closely related concepts include foreign aid, development assistance, official development assistance (ODA), development cooperation and technical assistance. See also Mariya Y. Omelicheva, "'Good' Samaritan? The Geopolitics of Russia's COVID-19 Assistance," *Canadian Journal of European and Russian Studies* 16, no. 1 (2020): 1–25.

national security of the donor states, assist recipient governments in deterring or combatting security threats, and foster international stability. For some governments, military aid is also a means of diplomacy to cultivate goodwill and persuade foreign governments to act consistent with the donor's interests.[3]

Humanitarian aid has been regarded as a distinct form of assistance due to its intent and ethical foundations. The goal of humanitarian aid is to alleviate human suffering in the wake of natural disasters, technological catastrophes, and conflicts, often classified as "complex emergencies."[4] Designed to offer short-term rapid relief in response to events threatening human lives, humanitarian assistance has been envisioned as different from development and security assistance.[5] With its roots in international humanitarian law, the modern thinking about humanitarian aid has been shaped by the principled ideas of humanity, neutrality, impartiality, and independence.[6] Often taken at their face value as universally applicable, these principles are said to remove political conditionality from the donor governments' considerations of humanitarian assistance.

Consistent with these humanitarian principles, donors' decisions concerning emergency relief aid must be guided exclusively by the needs of recipient countries, usually measured by the total number of people affected by a natural disaster or the number of casualties and displaced persons in a conflict.[7]

---

3   Emily M. Morgenstern and Nick M. Brown, "Foreign Assistance: An Introduction to U.S. Programs and Policy," (Congressional Research Service, R40213, 2022).

4   Günther Fink, and Silvia Redaelli, "Determinants of International Emergency Aid - Humanitarian Need Only?" *World Development* 39, no. 5 (2011): 741–757.

5   In practice, the distinction between different types of aid can be blurred. Military equipment and personnel, for example, can be used in the delivery and administration of humanitarian assistance. Humanitarian disasters can spread over months and medical facilities established during these kinds of events, for example, can become part of the health infrastructure of the recipient nations.

6   The International Committee of the Red Cross, "The Fundamental Principles of the Red Cross and Red Crescent Movement," ICRC, 2022, https://www.icrc.org/sites/default/files/topic /file_plus_list/4046-the_fundamental_principles_of_the_international_red_cross_and _red_crescent_movement.pdf; United Nations General Assembly, Resolution A/RES/46/182 "Strengthening of the Coordination of Humanitarian Emergency Assistance of the United Nations," December 19, 1991, https://documents-dds-ny.un.org/doc/RESOLUTION/GEN/NR0 /582/70/IMG/NR058270.pdf?OpenElement.

7   A. Cooper Drury, Richard S. Olson and Douglas A. Van Belle, "The Politics of Humanitarian Aid: U.S. Foreign Disaster Assistance, 1964–1995," *Journal of Politics* 67, no. 2 (2005): 454–473; Paul A. Raschky and Manijeh Schwindt, "On the Channel and Type of Aid: The Case of International Disaster Assistance," *European Journal of Political Economy* 28, no. 1 (2012): 119–131; David Strömberg, "Natural Disasters, Economic Development, and Humanitarian Aid," *Journal of Economic Perspectives* 21, no. 3 (2007): 199–222.

The greater the human suffering, the more humanitarian aid is expected to flow to alleviate it.[8] Donors, however, have been frequently caught between a desire to "do good" and making the hard choices about the allocation of scarce resources. In other words, the principled language of universal and impartial protection of human life has obscured the underlying challenges and questions facing all donors, namely, which lives are worth saving.[9]

Empirical studies of humanitarian aid in the post-Cold War period have recorded a worrisome trend toward a more political approach to disaster relief aid at the cost of foundational principles for humanitarian assistance. The politicization of aid unfolded through four related processes of instrumentalization, securitization, militarization, and developmentalization of humanitarian assistance. Instrumentalization occurred when donors explicitly used humanitarian aid as a tool of foreign policy to advance specific political, economic, and security interests.[10] Thus, studies have shown that donors provide more assistance to countries that are of strategic interest to them, to include their allies, former colonies, and politically-aligned countries.[11] Other donors have given more aid to geographically proximate, oil exporting, and ethnically homogeneous countries.[12] Still others have allowed their commercial interests[13] and domestic

---

8   Andreas Fuchs and Nils-Hendrik Klann, "Emergency Aid 2.0," *Beiträge zur Jahrestagung des Vereins für Socialpolitik* (2013), https://papers.ssrn.com/sol3/papers.cfm?abstract_id =2519635.

9   Joe Bryan, "War Without End? Miliary Humanitarianism and the Limits of Biopolitical Approaches to Security in Central America and the Caribbean," *Political Geography* 47(2015): 33–42.

10   Alan Ingram, "The New Geopolitics of Disease: Between Global Health and Global Security, *Geopolitics* 10, no.3 (2005): 522–545.

11   Alberto Alesina and David Dollar, "Who Gives Foreign Aid to Whom and Why?" *Journal of Economic Growth* 5, 1 (2000): 33–63; A. Cooper Drury and Richard Stuart Olson, "Disasters and Political Unrest: An Empirical Investigation," *Journal of Contingencies and Crisis Management* 6 (1998): 153–161; Constantine Boussalis and Caryn Peiffer, "Health, Need and Politics," p. 1801.

12   Günther Fink and Silvia Redaelli, "Determinants of International Emergency Aid"; Eric Neumayer, "Is the Allocation of Food Aid Free from Donor Interest Bias?" *The Journal of Development Studies* 41, no. 3 (2005): 394–411.

13   Axel Dreher and Andreas Fuchs, "Rogue Aid? The Determinants of China's Aid Allocation," *The Determinants of China's Aid Allocation, Courant Research Centre Discussion Paper* 93, September 6 (2011); Alex Dreher, Peter Nennenkamp and Reiner Thiele, "Are 'New' Donors Different? Comparing the Allocation of Bilateral Aid Between non-DAC and DAC Donor Countries," *World Development* 39 (2011): 1950–1968; Robert Fleck and Christopher Kilby, "How Do Political Changes Influence US Bilateral Aid Allocations? Evidence From Panel Data," *Review of Development Economics* 10, no. 2 (2006): 210–223; Andreas Fuchs and Krishna Chaitanya Vadlamannati, "The Needy Donor: An Empirical Analysis of India's Aid Motives," *World Development* 44 (2013): 110–128; Anke Hoeffler and Verity

political processes, such as election cycles and budgetary situations, to influence their decisions about humanitarian aid.[14]

A process of securitization of humanitarian issues refers to framing them into threats to donors' national security interests. Securitization of humanitarian concerns have increased their saliency on the donors' agendas and created the urgency of intervention on the premise that disaster-stricken or disease-afflicted societies were prone to social, health, political, and economic crises. These crises posed the risk of spillover into the donors' territory (in the form of a new disease vector or irregular migration[15]) and threatened stability, security, and development over the medium to long term.[16] Framing natural disasters and health issues as threats to national security opened doors to new types of interventions and access by the donor states. One of the byproducts of securitization of humanitarian issues is the militarization of humanitarian aid whereby activities of humanitarian and military actors become increasingly blurred as aid is integrated into counterterrorism and counterinsurgency strategies, as frequently happened during the "global war on terror."[17]

The developmentalization of humanitarian aid is another process of blurring the lines between saving lives and pursuing the broader issues of development in the administration of humanitarian assistance. The scholarship on humanitarian assistance has recorded the broadening of the scope of the disaster relief aid to include longer-term development goals. Many humanitarian agencies have incorporated market reforms, liberalization of the recipient countries' economies, human rights, and rights to property into their activities, thus compromising the principles of neutrality as their increasingly

---

Outram, "Need, Merit, or Self-Interest - What Determines the Allocation of Aid?" *Review of Development Economics* 15, no. 2 (2011): 237–250.

14   Thomas Eisensee and David Strömberg, "News Droughts, News Floods, and U.S. Disaster Relief," *Quarterly Journal of Economics* 122, no. 2 (2007): 693–728.

15   Erin Collinson and Jocilyn Estes, "A Global Pandemic Needs a Global Response: US Contributions to COVID Relief," Center for Global Development, 2021, https://www.cgdev.org /blog/global-pandemic-needs-global-response-us-contributions-covid-relief.

16   The framing of and responses to HIV/AIDS epidemic in Africa is a particularly instructive case of securitization of a health issue. As Ingram (2007) writes, the high rates of HIV/AIDS were deemed responsible for tearing the social and political fabric of African countries and undermining the combat effectiveness of their military and security forces (Alan Ingram, "HIV/AIDS, Security and the Geopolitics of the US-Nigerian Relations," *Review of International Political Economy* 14, no. 3 (August 2007): 510–534).

17   Charlotte Dany, *Beyond Principles vs. Politics: Humanitarian Aid in the European Union.* ARENA Working Paper 11, 2014, https://www.sv.uio.no/arena/english/research/publications /arena-working-papers/2014/wp11-14.pdf.

political agendas brought them into close contact with the governments of aid-recipient states.[18]

Furthermore, a growing concern with the effectiveness of humanitarian assistance has led some donor governments to favor a smaller pool of aid recipients characterized by a better quality of governance and the strength of their institutions. The presence of humanitarian stakeholders – international humanitarian agencies and non-governmental organizations – have begun to play a greater role in the donors' decisions for allocations of aid.[19] All in all, whether in general or in sector-specific types of assistance, such as food aid and health aid,[20] humanitarian principles, alone, have not been enough to motivate state donors to deliver the needed humanitarian assistance. The consideration of "merit" and "interest" have played a critical role in donors' decisions about aid allocations.[21] The motives for foreign aid have varied not only across the donor countries but also for the same donor over time.

We ascribe this variation in donors' motives for humanitarian assistance to different conceptual architectures of humanitarianism that are shaped by both donors' experiences with foreign aid and their positioning vis-à-vis the dominant humanitarian regime. To tap into these structures of meanings that uniquely shape donors' decisions to allocate humanitarian assistance, we draw on the theoretical repertoire of the critical geopolitics perspective. Instead of assuming the content of "need," "interest" or "merit" in relation to humanitarian assistance a priori, critical geopolitics maintains that there is multiplicity of possible political constructions of space, including the conceptual renderings of spaces.[22] An approach suggested by critical geopolitics allows for greater awareness of the historically contingent and power-laden nature

---

18   Charlotte Dany, *Beyond Principles vs. Politics.*

19   Gorm Rye Olsen, Nils Carstensen, and Kristian Høyen, "Humanitarian Crises: What Determines the Level of Emergency Assistance? Media Coverage, Donor Interests and the Aid Business," *Disasters* 27, no. 2 (2003): 109–126.

20   Eric Neumayer, "Is the Allocation of Food Aid Free from Donor Interest Bias?"; See also Constantine Boussalis and Caryn Peiffer, "Health, Need and Politics."

21   Alberto Alesina and David Dollar, "Who Gives Foreign Aid to Whom and Why?"; A. Maurits van der Veen, *Ideas, Interests and Foreign Aid* (Cambridge University Press, 2011), p. 10. Professor Michael Barnett who has emerged as the most thoughtful scholarly voice on the dilemmas of humanitarianism acknowledged that humanitarian actions cannot escape politics, even though its foundational purpose is apolitical (Michael Barnett, "Evolution Without Progress? Humanitarianism in a World of Hurt," *International Organization* 63, no.4 (2009).

22   Gearóid Ó. Tuathail and Simon Dalby, "Introduction: Rethinking Geopolitics: Towards a Critical Geopolitics," in *Rethinking Geopolitics* eds. Gearoid O Tuathail and Simon Dalby (London: Routledge, 1998), pp. 1–15.

of the principles of humanity, impartiality, and universality of humanitarian aid and considers how geopolitics inform the decisions about humanitarian assistance.[23] The application of the critical geopolitics lens allows us to probe the systems of meanings within China's, Russia's, and America's humanitarian discourse. These meanings, in turn, shape the donors' reasoning about humanitarian aid allocations.

2   **Humanitarianism as a Geopolitical Discourse: Alternative Geopolitical Logics for Humanitarian Assistance**

Immensely diverse in its application and emphasis, critical geopolitics, at its core, is an approach that views politics, including foreign policy decisions, as a social, cultural, discursive, and political practice of "construction of ontological claims."[24] According to this perspective, the seemingly universal categories describing the normative structure of the modern-day humanitarianism are constituted through specific discourses that structure humanitarian claims, human and state agency, and conduct within international relations.[25] States, through their top decision makers, are continuously engaged in constructing, defending, and experiencing the alternative claims about the "truths" of global politics, whether those pertain to their reasoning about humanitarian assistance, interventions, border security, or nation-building. Critical geopolitics engages with and interrogates the production of geopolitical knowledge and power hierarchies that uphold the dissemination of dominant "truths."

Consistent with the critical geopolitics lens, our point of departure is that states' motivations for humanitarian aid are shaped by alternative geopolitical logics composed of sets of meanings about the states, themselves, and their place in the spatial constructions of the world. These ideas give rise to specific geopolitical constructions of national identity and imagery of the others, and they ultimately define states' experiences in the field of humanitarianism (see Table 1).[26] Through their incorporation into the terms of political debate and institutionalization in domestic and international politics, these ideas become

23   Thomas Moore, "Saving Friends or Saving Strangers? Critical Humanitarianism and the Geopolitics of International Law," *Review of International Studies* 39, no. 4 (2013): 925–947.
24   Merje Kuus, "Critical Geopolitics," in *The International Studies Encyclopedia*, ed. R. Denemark, Vol. II (Oxford: Blackwell, 2010), pp. 863–670.
25   Thomas Moore, "Saving Friends or Saving Strangers?"
26   Thomas Moore, "Saving Friends or Saving Strangers?"

TABLE 1 A snapshot of alternative geopolitical logics of humanitarian assistance

	China	Russia	US
How does humanitarian aid fit into a state's conception of itself and its relations with people?	– State is a primary moral agent in a hierarchical social order based on subordination of individuals to state authority. – State authority depends on successful economic performance through development projects at home and abroad. – Aid serves state interests but is also mutually beneficial to the recipients of aid as development (through aid) promotes peace and prosperity.	– Russia is a great power state. – Great power identity comes with rights (e.g., claims to the "privileged sphere of influence") and responsibilities. – Aid is a responsibility of a modern great power. – Aid is also a tool to defend a great power's interests. – The commitment to the state and to its interests and strength stems from a belief that individuals are subordinate to the state.	– Individuals are the primary moral agents. – States bear responsibility for those in despair. – Impartiality, neutrality, and universality are the guiding principles for aid. – Tensions between a humanitarian ethos viewing the world as united in its humanity and transcending the physical geography of states and state interests linking humanitarianism to American global leadership, security, and prosperity.
How does humanitarian aid fit into a state's conception of the global order?	– The current global order and humanitarian regime embedded in it are unjust and threatening to China's interests.	– Tensions with the US-led global normative order and humanitarian regime. – Criticism of the dominant regime as US-serving and disruptive.	– US is an architect, participant, and enforcer of the liberal international order organized around a group of leading nations distinguished by their economic and military superiority that buttresses their claims to normative (liberal) superiority.

TABLE 1   A snapshot of alternative geopolitical logics of humanitarian assistance (*cont.*)

	China	Russia	US
	– An alternative order that mimics a system of "hierarchical harmony" practiced domestically and centering on China's global power and virtues is more conducive to Beijing's interests and global prosperity and security.	– Advancing a vision of the world divided into the spheres of influence of a handful of great power states capable of pursuing their interests without interference from others.	– Humanitarian aid contributes to expanding and sustaining this order favorable to countries that share characteristics of the US (democracy, market economy). – Development and participatory democracy are solutions to global security threats.
Motives for humanitarian aid	– Development assistance and humanitarian aid are the tools in the larger foreign policy toolkit that serves domestic economic interests by contributing to peace and prosperity abroad.	– Humanitarian need, prestige, and support for foreign policy goals are integrated motives for aid. – The normative and power contestation at the global level has added a reactionary dynamic to decisions about humanitarian aid by linking aid allocations to US moves and decisions.	– The US reasoning about humanitarian assistance has been constitutive of the political rationality of liberalism. – Humanitarian need, but also contributions to development and democratization have motivated US aid. – In the post-Cold War era, the US has allowed strategic objectives and economic concerns to pollute humanitarian obligations.

important parameters constraining and ordering the options available to states and shaping the course of their policies in the field of humanitarian action.[27]

Modern humanitarian principles of neutrality, impartiality, and universality that inform the US approach to humanitarian aid have their roots in the Enlightenment ideas about personhood and humanity. Etymologically, the French word *humanité* encompasses these two meanings. In the first connotation, it means that "all human beings form the basis for a shared world."[28] It can also be interpreted as an "emotional movement toward others" that translates into "sympathy for their suffering."[29] The historical roots of these ideas can be traced to the mid-eighteen-century Enlightenment thinking in Europe and in the US (although the notions of charity, benevolence, and compassion are not inimical to other religious, philosophical, and cultural traditions).[30] The European intellectuals such as John Locke and Jean-Jacques Rousseau penned ideas that state authority was derived not from God but from the people, and individuals held some inalienable rights to life, liberty, and property. Enlightenment, in short, elevated humans above all other political and societal considerations.[31]

The humanitarian principles of universality and impartiality are the offshoots of these liberal ideas. Because all individuals are believed to be equal in their inherent moral value, assistance to those in despair must be universally offered, regardless their political, religious, ethnic, or other backgrounds. Because the values and well-being of society are derivative of those of the individual, assistance must be rendered without prejudice to politics or place.[32] In this way a humanitarian ethos transcending the physical geography of the state system has emerged based on the new conception of the world as united in its humanity and recognizing a commonality between all people through their "human-beingness".

---

27   Judith Goldstein and Robert O. Keohane, *Ideas and Foreign Policy: Beliefs, Institutions, and Political Change* (Ithaca: Cornell University Press, 1993).

28   Didier Fa Fassin, "The Predicament of Humanitarianism," *Qui Parle: Critical Humanities and Social Sciences* 22, no. 1 (2013), p. 38.

29   Didier Fa Fassin, "The Predicament of Humanitarianism."

30   Michael Barnett, *Empire of Humanity: A History of Humanitarianism* (Cornell University Press, 2011), p. 50; Daniel Laqua, "Inside the Humanitarian Cloud: Causes and Motivations to Help Friends and Strangers," *Journal of Modern European History* 12, no. 2 (2014): 175–185; Bertrand Taithe, "Reinventing (French) Universalism: Religion, Humanitarianism and the 'French Doctors,'" *Modern & Contemporary France* 12, no. 2 (2004), p. 156.

31   Shane J. Ralston, "American Enlightenment Thought," *Internet Encyclopedia of Philosophy*, 2011, https://iep.utm.edu/american-enlightenment-thought/.

32   Daniel Laqua, "Inside the Humanitarian Cloud."

While not completely impervious to Western ideas, China has been in active confrontation with the Western-based order for centuries. Its official ideologies, therefore, have featured a curious amalgam as well as perennial tension between the Sino-centric views illuminating China's uniqueness and borrowed conceptions.[33] Yet, the Western liberal ideas that elevate human agency above state has not entered this amalgam of borrowed and indigenous thinking, with the latter strongly affected by Marxist-Leninist-Mao Zedong philosophy.[34] Foundational to China's approach to humanitarian aid is Beijing's beliefs in the primacy of the state, which legitimacy (and agency) hinges on successful economic performance through development projects at home and abroad. The physical isolation of China from the rest of the world and its unforgiving geography have turned self-reliance and extensive state involvement in political economy, including through the management of natural disasters, into the prerequisites of state rule. Classical Marxist thought does not treat individuals as abstract moral entities, but as political subjects who receive their rights from the state, and the state can ascribe individuals certain responsibilities and duties. As explained in *Red Flag* (Chinese: 红旗; pinyin: Hóngqí), an official journal on Chinese political theory published by the Chinese Communist Party (CCP) in 1960s–70s, "human rights are not 'heaven-given,' they are given and regulated by the state and by law; they are not universal, but have a clear class nature; they are not abstract but concrete; they are not absolute but limited by law and morality."[35]

While seemingly Westphalian at its core, Chinese conception of the state is nevertheless distinct in its emphasis on a hierarchical social order based on authority and subordination of the individual political subjects to the state. It is further shaped by China's own history of humiliation but also conquest and subordination of others. China's Sino-centric cosmology that imbues state identity with civilizational qualities has also left an imprint on its modern identity of a great power state.[36] The supremacy of the state over the individual, the primacy of state sovereignty over popular sovereignty, and state's

33   John Agnew, "Emerging China and Critical Geopolitics: Between World Politics and Chinese Particularity," *Eurasian Geography and Economics* 51 no. 5 (2010): 569–582.

34   Ashley Kim Stewart and Xing Li, "Beyond Debating the Differences: China's Aid and Trade in Africa," in *China-Africa Relations in an Era of Great Transformations*, edited by Li Xing and Abdulkadir Osman Farah (Ashgate, 2013), pp. 23–48.

35   R. Randle Edwards, Louise Henkin and Andrew J. Nathan, *Human Rights in Contemporary China* (New York: Columbia University Press, 1986), p. 130.

36   John Agnew, "Emerging China and Critical Geopolitics"; William A. Callahan, "The Cartography of National Humiliation and the Emergence of China's Geobody," *Public Culture* 21, no. 1 (2009): 141–173.

unquestioned involvement in economic and social life have paved the way for a state-centric approach to humanitarian assistance, which has been regarded as a tool of foreign policy designed to strengthen state capacity and legitimacy to rule.

Russia's views on humanitarian aid have been anchored in its self-image of great power and a long-standing zero-sum perspective on global affairs. In Russia's geopolitical renderings, the great power state has been defined by certain claims to the neighboring territory as well as special rights and responsibilities regarding international security and peace. One of these responsibilities that stem from a modern identity of a great power state is the provision of foreign aid. Like China, Russia has premised its humanitarian activities on a belief about the state as the primary moral agent. The central role of the state has made politics and geopolitics integral to Russia's foreign aid. Foreign assistance has become another tool for protecting Russia's national interests and its great power status in the "near abroad" and international affairs. This juxtaposition of identity-based (linked to the great power image) and pragmatic (tethered to national interests) considerations for foreign assistance has defined Russia's approach to aid.

According to the critical geopolitics perspectives, states' conceptual maps of the world are never static. They are continuously shaped by relations among countries. Since these relations are carried out by political elites on behalf of the state, political leadership can elevate some spatial conceptions while downgrading others in reaction to the changing global and domestic context and within the constraints imposed by the dominant normative order and sector-specific regimes embedded in it. The transposition of ideas into practice takes place in an environment in which different types of domestic and international events, unintended consequences of past policies, and occasional crises lead governments to repackage original ideas or stretch their original content to fit the changing circumstances. Some of these events and crises can be thought of as "critical junctures," the types of geopolitical events and trends, which economic, political, and security implications have profound consequences at the global level. These critical junctures can motivate states to search for and embrace new ideas or modify the content of the existing ones to make them comport with the associated practices.[37]

In the late 19th–early 20th centuries, liberal ideas foundational to US humanitarian action were reinforced by the anti-slavery movement, the development of humanitarian law, and the fight for civil rights and rights of

37   Trine Flockhart, "Democracy, Security and the Social Construction of Europe," *Perspectives on European Politics and Society* 2, no. 1 (2001): 27–52.

minorities at home. After the second World War, these original humanitarian principles received confirmation in practices of the growing number of humanitarian NGOs, whose actions interlaced relief activities of Western state donors.[38] At the same time, in the politically and ideologically divided atmosphere of the Cold War, the United States, the Soviet Union, and China habitually exploited humanitarian rhetoric for advancing their geopolitical interests under the guise of foreign assistance illuminating the tension between the conception of the world as a "humanity" and the state-centric rendering of global space divided into spatially distinct sovereign political units. The new geo-spatial ideas linked to the new structures of global economic governance as well as the growing visibility of racial and class divides of the world in the post-World War II context engendered new ways of reasoning about assistance. "Developmentalism" became the new catchword denoting the duty of the rich countries to help the less fortunate ones by teaching them to fend for themselves following the example of the developed nations.[39]

China's post-independence experiences have taught Beijing the imperative of economic independence. When the PRC found itself in the political and economic isolation by the West and the Soviet Union, it sought to build a ring of friendly socialist countries through the provision of foreign aid. Simultaneously, the Chinese leadership projected their nation as "a champion of the world's oppressed against the depredations of an imperial West," a self-image that continues beckoning its leaders and intellectuals. Chinese political and academic elites eschew the monikers of "donor" and "recipient" countries as vestiges of the imperial occupation of colonies by the Western states. While ideology strongly dominated China's aid decisions during the post-World War II era, the PRC also considered assistance as a tool for expanding economic cooperation within the block of socialist states and bolstering its economic independence. Economic independence, in turn, was deemed essential to achieving political independence, maintaining sovereignty, and reinforcing the legitimacy of the communist regime.[40] The Deng Xiaoping's Reform and Opening Up policy launched in 1978 taught the Chinese leadership the virtues of economic development through rapid capital accumulation. As discussed in greater detail in Chapter 3, soon the Communist leadership

---

38   Michael Barnett, *Empire of Humanity;* Noora Kotilainen, "Resilience of the Humanitarian Narrative in US Foreign Policy," in *Contestations of Liberal Order* (London: Palgrave Macmillan, 2020), pp. 233–261.

39   Michael Barnett, *Empire of Humanity*, pp. 30–31.

40   Andreas Fuchs and Marina Rudyak, "The Motives of China's Foreign Aid," in *Handbook on the International Political Economy of China* (Cheltenham, UK: Edward Elgar Publishing, 2019), pp. 391–410.

began exporting these lessons abroad: China's experiences with development projects and responses to humanitarian disasters at home laid basis for its approach to development and humanitarian assistance abroad.

The breakup of the USSR became another watershed moment in the history of global politics, and a critical juncture in the evolution of humanitarian aid. For the United States, the collapse of the Soviet Union demonstrated the inferiority of the Communist ideology and a triumph of liberal ideas of multilateralism, collective security, market economy, and individual freedoms.[41] Enjoying the unipolar moment, Washington amplified its commitment to liberal principles, most notably, to the protection of human rights and democracy, in its foreign policy discourse, and elevated interventionalism in the name of these principles in its foreign policy toolbox. To create space for liberal development and participatory democracy, the US and other Western states turned their attention to saving "failed" states. Changing domestic conditions, such as poverty and despotism, in "fragile" political settings by means of military intervention, diplomacy, and foreign aid has become a new moral imperative for Washington. The 9/11 terrorist attacks on the World Trade Center and the Pentagon and the "War on Terror" that ensued have led to further blurring of humanitarian principles with political, security, and economic concerns of the US. One of the consequences of the saturation of American foreign policy with humanitarian rhetoric and incorporation of humanitarian agencies into complex emergencies and conflict settings has been the politicization of American humanitarian aid.

Both China and Russia have clamored about the US military interventions under the guise of humanitarianism. Watershed in this regard were the NATO Kosovo bombings in 1999, the 2003 invasion of Iraq, the 2005 institution of the UN Responsibility to Protect Principle (R2P), and the 2011 military invention in Libya on the grounds of R2P. Moscow and Beijing accused Washington in cooping humanitarian principles as a new political frame through which it [de]legitimized its own and other countries' foreign policy.[42] Beijing went even further by accusing Washington of causing humanitarian disasters through its military adventurism.[43]

41   Francis Fukuyama, "The End of History?" *The National Interest*, no. 16 (1989): 3–18; John G. Ikenberry, *Liberal Leviathan: The Origins, Crisis and the Transformation of the American World Order* (Princeton: Princeton University Press, 2012).

42   Noora Kotilainen, "Resilience of the Humanitarian Narrative in US Foreign Policy."

43   The Associated Press, "China Report Accuses US of Causing Humanitarian Disasters," ABC *News*, April 9, 2021, https://apnews.com/article/beijing-china-united-states-86b3f9d2b89 14f2f5d12d8a5f9719be3.

3   Contestations over the Conceptual Architecture of Global
        Humanitarian Regime

Donors' humanitarian experiences take place in the broader international context characterized by the prevailing normative order and supporting this order
power relations. As conceived in this book, a global normative order is a geopolitical construct that puts forth a certain spatial rendering of political subjects
as well as their hierarchy and describes constellations of norms, principles,
institutions, and power relations assisting in managing interactions among
political subjects. In the post-World War II context, this constellation of rules,
principles, and institutions included a web of international treaties and institutions promoting economic interdependence (e.g., GATT/WTO, IMF, World
Bank), foreswearing the use of force except in self-defense (e.g., UN Security
Council), and advocating for principled commitments to democracy, human
rights and the rule of law (e.g., UN Charter, the 1948 Universal Declaration of
human rights).[44] These institutions have played the role of gatekeepers, social-
izers of states into the dominant order, as well as the enforcers of its norms.

This order, which has been known as the "liberal international order" was
neither fully global nor truly liberal because it was grounded in the Westphalian thinking about the international system as consisting of sovereign states
organized around a group of leading nations distinguished by their power
preponderance that buttressed their claims to normative and even civilizational
superiority. The differences in relative economic and political power and
adherence to unique historically contingent ideas about the routes to modernity and development gave rise to divisions within the liberal international
order into the geospatial categories of the West versus the non-West, the liberal
versus the illiberal, and the civilian versus the backward and barbaric.[45] These
differences were encoded in the legal foundations and decision-making processes of the institutions established in the post-World War II context (such
as the UN, WHO, etc.). They shaped the character and direction of aid programs that were used in a way that allowed the donors to extend claims to
governance over the beneficiaries of their assistance.[46] Although highly non-
egalitarian, the post-World War II order evinced a degree of predictability in

---

44   Alexander Cooley and Daniel Nexon, *Exit from Hegemony: The Unraveling of the American
        Global Order* (Oxford: Oxford University Press, 2020).
45   Chenchen Zhang, "Right-wing Populism with Chinese Characteristics? Identity, Otherness
        and Global Imaginaries in Debating World Politics Online," *European Journal of Interna-
        tional Relations* 26, no. 1 (2020): 88–115.
46   Young-sun Hong, *Cold War Germany, the Third World, and the Global Humanitarian
        Regime* (Cambridege: Cambridge University Press, 2015).

interstate relations, especially among states recognized as rational and autonomous beings through their embrace of liberal ideas and neoliberal economic
principles.

The new order, however, was subject to multiple challenges. The Soviet
Union and other communist countries used their own extensive aid programs
to propagate a different vision for global order that was rooted in the ideas
of socialism. Socialist fraternal aid became a vehicle for inducing recipient
countries' collaboration with the Soviet bloc against capitalism and adoption
of the socialist model of development.[47] Yet, the growing rivalry between the
Soviet Union and communist China, and a unique approach to development
advanced by Beijing, weakened their ability to advance a unified alternative
vision for the global order.

The collapse of the Soviet Union and developmental challenges experienced by China in the early 1990s left the US without a peer rival for global
dominance. The fall of communism as a set of ideas describing a vision for a
socioeconomic and political order that is based on the common ownership of
the means of production that transcends class divisions led to the consolida-
tion and expansion of the values, institutions, and networks underpinning the
vision for the liberal international order. The United States used its unraveled
power position to project these values outward, at times with the use of force.
It provided a framework for US foreign policies and strategies, which it used
to justify disciplinary and punitive forms of power projection exercised upon
those viewed as "threats" or "others" in need of reforms and improvement to
integrate them into the western community of states.[48] Since ethics of human
rights and humanitarianism have been entwined with the norms and values
of liberal international order, the US has also found itself at the helm of global
humanitarianism that has become tied to America's power – its economy,
global leadership, and alliance system.[49]

Other countries had to work within the US-led global order or circumvent
or even challenge it. Neither China nor Russia has been able to completely
escape from the influence of the liberal international order. Both have had
to negotiate their relations with other states and international organizations
and participate in drawing boundaries in content and reach of international
norms. China's prosperity has depended on its ties to and participation in the

---

47   Young-sun Hong, *Cold War Germany, the Third World, and the Global Humanitarian
       Regime*.
48   Chenchen Zhang, "Right-wing Populism with Chinese Characteristics?"
49   John G. Ikenberry, "The End of Liberal International Order?" *International Affairs* 94, no. 1
       (2018): 7–23.

global economic institutions that facilitated its growth. The participation of China in the neoliberal global economy raised hopes that it, too, would gradually transform into a Western-like nation-state espousing the key principles of liberal international order, namely, the rule of law, free trade, multiculturalism, democracy, and human rights. Following the breakup of the Soviet Union, Russia was expected to democratize and liberalize to become a responsible stakeholder in the liberal international order. While embracing the Westphalian and certain neoliberal economic principles of global order, both Moscow and Beijing have eschewed liberal humanism that elevated the rights of individuals against their governments. American-led military humanitarianism have shaped Beijing's and Moscow's conviction that Washington has been seeking to weaken, if not overturn, the incompatible political systems, like China's communist government and Russia's authoritarian regime. Russia has views Western humanitarianism as a rhetorical disguise for a strategy of global influence and control over illiberal governments.[50] It has been rattled by human rights conditionalities and expectations of democratic reform and vetoed resolutions proposing sanctions or military action against authoritarian regimes in the UN Security Council on this basis. Both China and Russia have viewed the liberal international order as beneficial to the US but inimical to their interests and incompatible with their foundational ideas.

For Chinese leadership, who believes that economic underdevelopment is a key to global problems, the 2008 global financial crisis was another turning point. According to Beijing, the 2008 financial crisis, which originated in the "core of the capitalist world, the US,"[51] has led not only to economic and political stresses, but also damaged America's soft power by exposing the flaws of the system that Washington has built in its own image. The 2008 global economic downturn has also shifted the asymmetry of the US–China relations in favor of Beijing. As China's share of global economy and military has grown, it has become more vocal about its intent to revise the global order to make it more conducive to Beijing's interests.[52] This process has accelerated under the

---

50   Shi Jiangtao, "China Blames 'Aggressive US Wars' for Humanitarian Disasters around the World as It Hits Back at Criticism of Human Rights Record," *South China Morning Post*, April 9, 2021, https://www.scmp.com/news/china/diplomacy/article/3128982/china-blames-aggressive-us-wars-humanitarian-disasters-around.

51   Daniel Tobin, "How Xi Jinping's 'New Era' Should Have Ended U.S. Debate on Beijing's Ambitions," Testimony before the U.S.-China Economic and Security Review Commission, March 13, 2020, https://www.csis.org/analysis/how-xi-jinpings-new-era-should-have-ended-us-debate-beijings-ambitions.

52   Mira Rapp-Hooper, Michael S. Chase, Matake Kamiya, Shin Kawashima and Yuichi Hosoya. "Responding to China's Complicated Views on International Order," Carnegie

leadership of Xi Jinping, China's most powerful leader since Mao Zedong. First selected to become General Secretary of the CCP in 2012 and, then, the President of PRC in 2013, Xi Jinping declared that Beijing would "lead the reform of the global governance system" seeking to reshape international institutions and norms in ways that reflect China's own values and priorities.[53] With the Chinese-led geo-economic projects, such as the Belt and Road Initiative (BRI) and the Asian Infrastructure Investment Bank (AIIB), and new frameworks offering conceptual links between China and the world, Beijing's leadership has avowed to "push the reform of the unjust and unreasonable arrangements in global governance system" and offer alternative approaches to peace and development for other countries to emulate.[54] Far from being egalitarian, the Chinese alternative to global governance mimics a system of "hierarchical harmony" practiced at home and centers on China's global power and virtues.[55]

Humanitarian sector has become one area where Beijing and Moscow have ventured to improve their ability to project soft power to complement their emerging roles on the international scene and undermine the US leadership in the process. Under President Xi Jinping, China has considerably increased its support to countries experiencing natural disasters and become more actively involved in the humanitarian action in conflict settings.[56] Conceived in a different historical setting and rooted in a set of different foundational ideas, China's (and Russia's) approach to humanitarian aid has differed from those of the US and other traditional donors. Such differences have elevated concerns that China's and Russia's greater engagement in the humanitarian realm challenges the dominant humanitarian regime and threatens the foundations of the broader global order and US power standing. This contestation over the principles and norms informing approaches to humanitarian assistance and confrontation over the normative foundations and institutional infrastructure of the global regime has become a new driver in the US, Chinese, and Russian decisions about aid allocations.

Endowment for International Peace, 2019, https://carnegieendowment.org/files/China RiskOpportunity-Chinas_Complicated_Views.pdf.

53   Kevin Rudd, "Xi Jinping's Vision for Global Governance," *Foreign Affairs*, October 10, 2022, https://www.foreignaffairs.com/china/world-according-xi-jinping-china-ideologue -kevin-rudd.

54   Yun Sun, "China's Aid to Africa: Monster or Messiah?" The Brookings Institution, February 7, 2014, https://www.brookings.edu/opinions/chinas-aid-to-africa-monster-or-messiah/.

55   John Agnew, "Emerging China and Critical Geopolitics."

56   Lina Gong, "Humanitarian Diplomacy as an Instrument for China's Image-Building," *Asian Journal of Comparative Politics* 6, no. 3 (2021): 238–252.

To sum up, states' motives for humanitarian assistance are grounded in historically and culturally contingent ideas, which get tested by practical experiences with aid resulting in a complex and evolving logic of aid-related decisions. The US reasoning about humanitarian assistance has been constitutive of the political rationality of liberalism.[57] Confronted with the challenges of the Cold War era, novel threats in the post-Cold War period, and shifts in global power relations, the US has allowed strategic objectives and economic concerns to pollute humanitarian obligations. Both China and Russia have attached ethical weight to the state and state sovereignty, which had significant practical implications for their decisions about humanitarian aid. For Beijing, economic development has been regarded a chief pillar of state legitimacy. Domestic economic growth in China has been tethered to economic development in the global realm. According to this thinking, development assistance and humanitarian aid are the tools in the larger foreign policy toolkit that serves domestic economic interests by contributing to peace and prosperity abroad. Finally, Russia has placed a higher premium on projecting and defending its identity of a great power state. Humanitarian aid has become another means for Moscow to convey its great power self-image and pursue its interests abroad.

The shift in the distribution of global power has provided an opportunity to challenge principles of the dominant humanitarian regime buttressed by the material power of the US and other traditional donors. Both China and Russia have used this opportunity to alter or weaken the norms and institutions of global governance that they believe benefit the US. Concerned with China's and Russia's challenge to the global order and humanitarian regime, the US has sought to counter their influence military, economically, and through increased public diplomacy and humanitarianism. This normative and power contestation at the global level has added a reactionary dynamic to the states' decision-making processes about humanitarian aid by linking aid allocations to competitors' moves and decisions.

---

57   Daniel Laqua, "Inside the Humanitarian Cloud."

China's COVID-19 Humanitarianism: an Aid Model Rooted in the State-Centered Logic of Development Assistance

The turn of the 21st century was marked by China's meteoric rise in the field of foreign assistance. The outbreak of the COVID-19 pandemic generated further diplomatic pressure on Beijing creating an unexpected momentum for the elevation of humanitarian aid in China's strategy. The Chinese Communist Party's leadership initiated the largest global humanitarian effort in the country's history and used this opportunity to levy claims to China's leadership in the global health governance at a time of the perceived American retrenchment. Beijing's remarkable transition from an aid recipient to a major donor has become one of the most visible and widely discussed changes in the global development and humanitarian realms. Increased political scrutiny has been accompanied by concerns that the growing engagement of China in the provision of humanitarian and developmental aid will fundamentally change the character of global aid architecture consistent with the Sino-centric views of the world espoused by China's leader Xi Jinping and members of his political elite.

Taking inspiration from the deconstructive emphasis of critical geopolitics, this chapter probes the conceptual foundations of China's foreign aid, which are shaped by the dynamic and intersubjective processes of interactions between the physical (geographical) and imaginary (aspirational) worlds. The chapter begins with an overview of China's rising profile in the humanitarian field followed by conceptual mapping of its geopolitical logic underlying Beijing's decisions about humanitarian assistance. We develop these ideas and principles into testable expectations for China's COVID-19 aid allocations. The chapter discusses the levels, types, and administration channels of China's coronavirus aid and systematically examines its motivations for assistance. All in all, China's COVID-19 aid has become part of its broader vision of global health closely tethered to its approach to development. China has perceived a casual linkage between the lack of development and various humanitarian crises and viewed development assistance as a key component of the long-term solutions to humanitarian emergencies. In Beijing's logic of assistance, its contributions to developmental causes create a "win-win" situation for co-prosperity of China and the recipients of its aid. By investing in global development, peace, and resilience to humanitarian disasters, Beijing sees itself as contributing to economic growth and stability at home. Reversely, China's own economic prosperity and harmony at home is believed to be essential for global development and peace.

1   Background on China's Humanitarianism

In April 2005, the United Nations' World Food Programme (WFP), one of the leading global humanitarian agencies, delivered the final cargo of food to China. The shipment marked the end of a 25-year-long $1-billion UN aid program for Beijing designed to assist in alleviating hunger and malnourishment in the country.[1] The same year it stopped receiving aid from the WFP, China emerged as the world's third largest food donor contributing 577,000 tons of food to the WFP in 2005.[2] The PRC's transition from recipient to donor of humanitarian aid began on a small scale but quickly accelerated turning Beijing into one of the largest non-DAC contributors of emergency relief assistance (see Figure 1).

The size and scope of China's humanitarian assistance are still difficult to decipher. For historical, political, and ideological reasons, Beijing refrains from calling its donations "foreign aid." According to the Chinese government, the donor-recipient language symbolizes hierarchical and unequal power relations that harken back to the post-colonial period during which capitalist states used aid as a pretext for exploiting developing countries.[3] Beijing describes its aid as mutually beneficial two-way exchanges and "South-South cooperation" in economic, scientific, technological, educational, and cultural fields, and lumps assistance together with concessional loans, trade, and investments.[4] Beijing

---

1   United Nations News, "China Emerges as World's Third Largest Food Aid Donor, UN Agency Says," July 20, 2006, https://news.un.org/en/story/2006/07/186362-china-emerges-worlds-third-largest-food-aid-donor-un-agency-says.

2   Zhao Huanxin, "China Emerges as Major Food Donor," *China Daily*, July 21, 2007, https://www.chinadaily.com.cn/china/2006-07/21/content_645844.htm.

3   Miwa Hirono, "Three Legacies of Humanitarianism in China," *Disasters* 37 (2013), p. S208; Miwa Hirono, "Exploring the Links between Chinese Foreign Policy and Humanitarian Action," HPG Working Paper (London: Humanitarian Policy Group, 2018); The State Council of the People's Republic of China, "China's Foreign Aid," 2011, http://english.www.gov.cn/archive/white_paper/2014/09/09/content_281474986284620.htm.

4   W. He, "China's Aid to Africa: Views on Chinese Aid and Trade in Africa," in *Challenging the Aid Paradigm: Western Currents and Asian Alternatives*, edited by Jen Stilhoff Sörensen (London: Palgrave Macmillan, 2010), p. 147. China's first white paper on foreign aid (released in April 2011) clearly stated that "Chinese foreign aid belongs to South–South cooperation and the mutual assistance between developing countries" (The State Council of the People's

eschews reporting its levels of development assistance to the OECD-DAC and similar accounting mechanisms, and withholds information on its humanitarian spending from the United Nation's Financial Tracking Service (FTS). The variance in definitions and approaches to aid, coupled with the limited and haphazard disclosure of aid amounts by China,[5] makes it challenging to assess the scope of its foreign aid and differentiate development and humanitarian assistance.[6]

Even allowing for these limitations, the available data suggests rapid growth in China's humanitarian contributions in the two decades preceding the COVID-19 pandemic (see Figure 1). In 2000–2009, China's average annual humanitarian contributions were $9.48 million. During the next ten years, the average annual humanitarian contributions were $43.8 million, a nearly 5-fold increase, not counting the cost of deploying China's international search and rescue teams during the same period.[7] Notwithstanding rapid growth in China's humanitarian spending, its disaster relief had not caught up with its GDP growth, which increased by nearly 10% every year from 2004 to 2015. The pace of emergency relief contributions has also trailed behind increases in China's net development aid, which increased, on average, 24 percent every year from 2004 to 2011.[8]

Republic of China, "China's Foreign Aid"; Denghua Zhang, *A Cautious New Approach* (ANU Press, 2020), p. 6).

5   Until 2018, there were several dozen ministerial-level agencies involved in China's aid management (Zhang, *A Cautious New Approach*, p. 8).

6   The Chinese discourse has occasionally distinguished humanitarian assistance (*rendao zhuyi yuanzhu*) from the broader concept of assistance in disaster areas (*jiuzai*). The former involves short-term provision of food, goods, materials and personnel to countries or regions suffering severe natural or humanitarian disasters, while the latter includes not only emergency relief but also domestic and international reconstruction effort (Hirono, "Exploring the Links between Chinese Foreign Policy and Humanitarian Action"; Information Office, "China's Peaceful Development," *China's Cabinet*, 2011, http://english1.english .gov.cn/official/2011-09/06/content_1941354.htm; Denghua Zhang, "Positive Disruption? China's Humanitarian Aid, (Humanitarian Horizons Practice Paper Series, December, 2019), https://www.icvanetwork.org/uploads/2021/09/Positive-Disruption_-Chinas-Humanitarian -Aid-December-2019.pdf).

7   China's International Search and Rescue (CISAR) team was created in April 2001. Since its first international mission, in response to the earthquake in Algeria in May 2003, the team has been deployed to disaster responses in Iran, Pakistan, Indonesia, Haiti, New Zealand, Japan, and Nepal, among others (Hirono, "Exploring the Links between Chinese Foreign Policy and Humanitarian Action").

8   Naohiro Kitano and Yumiko Miyabayashi, "Estimating China's Foreign Aid 2001–2013, JICA-Research Institute Working Paper: Comparative Study on Development Cooperation Strategies: Focusing on G20," *Emerging Economies*, no. 78, 2014, https://www.jica.go.jp/Resource/jica -ri/publication/workingpaper/jrft3q00000025no-att/JICA-RI_WP_No.78_2014.pdf;   Naohiro

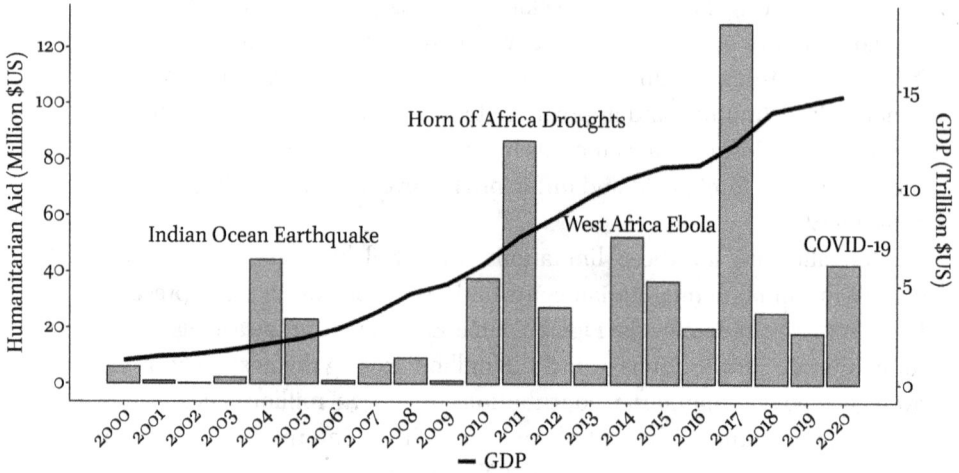

FIGURE 1   China's humanitarian spending and GDP, 2000–2020
SOURCES: UNOCHA FTS (HTTPS://FTS.UNOCHA.ORG); THE WORLD BANK (HTTPS://DATA
.WORLDBANK.ORG/INDICATOR/NY.GDP.MKTP.CD?LOCATIONS=CN)

In support of its growing humanitarian involvement, China developed a sprawling institutional architecture for international emergency relief with the involvement of key national ministries, including the Ministry of Commerce, Ministry of Foreign Affairs, and Ministry of Finance. The Chinese People's Liberation Army (PLA) and China's International Search-and-Rescue Team (CISAR) have also expanded their involvement in humanitarian assistance and disaster relief missions overseas.[9] In 2018, the Chinese government consolidated its diverse foreign aid programs in the new International Development Agency (CIDCA) that replaced an inter-agency liaison mechanism coordinating aid initiatives of over 40 agencies. Overseen by the State Council, CIDCA has signaled a notable shift in the Chinese aid system. The institutional reform gives greater weight to diplomacy under the auspices of the Ministry

Kitano, Naohiro, and Yumiko Miyabayashi, "Estimating China's Foreign Aid: 2019–2020 Preliinary Figures," JICA Ogata Sadako Research Institute for Peace and Development, 2020, https://www.jica.go.jp/Resource/jica-ri/publication/other/l75nbgooo01900pq-att/Estimating-Chinas_Foreign_Aid_2019-2020.pdf.

9   Peng Lin, "China's Evolving Humanitarian Diplomacy: Evidence from China's Disaster-Related Aid to Nepal," *Asian Journal of Comparative Politics* 6, no. 3 (2021): 221–237; Matthew Southerland, *The Chinese Military's Role in Overseas Humanitarian Assistance and Disaster Relief: Contributions and Concerns* (US-China Economic and Security Review Commission, 2019); Zhang, "Positive Disruption?".

of Foreign Affairs in the aid system, previously dominated by the Ministry of Commerce.[10]

The growing importance of humanitarian aid in China's foreign policy and diplomatic affairs coincided with the rise of Xi Jinping as China's paramount leader since 2012. President Xi elevated the normative and ideological aspects of foreign aid and humanitarian assistance in PRC's foreign policy declaring aid a moral obligation of China as a rising great power.[11] While recognizing that mutually beneficial and "win-win" aid packages serve Chinese national interests, President Xi, nevertheless, has avowed that China would "refrain from seeking interests at the expense of justice."[12] Many scholars and observers of Chinese foreign policy have dismissed these appeals as a rhetorical cover-up for PRC's geopolitical objectives ranging from access to the markets of raw materials to feed the growth of its slowing economy to rewriting the rules of global order in Asia and beyond. China has been charged with exploiting the tools of foreign aid for courting aid recipients, projecting its favorable image, and altering aid practices to suit the national interests of Beijing.[13]

Yet, looking at Beijing's humanitarian aid through the binary logic of pragmatic versus normative motives has several limitations. The normative reasoning stipulates a moral obligation to supply humanitarian aid to people in need. However, it does not explain how the Chinese government makes

---

10   Zhang, *A Cautious New Approach*, pp. 246–247.

11   Denghua Zhang and Y. Huang, "Zhongguo he xifang zai duiwai yuanzhu linian shang de chaiyixing bianxi [Analysis of different aid conceptions between China and the West]," *Contemporary International Relations*, 2 (2012): 41–47; H. Zhou, "Zhongguo yuanwai liushinian de huigu yu zhanwang [Look back and look forward: Sixty years of China's foreign aid]," *Foreign Affair Review*, 5 (2010): 3–11. The term "responsible state" had been a prominent feature of Chinese foreign policy discourse and analysis even before Xi's ascent to power (for further discussion, see Hirono, "Exploring the Links between Chinese Foreign Policy and Humanitarian Action").

12   See, for example, Ministry of Foreign Affairs of the People's Republic of China, "Xi Jinping Delivers Important Speech at UN Sustainable Development Summit, Stressing to Realize Common Development of All Countries from New Starting Point of Post-2015 Development Agenda," 2015, http://lt.china-office.gov.cn/eng/zt/UN/201512/t20151219 _2910425.htm; Xinhua Net, "Xi Jinping Attended the Central Foreign Affairs Work Conference and Delivered an Important Speech," 2014, http://www.xinhuanet.com//politics /2014-11/29/c_1113457723.htm.

13   See, for example, Anne-Marie Brady, *Looking North, Looking South: China, Taiwan and the South Pacific*, Vol. 26 (Singapore, Malaysia: World Scientific Pub. Co. Inc., 2010); John Henderson and Benjamin Reilly, "Dragon in Paradise: China's Rising Star in Oceania," *The National Interest* 72 (2003): 94–105; Thomas Lum and Bruce Vaughn, "The Southwest Pacific: US Interests and China's Growing Influence," (Library of Congress Washington, D.C.: Congressional Research Service, 2007).

determination about which lives of people in need are worth saving through the supply of aid when demand for disaster relief exceeds the supply and resources available for humanitarian assistance. The track record of China's humanitarian allocations also appears to be more ad hoc than the interest-based explanations would suggest. In some years, Beijing's humanitarian allocations have been consistent with aid contributions of traditional donors. For example, consistent with the global humanitarian trends, China prioritized earthquake-struck Haiti and Pakistan affected by disastrous floods in its humanitarian aid in 2010. In 2014, China and traditional donors prioritized humanitarian assistance to countries in West Africa fighting an Ebola outbreak (see Table 2). In other periods, China's disaster relief aid has departed from the global funding trends. In contravention of "One China" policy, Beijing has sent humanitarian aid to a handful of countries maintaining diplomatic relations with Taiwan. It became the largest contributor of peacekeeping troops

TABLE 2   Top recipients of China's humanitarian aid compared to the top recipients of the global humanitarian aid

2020
China's total funding: $42.6 million
1. WHO COVID assistance (62.1%)
2. Tropical Cyclone Idai in Zimbabwe (10.3%)
3. COVID assistance to Libya (8.8%)
4. COVID assistance to DRC (5.6%)
5. COVID assistance to Cameroon (5.3%)

Global humanitarian spending: $27.89 billion
1. Food security (21.8%)
2. Health (10.3%)
3. Syria (9.5%)
4. Yemen (8.0%)
5. Lebanon (5.7%)

2017
China's total funding: $128.6 million
1. Kenya (20.8%)
2. Ethiopia (16.3%)
3. South Sudan (15.2%)
4. Somalia (10.1%)

2011
China's total funding: $86.9 million
1. Ethiopia (26.8%)
2. Kenya (23.2%)
3. World Food Programme (19.6%)
4. Djibouti (10.7%)
5. Cambodia (9%)

Global humanitarian spending: $13.65 billion
1. Somalia (10.2%)
2. Sudan (6.9%)
3. Afghanistan (6.6%)
4. Ethiopia (6.0%)

2010
China's total funding: $37.6 million
1. Pakistan (47.3%)
2. Haiti (30.5%)
3. Chile (5.3%)

TABLE 2   Top recipients of China's humanitarian aid compared to the top recipients (*cont.*)

Global humanitarian spending: $21.74 billion
1. Syria (11.5%)
2. Yemen (11.3%)
3. South Sudan (7.1%)
4. Iraq (6.9%)

Global humanitarian spending: $16.04 billion
1. Haiti (22.4%)
2. Pakistan (20.1%)
3. Sudan (8.7%)

2014
Total funding: $55.2 million
1. Ebola in West Africa (85.2%)
2. Typhoon Halyan in the Philippines (3.3%)

2004
Total funding: $44.2 million
1. North Korea (22.9%)
2. Sri Lanka (15.4)
3. UN Food & Agriculture Organization (10%)

Global Humanitarian Spending: $21.73 billion
1. Global Health (including fight with Ebola) (22.3%)
2. Syria (9.4%)
3. South Sudan (8.4%)

Global Humanitarian Spending: $4.62 billion
1. Sudan (22%)
2. Palestine (6.6%)
3. North Korea (6.5%)
4. The Democratic Republic of the Congo (5%)

SOURCE: FINANCIAL TRACKING SERVICE OF THE UN OFFICE FOR COORDINATION OF HUMANITARIAN AFFAIRS (HTTPS://FTS.UNOCHA.ORG/HOME/2023/DONORS/VIEW)

among the five permanent members of the United Nations Security Council, and the second largest financial contributor to the UN peacekeeping budget.[14]

To decipher China's motives for humanitarian aid, we have traced its own thinking about the roots of obligations in aiding other countries. China has developed its own approach to humanitarian assistance informed by a long history of dealing with natural disasters,[15] China's own experience as an aid

---

14   Andrew Garwood-Gowers, "China's 'Responsible Protection' Concept: Reinterpreting the Responsibility to Protect (R2P) and Military Intervention for Humanitarian Purposes," *Asian Journal of International Law* 6, no. 1 (2016): 89–118; Richard Gowan, "China's pragmatic approach to UN peacekeeping," (The Brookings Institution, September 14, 2020), https://www.brookings.edu/articles/chinas-pragmatic-approach-to-un-peacekeeping/; Richard Salmons, "Disaster Relief, International Status and Regional Order: A Case Study of Typhoon Haiyan," *Global Change, Peace & Security* 31, no. 3 (2019): 283–301.
15   Due to its geographical location, China is prone to natural disasters – typhoons, tsunamis, floods, earthquakes, and droughts.

recipient, and a degree of pragmatism of Chinese leadership in using select historiographies of Beijing for rationalizing its approach humanitarian assistance. The politically and historically bound principles of humanitarian aid have provided the intellectual footing for the unique geopolitical logic that shaped China's decisions in the provision of the COVID-19 aid.

2   Elements of China's Geopolitical Logic about Humanitarian Assistance

China's principles of humanitarian assistance have been remarkably consistent over its long history of aid, despite the persistent and unresolved ambiguity in Chinese leadership's ideology about their country's unique place in the world.[16] Upon its entry into the humanitarian assistance space, Beijing has repurposed some of the same ideas buttressing its involvement in the development assistance to guide its engagement in the disaster relief field. Articulated by China's first premier Zhou Enlai in 1964,[17] these foundational ideas include a state-centric approach to assistance, which translates into the avowed respect for the recipient states' political sovereignty and commitment to non-interference in their domestic affairs. This also includes a belief in development and humanitarian aid being mutually reinforcing, and a focus on high-yield in-kind humanitarian projects that bring mutual benefit for China and recipient states. Strategically linking its aid focus to its own development practices and experiences with humanitarian disasters has enabled China to promote its state-centric development logic informing its humanitarian assistance as a rival to the neoliberal economic development agenda and Western framework for humanitarian aid.

2.1   State-Centric Humanitarianism
Compared to the DAC-centered humanitarian system that integrates diverse actors ranging from states to international organizations, civil society groups, and private businesses, China's humanitarian project pivots around the state. The state-centric logic of Chinese humanitarian aid is manifested in the predominantly government-to-government channel of bi-lateral assistance

---

16   John Agnew, "Emerging China and Critical Geopolitics: Between World Politics and Chinese Particularity," *Eurasian Geography and Economics* 51, no. 5 (2010): 569–582.

17   Zhou Enlai, "China's Eight Principles for Economic Aid and Technical Assistance to Other Countries," 1964, http://www.china.org.cn/government/whitepaper/2011-04/21/content _22411843.htm.

delivered based on a request by, and agreement with, a recipient state.[18] In recent years, Beijing has forged deeper partnerships with international organizations[19] and allowed private enterprises' involvement in the provision of emergency relief aid. Still, the government of China and the Chinese Red Cross, which is recognized as a government-organized non-governmental organization (GONGO), are the main providers of Chinese humanitarian assistance. Chinese civil society groups are limited in their ability to partake in disaster relief activities outside China. Even within the Chinese territory, the state maintains strict control over disaster relief and assistance by non-state actors.[20]

The ideas of state-centric humanitarianism are shrouded in Chinese mythology and Confucian tradition, and bolstered by socialist and communist interpretations of the relationships between individual, society, and state.[21] Due to its geographic location, China has experienced frequent natural disasters - floods, earthquakes, plagues, and droughts. The state has traditionally played a key role in dealing with these calamities. In fact, the Great Flood dated to the third millennium BC and the heroic attempts of Chinese rulers to control it is one of the foundational events in the Chinese mythology. The successful disaster management by a leading character – Yu – propelled him to the Emperorship leading to the establishment of the Xia dynasty in China.[22] The legacy of Yu and state in disaster management has endured in Chinese history and can still be found in popular myths and folklore. One of the Chinese proverbs, for example, reads, "those who govern water also govern the world."[23]

The state-centric nature of Chinese humanitarianism has been reinforced through interpretations of the classics of Confucian and Taoist traditions, and

---

18   Hirono, "Three Legacies of Humanitarianism in China."
19   Hirono, "Exploring the Links between Chinese Foreign Policy and Humanitarian Action"; Lin, "China's Evolving Humanitarian Diplomacy". The 2004 Indian Ocean tsunami became a watershed moment in China's engagement with multilateral humanitarian initiatives (Sisira Jayasuriya and Peter McCawley, "The Asian Tsunami Aid and Reconstruction After a Disaster," (Asian Development Bank Institute and Edward Elgar Publishing, 2004); Richard Salmons, "Disaster Relief." Beijing's increased participation in humanitarian disasters was marked by its involvement in the 2005 South Asian earthquake, the 2010 Haiti earthquake, the 2011 Libya refugee crisis; food insecurity in Africa in 2011–2012; the 2012 Syria refugee crisis, and the 2014 West Africa Ebola epidemic, among others. China has begun making consistent, albeit insignificant, donation to the Central Emergency Response Fund under the OCHA (Lin, "China's Evolving Humanitarian Diplomacy").
20   Hirono, "Three Legacies of Humanitarianism in China."
21   Hirono, "Three Legacies of Humanitarianism in China."
22   Lihui Yang, Deming An, and Jessica Anderson Turner, *Handbook of Chinese Mythology* (Abc-clio, 2005).
23   Hirono, "Three Legacies of Humanitarianism in China."

ideas expressed in Marxism-Maoism. Confucianism, for example, advocates that the ruler should put people first by taking care of the population in times of disasters and crises. The purpose of doing so, however, is to consolidate his rule believed to be necessary for unity of the Chinese territory, known as Tianxia ("all under heaven"). This premise of unity and a sole political authority has remained an unquestioned ideological pillar of state-centric governance (centered in the emperor or Communist party).[24] In this way, the Chinese Confucian tradition reinforces the primary role of a well-ordered state in dealing with disasters.[25] The establishment of communism in the PRC further solidified the preeminence of the state in aid. The Marxist-Leninist-Mao Zedong thinking regarded humans as political subjects who were afforded their rights by the state in accordance with their socio-economic class. Contrary to the Western liberal philosophy that ascribes human beings with a final moral value, Chinese political philosophy deems the state as the primary moral agent. State involvement in humanitarian crises furnishes its action with legitimacy.[26]

It is important to underscore that in China's cosmology of the state, state is imagined in both material (geographic) and ethical (ideological) terms. State power is construed as both moral and material because it stems from the possession of virtue. The premise of unity of duty and power in a sole political authority has become the ideological basis of the Chinese empire and remained unquestioned for centuries. China's geo-imagery of the state does not conceive of any other power hierarchy but the one that vests all power in the state represented by the all-powerful (omnipotent) ruler.[27]

An important implication of China's state-centric logic of humanitarianism is the politicization of humanitarian assistance. According to Chinese thinkers, the infusion of politics into decisions about foreign aid is not an aberration but an inherent (prudent and virtuous) feature of assistance. The state, by definition, is a political actor. The central role of the state in humanitarian aid makes politics integral to China's humanitarian project. Humanitarian aid has been viewed as one of the many foreign policy tools leveraged in support of China's economic development that is regarded as an essential function of the state and a key to its flourishment and preservation.

---

24   Daniel Lemus Delgado and Jose Jesus Bravo Vergara, "Geopolitics, Real and Imagined Spaces: China and Foreign Policy in the Context of East Asia," *International Journal of China Studies* Vol. 8, No. 3 (2017): 397–421.

25   Sarah Teitt, "Atrocity or Calamity?" (Cultures of Humanitarianism: Perspectives from the Asia-Pacific Project, 2013), https://www.nottingham.ac.uk/iaps/documents/project/teitt.pdf.

26   Teitt, "Atrocity or Calamity?"

27   Delgado and Vergara, "Geopolitics, Real and Imagined Spaces."

A second implication of state-centric humanitarianism is a humanitarian policy that centers on the principle of non-interference and respect for state sovereignty. For the Chinese government, respect for an affected country's political sovereignty, territorial integrity and national unity is the declared basis for legitimate humanitarian action.[28] Because sovereignty assumes such a central place in China's humanitarian imaginations, there is limited room for humanitarian intervention or emergency assistance in conflicts where the governments, themselves, may be responsible for keeping "complex emergencies" alive. From an operational standpoint, respect for state sovereignty translates into Beijing's preferences for bilateral (government-to-government) assistance based on the host country's requests or an official acceptance of assistance.[29] It is important to note that non-interference is construed narrowly in Chinese thinking as limited to politics, and revolving around the issues of regime, corruption, accountability, and governance. As discussed in greater detail below, China's foreign aid has strong economic conditionality with many of its development assistance projects tied to investments and trade in Chinese goods.[30]

2.2 *Interdependence of Humanitarian Aid and Development Assistance*

In China's conception of foreign aid, humanitarian assistance is inextricably linked to development assistance. As succinctly expressed by China's Deputy Representative to the United Nations Wu Haitao, development is a "fundamental solution" to most of the global problem and needs.[31] Speaking at the UN General Assembly on 8 December 2017, the Chinese diplomat maintained that "helping developing countries realize development represents the

---

28   Liselotte Odgaard, *China and Co-Existence: Beijing's National Security Strategy for the Twenty-First Century* (Washington, D.C.: Woodrow Wilson Centre Press, 2012); Aglaya Snetkov and Marc Lanteigne, "'The Loud Dissenter and its Cautious Partner' – Russia, China, Global Governance and Humanitarian Intervention," *International Relations of the Asia-Pacific* 15, no. 1 (2015):113–146.

29   Ashley Kim Stewart and Xing Li, "Beyond Debating the Differences: China's Aid and Trade in Africa," in *China-Africa Relations in an Era of Great Transformations*, edited by Li Xing and Abdulkadir Osman Farah (Ashgate, 2013), pp. 23–48.

30   Hirono, "Three Legacies of Humanitarianism in China"; Yun Sun, "China's Aid to Africa: Monster or Messiah?" (The Brookings Institution, February 7, 2014), https://www.brookings .edu/opinions/chinas-aid-to-africa-monster-or-messiah/.

31   Haitao Wu, "Statement by Ambassador Wu Haitao at the 71st Session of the UN General Assembly on Agenda Item 69: Strengthening of the Coordination of Humanitarian and Disaster Relief Assistance of the United Nations, Including Special Economic Assistance," December 8, 2016, http://www.china-un.org/eng/chinaandun/economicdevelopment /humanitarian/t1422694.htm.

fundamental way to reduce the need for humanitarian relief."[32] Development, therefore, has been viewed as a tool for addressing humanitarian issues, while humanitarian aid has been seen as a method for building state capacity to deal with disasters. Given the tight relationship between humanitarian aid and development in China's geopolitical logic, to better understand humanitarian aid requires a closer consideration of China's experiences with and views on development and development assistance.

Following its independence in 1949, the People's Republic of China became politically and economically isolated by the US and other Western nations who recognized the Republic of China (Taiwan) at the UN. The Sino-Soviet split caused by the divergent interpretations and practical applications of Marxism-Leninism resulted in the withdrawal of Soviet aid from China and heightened competition between the PRC and Soviet Union over the leadership of communist world.[33] Yet, China's drive to diminish and contain the influence of hegemonic powers – the US and the USSR – around the world was restrained by its limited capabilities. The lack of the "economic muscle" prevented Beijing from carrying out an effective diplomatic and economic offensive against "hegemonism."[34]

To end decades of isolation and economic stagnation and carve out the deserved place for China in the world, then-leader Deng Xiaoping launched Reform and Opening Up policy in 1978 that ushered in a new era of spectacular economic growth in China. Domestic economic development became the top priority for the CCP that built its legitimacy on a promise of the continued economic growth in exchange for public support of its dominant position at home.[35] At the heart of what became known as the "China model" of development was rapid capital accumulation – the growth in the country's capital assets, such as new industrial enterprises, transportation and communication systems, and manufacturing industries.[36] China's accession to the World Trade Organization induced further domestic reforms and economic liberalization laying the framework for Beijing's deeper integration into the global economy and enabling it to dramatically expand its global share of trade. By 2010, China

---

32   Wu, "Statement by Ambassador Wu Haitao."

33   Lorenz Lüthi, *The Sino-Soviet Split: Cold War in the Communist World* (Princeton University Press, 2008).

34   Marcus Power and Giles Mohan, "Towards a Critical Geopolitics of China's Engagement with African Development," *Geopolitics* 15, no. 3 (2010): 462–495.

35   Roy Wye, "China's Leadership Transition," in *Charting China's Future: Domestic and International Challenges*, edited by D.L. Shambaugh (New York, NY: Routledge, 2011), pp. 22–32.

36   Zuliu Hu and Mohsin S. Khan, "Why Is China Growing So Fast?" (International Monetary Fund, June 1997), https://www.imf.org/EXTERNAL/PUBS/FT/ISSUES8/INDEX.HTM.

became the world's undisputed export champion, and its investments and loans supplanted grants in the structure of foreign assistance.[37]

Suffice it to say that the singularity and coherence of the so-called "Chinese model" of development has been overstated. The term has been deployed to describe an approach to development in China (which has been offered as a template for other countries to emulate), a model of development applied toward other developing countries (an alternative to the "Washington Consensus"), and a framework for development cooperation with other international actors.[38] Recognizing contradictions and variations in what has been known as the "Chinese model," it is possible to single out several elements of the Chinese approach to development that are relevant for understanding its logic of humanitarian assistance. First, China's model of development is not about aid. Instead, it encompasses a wide range of state-backed commercial engagements, including investments in large infrastructural projects and loans on preferential terms. Second, coupled with the liberalization of trade and investments, relaxation of state regulations, and education of the workforce, it features the blend of state control and ownership of critical resources with economic activities dominated by private businesses."[39]

Many of these elements of China's approach to development were reinforced in the wake of the 2008 financial crisis. To soften the impact of the global economic downturn, the Chinese government boosted public investments in a wide array of large-scale infrastructure projects to spike up demand for state-owned heavy industry. The artificially created state-backed industrial growth at home prompted the Chinese government under the leadership of Xi Jinping to export these experiences in the construction and infrastructure sectors abroad. Chinese public and private firms scaled up their overseas operations in what became known as the Belt and Road Initiative (BRI).[40] A signature project of President Xi who unveiled it in 2013, the BRI was envisioned

37   Alessandro Nicito and Carlos Razo, "China: The Rise of a Trade Titan," (UNCTAD, April 27, 2001), https://unctad.org/news/china-rise-trade-titan; Jiantuo Yu and Evan Due, "Mutual Learning in Development Cooperation: China and the West," *IDS Bulletin* 52, no. 2 (2021): 19–36.

38   Power and Mohan, "Towards a Critical Geopolitics of China's Engagement with African Development."

39   Wayne M. Morrison, *China's Economic Rise: History, Trends, Challenges, and Implications for the United States* (Washington, DC: Congressional Research Service, 2019), https://sgp.fas.org/crs/row/RL33534.pdf.

40   Seth Schindler and Jessica DiCarlo, 2022. "Towards a Critical Geopolitics of China – US Rivalry: Pericentricity, Regional Conflicts and Transnational Connections," *Area* 54, no. 4 (2022): 638–645; see also David M. Lampton, Selina Ho and Cheng-Chwee Kuik, *Rivers of Iron: Railroads and Chinese Power in Southeast Asia* (University of California Press,

as a series of terrestrial and maritime corridors for trade, development, and investment initiatives radiating outwards from China to East Asia, Europe, Africa, and Latin America.[41] Seen by many analysts and participating countries as a display of unsettling extension of China's power, the BRI has become an umbrella strategy for ongoing activity of Chinese public and private companies abroad relying on the "commerce-is-development" approach in an effort to create an expanded global market for China and protect it from the influence of the US.[42] In this way, a model of development applied at home has been translated into China's foreign realm.[43] The "commerce-is-development"[44] approach has led to the merger of trade and investment deals with foreign aid blurring the line between economic interchanges and development and humanitarian assistance. The roll-out of the BRI has coincided with increased humanitarian spending by China in countries along the BRI route vulnerable to natural hazards and internal conflicts. Consistent with Chinese views on interdependence of development and humanitarian aid, Beijing's economic stakes in BRI-participating countries have stimulated China's greater participation in humanitarian response in these territories.[45]

2020); Min Ye, *The Belt Road and Beyond: State-Mobilized Globalization in China, 1998–2018* (Cambridge University Press, 2020).

41 Leah Lynch, Sharon Andersen, and Tianyu Zhu, "China's Foreign Aid: A Primer for Recipient Countries, Donors, and Aid Providers," (Center for Global Development, July 9, 2020), https://www.cgdev.org/publication/chinas-foreign-aid-primer-recipient-countries -donors-and-aid-providers.

42 Yu Jie and Jon Wallace, "China's Belt and Road Initiative (BRI)," The Chatham House (September 13, 2021), https://www.chathamhouse.org/2021/09/what-chinas-belt-and-road -initiative-bri.

43 Jaewoo Choo, "Ideas Matter: China's Peaceful Rise," *Asia Europe Journal* 7, no. 3 (2009): 389–404. This unity of thinking about domestic and foreign policy was articulated by President Hu Jintao (2005) in a series of speeches to the Chinese and foreign audiences in 2004–2005 where he expounded on ideas of building a "harmonious world" with lasting peace and common prosperity after Chinese experience with "harmonious society" at home (Hu Jintao, "Build Toward a Harmonious World of Lasting Peace and Common Prosperity," Statement by H.E. Hu Jintao, President of the People's Republic of China. [Translation]. New York, September 15, 2005, https://www.un.org/webcast/summit2005 /statements15/china050915eng.pdf; See also Xiaoxiong Yi, "Chinese Foreign Policy in Transition: Understanding China's Peaceful Development," *The Journal of East Asian Affairs* (2005): 74–112; Zhang, *A Cautious New Approach*).

44 Jusin Yifu Lin and Yan Wang, *Going Beyond Aid: Development Cooperation for Structural Transformation* (Cambridge University Press, 2017).

45 Lina Gong, "The Belt and Road Initiative: Vehicle for China's Humanitarian Action?" (Policy Report. Nanyang Technological University, Singapore, 2021), https://www.rsis .edu.sg/wp-content/uploads/2021/06/PR210628_The-Belt-and-Road-Initiative-Vehicle -for-China's-Humanitarian-Action_V2.pdf.

2.3 *"Mutual Interest" as a Principle and Operational Signpost for Assistance*

"Mutual interest" has been another pillar in China's logic for foreign assistance articulated in numerous official documents and statements by China's leaders. Conceptually, the idea of "mutually beneficial" assistance is linked to the Chinese understanding of development, whereby development assistance furnished by Beijing contributes to global prosperity and peace, and global development furthers China's own economic growth. Prosperity is viewed as a prerequisite for China's "peaceful" global rise, and as a necessary condition for maintaining the Communist regime's legitimacy at home.[46] In short, China's own and foreign development are in a "win-win" relationship enhancing co-prosperity from which everyone profits. According to this thinking, development assistance and humanitarian aid are the tools in the larger foreign policy toolkit that serve domestic economic interests by contributing to peace and prosperity abroad.

Operationally, "mutually beneficial" Chinese foreign aid has been tied to the provision of material (in-kind) donations of Chinese machinery, equipment, labor, and concessional loans often tethered to the purchase of materials from China. The PRC first provided foreign aid to the North Korea and Vietnam in the early 1950s, but quickly extended it to other countries in South and Southeast Asia and Sub-Saharan Africa. The aid came in the form of transfers of materials, provision of labor, reconstruction and building of plants, technology transfers, and the education of specialists and students.[47] China's first Premier Zhou Enlai who named "mutual benefit" the guiding principle of Chinese aid in 1956 linked it to the Soviet aid model, in which China was a recipient of assistance. The Soviets tied their loans to the purchase of commodities and materials from the USSR, which also sent its technical experts to operate the Soviet machinery and the military to work on the infrastructural projects funded by the USSR.[48] These experiences shaped China's own approach to aid. In the late 1950s, the PRC began providing aid in the form of complete "turnkey" projects, in which it managed all aspects of a project - from the budget and design to machinery and workers. The majority of these "turnkey" projects were large infrastructure development ventures as the Chinese government believed that investments

---

46   Andreas Fuchs and Marina Rudyak, "The Motives of China's Foreign Aid," in *Handbook on the International Political Economy of China* (Edward Elgar Publishing, 2019), pp. 391–410.

47   Salvador Santino F. Regilme, Jr. and Obert Hodzi, "Comparing US and Chinese Foreign Aid in the Era of Rising Powers," *The International Spectator* 56, no. 2 (2021): 114–131.

48   Fuchs and Rudyak, "The Motives of China's Foreign Aid."

in infrastructure were essential for economic growth and building capacity of the recipient states.[49]

Despite its embrace of foreign aid as an essential foreign policy tool, the PRC has always had limited resources for assistance. With insufficient funds to compete with the US or the Soviet Union during the Cold war era, the PRC chose to invest in the high-yield and headlines-worthy initiatives that benefitted China economically and raised its international prestige. The Tanzania-Zambia Railway (TAZARA) Construction Project, for example, was the largest single-item project financed and executed by the Chinese government, which significantly raised international prestige of the PRC among the African nations in the 1970s-1980s. High-profile sports stadiums, conference halls, and friendship palaces have also been a common feature of the PRC's aid programs.[50] This principle of mutually beneficial assistance remains to this day manifested in the use of Chinese-manufactured equipment, material, labor, and technical assistance on highly visible development support and humanitarian projects.

2.4   *Humanitarianism and Great Power Competition*

China's decisions about humanitarian aid can't be understood without considering a broader context of international relations, in which these decisions are made, including the distribution of power that underpins structures, meanings, norms, and institutions of global governance. From its inception, China's foreign aid had an anti-Western tint. In the 1950s, Beijing assisted other socialist and developing countries to build a united front against the West and, later, the Soviet Union. China's foreign aid was used to countervail the Western humanitarian assistance regarded as a tool of imperialists and "bourgeoisie" "seeking merciless exploitation and oppression" of the working people.[51]

Following the opening of China to the world with Deng Xiaoping's Reform and Opening Up policy, China's aid became less ideologically-driven but it retained a distaste for the Western humanitarian norms and democratization initiatives advocated by the US and European donors. The Chinese anti-Western sentiment was matched by corresponding hostility of Western countries toward Beijing caused by the deplorable human rights record of Beijing that was revealed by the 1989 Tiananmen incident.[52] As China's confidence swelled bolstered by the weight of its economy and military, it began

---

49   Hirono, "Three Legacies of Humanitarianism in China"; Information Office, "China's Peaceful Development."

50   OECD, *The Aid Programme of China* (Paris: OECD Publishing, 1987).

51   Hirono, "Three Legacies of Humanitarianism in China," p. S208.

52   Hirono, "Exploring the Links between Chinese Foreign Policy and Humanitarian Action."

jostling against the norms and institutions of the liberal international order that Beijing deemed threatening to its political system and constraining its "peaceful evolution."[53]

This process of contestation of US-led global order accelerated under President Xi who has called for greater Chinese leadership in global affairs. The conceptual architecture of the world advanced by politicians and ideologues in Beijing takes China's historical experiences, or rather its leadership's renditions of history, as a reference point from which the government has defined Beijing's role in global affairs.[54] While there are several alternative readings of China's history including those maintaining that China's development cannot be understood apart from the external environment and China's relations with other states, including the US, the Chinese government led by Xi Jinping has appropriated a Sinocentric world vision rooted in the Chinese imperial history. This historical account depicts China as a Central Kingdom constituting the core of Tianxia (the realm under heaven or "all under heaven").[55]

A new concept of the "community of common destiny for mankind" promulgated by Xi has been elevated to a modern-day derivative of the Sinocentric world vision.[56] While this worldview has been wrapped in the language of harmony, peace, inclusivity, and respect for differences, the "community of common destiny" is not an egalitarian vision. Instead, it perpetuates a system of hierarchical harmony, in which each state assumes a specific role that corresponds to its positioning in the hierarchical ordering of state relations. According to this logic of thinking, China has been predestined to hold a unique position due to its self-image as a Central Kingdom and virtues located in China. In this conception, the world order reflecting the achievements and character of the Chinese civilization is both a political and ethical phenomenon. From the Chinese leadership's standpoint, China's rise on the global scene simply manifests the reclaiming of the privileged position that China has

---

53 Xi Jinping's speech at the Communist Party of China's 19th National Congress (Daniel Tobin, "How Xi Jinping's 'New Era' Should Have Ended U.S. Debate on Beijing's Ambitions," Testimony before the U.S.-China Economic and Security Review Commission, March 13, 2020. https://www.csis.org/analysis/how-xi-jinpings-new-era-should-have-ended-us-debate-beijings-ambitions).

54 Chih Yuan Woon, "China's Contingencies: Critical Geopolitics, Chinese Exceptionalism and the Uses of History," *Geopolitics* 23, no. 1 (2018): 67–95.

55 Li Dalong, 2008. "'The Central Kingdom' and 'the Realm Under Heaven' Coming to Mean the Same: The Process of the Formation of Territory in Ancient China," *Frontiers in History of China* 3, no. 3 (2008): 323–352.

56 Xi did not coin the term but the Chinese media credit him for introducing and promoting the concept to the global audiences (Tobin "How Xi Jinping's 'New Era' Should Have Ended U.S. Debate on Beijing's Ambitions," pp. 39–40).

aspired to and enjoyed throughout its history.[57] Frequently articulated in President Xi's speeches to international audiences, these assertions signal a "change in the historical consciousness of Chinese leaders as they have become more willing to celebrate the glories of imperial China to boost national pride and redefine China's [(re)emerging] position in the world."[58]

Suffice it to say that the CCP has embraced the "community of common destiny for mankind" as China's brand for foreign affairs. The new concept promotes global economic development as a chief solution for global problems. The BRI, which seeks to build "policy, infrastructure, trade, financial, and people-to-people connectivity," has become the main vehicle for implementing China's new concept for global order.[59] The infrastructure component of BRI has been augmented with a cyber component ("The Digital Silk Road") and space assets. With the addition of the "Health Silk Road" to the BRI, Beijing has extended a debate over the best approaches to global governance and the validity of competing development models to the humanitarian regime and health sector. With its COVID-19 aid, China has followed a model of humanitarian assistance and an approach to global health rooted in the Sinocentric approach to global affairs that Beijing deems to be best suited to deal with humanitarian challenges in the post-COVID world.

To summarize, China's humanitarian assistance has been informed by the ideas of state as a chief moral agent and final authority for foreign aid. Decisions about humanitarian aid have been embedded in Chinese thinking about the mutually beneficial economic development and assistance. The state-centric position on humanitarian assistance has spun off the principles of respect for state-sovereignty and political non-interference in aid administration. State centrism combined with beliefs in development as the main pillar of state sovereignty and legitimacy has contributed to the transformation of aid into a foreign policy tool for attaining prosperity at home. The principle of mutually beneficial assistance has fathered projects yielding quick results and involving the provision of Chinese materials, equipment, personnel, and technical assistance.[60] Chinese aid has also challenged the dominant liberal development and humanitarian agenda of the United States

57   Delgado and Vergara, "Geopolitics, Real and Imagined Spaces."

58   Suisheng Zhao, "Rethinking the Chinese World Order: The Imperial Cycle and the Rise of China", *Journal of Contemporary China* 24, no. 96 (2015): 961- 982.

59   Ministry of the Foreign Affairs of the People's Republic of China, "Building an Open, Inclusive and Interconnected World for Common Development," Keynote Speech by H.E. Xi Jinping (October 18, 2023), https://www.fmprc.gov.cn/mfa_eng/zxxx_662805/202310/t20231018 _11162854.html.

60   Fuchs and Rudyak, "The Motives of China's Foreign Aid."

As discussed in greater detail below, Beijing's COVID-19 aid has followed a similar pattern of mostly bi-lateral (state-to-state) in-kind assistance involving the transfer of Chinese medical supplies and equipment, and the dispatch of Chinese doctors and other medical personnel. China's COVID-19 aid, and vaccine allocations have also trailed its development assistance. Furthermore, China's decisions about coronavirus aid have evinced an element of competition with the United States in that the patterns of Beijing's assistance have been correlated with the patterns of Washington's foreign aid.

3   Where Did China Send Its COVID-19 Aid and Why

By our accounts, China delivered $759.8 million worth of COVID-19 aid (the lowest estimate) in mostly bi-lateral, state-to-state assistance in 2020.[61] Of the total amount, $111.05 million or 15.6% was in private donations. In addition, it delivered or committed $195.4 million in total contributions to the World Health Organization, with most of the funding dedicated to the WHO's fight with the global COVID-19 crisis.[62]

China's aid has reached over 151 countries and 14 international organizations (see Map 1.).[63] As the world's largest manufacturer of medical protective equipment, China prioritized the delivery of medical supplies, mainly masks and PPE (gloves, face shields, protective suits, etc.) as well as test kits, thermometers, and ventilators. The second category of China's COVID-19 aid involved sharing its experience and expertise in COVID-19 control and prevention as well as testing, diagnosis, and treatment, including by sending teams of civilian or military medical personnel.

Most COVID-19 donations were announced by the Chinese Ministry of Foreign Affairs and delivered through its channels. However, the Ministry of Defense and People's Liberation Army (PLA) have also delivered medical supplies to no less than 46 countries in Southeast Asia, Sub-Saharan Africa, and the Middle East.[64] Another notable feature of Chinese aid patterns was the high level of involvement of municipalities in the delivery of COVID-19 aid based

---

61   On the high end, our estimate is considerably higher – $11.5 billion, including 1.26 billion in private donations.

62   World Health Organization, "Contributors," (2021), http://open.who.int/2020-21/contributors/contributor?name=China.

63   See also Xinhua Net, "China Provides Anti-Epidemic Assistance to 151 Countries: White Paper," (2021), http://www.xinhuanet.com/english/2021-06/24/c_1310025458.htm.

64   Matthew Southerland, *The Chinese Military's Role in Overseas Humanitarian Assistance and Disaster Relief.*

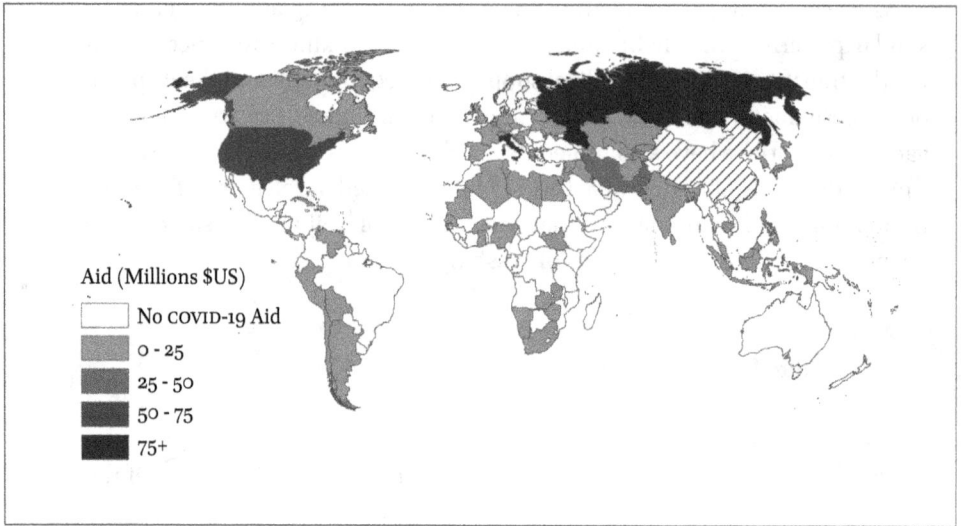

MAP 1   China's COVID-19 aid allocations

on the twin-cities agreements and cooperative partnerships in trade, investments, and tourism.[65] A few examples demonstrate the depth and breadth of
ties between China's provinces and towns with municipalities of other countries. Guangxi Autonomous Region sent a medical team to Cambodia in March
2020 in support of the existing cooperative agreement.[66] A sister-city relationship between Tai'an (Shandong Province) and Francistown (Botswana) paved
the way for multiple donations by China's Shandong Province to Botswana.[67]
China's northwest Gansu province donated medical supplies to Zimbabwe
in a transfer birthed through the twinning agreement between Mashonaland

---

65   Andreas Fuchs, Kaplan Lennart, Kis-Katos Krisztina, Sebastian S. Schmidt, and Turbanisch
       Felix, "China Sent Masks, Gloves and Gowns to Many U.S. States. Here's Who Bene-
       fited," *Washington Post* (January 29, 2021), https://www.washingtonpost.com/politics
       /2021/01/29/china-sent-masks-gloves-gowns-many-us-states-heres-who-benefited/;
       Diego Telias and Francisco Urdínez, "China's Foreign Aid Determinants: Lessons from a
       Novel Dataset of the Mask Diplomacy During the COVID-19 Pandemic," *Journal of Current
       Chines Affairs* 51, no. 1 (2021): 108–136.
66   Xinhua Net, "Cambodia, China's Guangxi Pledge to Broaden Cooperation," (June 13, 2013),
       http://news.xinhuanet.com/english/china/2013-06/13/c_132453081.htm.
67   Embassy of the People's Republic of China in the Republic of Botswana, "China's Shan-
       dong Province Donates Anti-Pandemic Materials to Botswana," 2020, http://bw.china
       -embassy.gov.cn/eng/xwdt/index_1.htm.

West and Gansu Provinces signed in 2004,[68] and Jiangsu province sent medical donations to New York.[69]

The observed trend in the private COVID-19 donations shows the growing importance of the Jack Ma Foundation, a philanthropic company established by the Chinese business magnate Jack Ma in 2014 with the goal of supporting projects in the areas of education, entrepreneurship, environmental protection, and women's leadership. The Jack Ma Foundation along with the Alibaba Foundation and the Joe and Clara Tsai Foundation accounted for nearly three-quarters of all private COVID-19 donations from China. Huawei – a Chinese tech giant at the heart of the international controversy with China's expanding global footprint in 5G technology and equipment – has also contributed COVID-19 aid, but on a significantly lesser scale. In March 2020, Huawei scaled back its donation program following remarks by the EU's Foreign Chief Josep Borrell accusing the tech giant in the "politics of generosity."[70] Striving to stay out of the "global battle of narratives," Huawei put an end to its mask donations in Europe, but continued delivering PPE and tech devices for medical personnel to multiple countries in Latin America, Africa, and Canada.[71] It has also promoted and delivered multiple packages of new artificial intelligence diagnostic systems and thermal scanning systems to detect COVID-19 through computerized tomography images using Huawei Cloud platform.[72] Finally, there were a small number of Chinese civil society groups, chambers of commerce, and enterprises that have made individual and collective small-scale donations. All this reflect the growing complexity of the humanitarian aid system in China and the difficulties in tracking hundreds of donations made to countries around the world in a short period of time.

Looking at the disaggregated patterns of aid at the national level, the top 10 recipients of official COVID-19 assistance included a diverse group of countries from all regions of the world - Italy, Russia, Pakistan, Iran, Kuwait, UK, Egypt,

---

68   National Health Commission of the People's Republic of China, "China Committed to Facilitating Equitable Vaccine Distribution Globally," 2021, http://en.nhc.gov.cn/2021-06 /24/c_83960.htm.

69   Fuchs, et al., "China Sent Masks, Gloves and Gowns to Many U.S. States."

70   Samuel Stolton, "Huawei to 'Scale Down' Supply of COVID-19 Masks, after Borrell Comments," EURACTIV (March 26, 2020), https://www.euractiv.com/section/digital/news /no-more-coronavirus-masks-from-us-huawei-says/.

71   Telias and Urdínez, "China's Foreign Aid Determinants."

72   Huawei, "Fighting COVID-19 with Technology," 2020, https://activity.huaweicloud.com /intl/en-us/fight-covid-19.html; Huawei, "Huawei's Cloud and Artificial Intelligence Solution to Boost SA's COVID-19 Fight," (2020), https://www.huawei.com/za/news/za /2020/huaweis-cloud-and-artificial-intelligence--solution-to-boost-sas-covid-19-fight.

COVID-19 Aid (Million SUS)

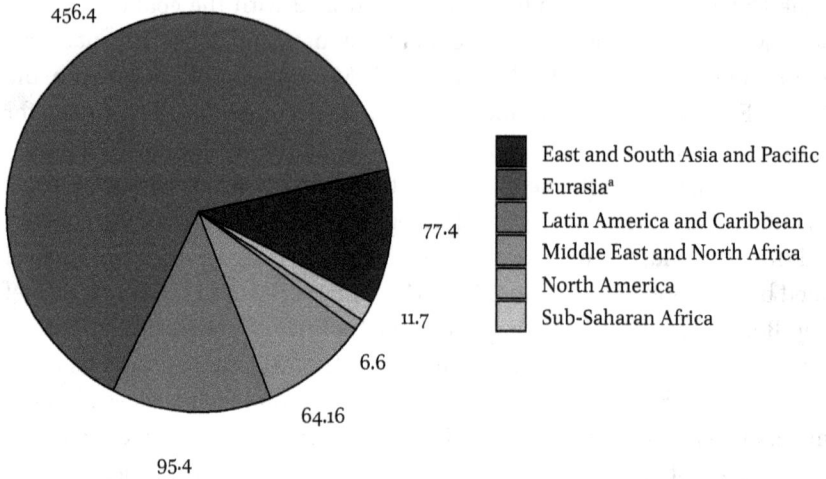

FIGURE 2   Regional distribution of China's COVID-19 assistance
[a]Eurasia includes all countries in Europe in addition to Russia and Central Asia.

Serbia, Czech Republic, and Venezuela. The fact that Russia, Iran, and Venezuela were among the largest recipients of aid from China is not surprising (see Figure 2.).[73] These three countries are under US sanctions and embargoes, and all are vocal in their anti-American positions. Both Venezuela and Iran have experienced humanitarian emergencies due to economic crises exacerbated by COVID-19. Overall, though, Eurasia, which includes all countries on the European continent, Russia, and the Central Asian republics, accounted for 64 percent of China's global aid. Latin America and the Caribbean was a distant second with 13.4 percent of COVID-19 aid. South and East Asia accounted for 11 percent of China's coronavirus assistance, MENA – 9 percent, Africa – 1.6 percent and North America - 1.6 percent. Certainty, it is not merely the quantity but also the types of assistance provided by China that matter. Some countries, such as Myanmar and Laos, received military medical teams from the

73   Looking at the high-end estimates, the relative distribution of aid across regions stays the same but the volumes are considerably higher: Eurasia – $7.6 billion; Latin America and Caribbean – $1.98 billion; East and South Asia – $982.8 million; Sub-Saharan Africa – $331.45 million; MENA – $1.13 billion; North America – $6.6 million.

PLA. Beijing sent teams of civilian medics to others. In some cases, military teams have brought unspecified amounts of military supplies and equipment.[74]

The preliminary observations on China's COVID-19 allocations comport with several elements of its geopolitical logic that have informed its foreign aid. First, China continues prioritizing a state-centric and bilateral approach, which has limited its engagement with the broader humanitarian community, despite its involvement in the WHO and other international humanitarian organizations. Beijing has favored the delivery of contextually important and China-manufactured materials and resources, such as medical aid, equipment, and supplies. And, all aid transfers have been accompanied with information fanfare. China's Ministry of Foreign Affairs, SCIO (State Council Information Office) and websites of private companies advertised China's contributions to helping other countries fight COVID-19 and highlighted the gratitude these states have expressed to Beijing for assistance.[75]

4 Statistical Analysis of China's COVID-19 Assistance

Decisions about humanitarian aid allocations encompass two distinct stages.[76] During the first "selection" stage, a donor decides which countries will receive aid, and which ones will be bypassed. In the second "outcome" stage, a donor makes decisions about the amount of aid that will be allocated to countries identified as aid recipients in the first round. Consistent with this decision-making pattern, we tested the determinants of China's COVID-19 allocations in two stages. In the "selection" stage, the dependent variable is whether the COVID-afflicted country received any coronavirus aid from Beijing. It is a binary (yes/no) measure with "1" assigned to those countries, which received any amount of COVID-19 aid from China, and "0" otherwise. In the second "outcome" stage, the dependent variable is the total amount of

---

74　Lye Liang Fook, "China's COVID-19 Assistance to Southeast Asia: Uninterrupted Aid Amid Global Uncertainties," *Perspective* 58 (June 2020): 1–13.

75　Jabin T. Jacob, "'To Tell China's Story Wel;': China's International Messaging during the COVID-19 Pandemic," *China Report* 56, no. 3 (2020): 374–392.

76　See, for example, Constantine Boussalis and Caryn Peiffer, "Health, Need and Politics: the Determinants of Bilateral HIV/AIDS Assistance," *Journal of Development Studies* 47, no. 12 (2011): 1798–1825; Rob Kevlihan, Karl DeRouen Jr. and Glen Biglaiser, "Is US Humanitarian Aid Based Primarily on Need or Self-Interest?" *International Studies Quarterly* 58, no. 4 (2014): 839–854.

coronavirus aid allocated by China (in US dollars) if the country was selected to receive coronavirus assistance.

Using a LexisUni news search and announcements posted by China's Ministry of Foreign Affairs, we identified COVID-19 aid transfers by Chinese entities to countries around the world. Only aid deliveries (rather than aid requests and promises of future aid) were included. All non-monetary aid transfers were converted into dollars using market prices in 2020. Since prices on medical supplies and equipment varied, we created a price bracket with the lowest and highest known market price for each type of medical equipment and supplies. Then, we calculated the total volumes of the COVID-19 assistance in 2020 US dollars based on these price brackets of market values of medical supplies. The findings of analyses performed on the lowest estimates are reported in this chapter.

Our main expectation is that China's COVID-19 aid allocations follow the patterns of its development decisions and, therefore, trail Chinese investments, development assistance and trade. Therefore, our statistical analysis includes measures of China's trade and development assistance allocations to countries in the previous years (see Table 3). We have also created two

TABLE 3   Independent and control variables used in the analysis of China's COVID-19
            assistance

Independent and control variables	Definition	Source
BRI	Countries that have signed a MOU on the BRI with China are coded "1," and all other COW countries are coded "0"	Lynch, Andersen, and Zhu 2020.
CIDCA	Countries that have signed agreement with China's International Development Cooperation Agency (CIDCA) in 2018–2019 are coded "1" and all others are coded "0"	Lynch, Andersen, and Zhu 2020.
Trade Balance (2014–2019)	An average trade balance (exports minus imports) for 2014–2019	United Nations Statistics Division 2020.
Development Assistance	The total amount of known foreign aid provided by China bilaterally between 2000 and 2014 in USD	Dreher, Fuchs, Parks, Strange, and Tierney 2022.

TABLE 3   Independent and control variables in China's COVID-19 assistance (*cont.*)

Independent and control variables	Definition	Source
Hospital Beds	Hospital beds per 1,000 people, most recent year available since 2010	Appel, et al. 2020.
Recognition of Taiwan	An ordinal measure denoting whether a country recognizes Taiwan (coded "3"), has non-diplomatic relations with Taiwan (coded "2"), and "1" otherwise	Coded based on online sources.
Total COVID-19 Deaths	The number of reported deaths in a country as of June 30, 2020, per million population	The Center for Systems Science and Engineering at Johns Hopkins University 2020.
Membership in Alliances	The recorded number of alliances that a country has with China. Countries with no recorded alliances are coded "0"	Leeds et al. 2002.
Distance to Capital	A measure of distance from the donor capital to the capital of the recipient country (in km)	Gleditsch and Ward 2001.
Liberal Democracy	A composite index that measures the extent to what an ideal liberal democracy is achieved in the country (0–1 scale)	Coppedge et. al., 2021.
GDP per Capita	Per capita values for gross domestic product (GDP) expressed in millions of current international dollars (for 2019) converted by purchasing power	World Bank 2019.
Population	Total population	United Nations Population Division 2019.
US COVID-19 Assistance	A binary measure of whether a country received any COVID-19 assistance from the US	Data collected by the authors

variables to measure Beijing's development-trade-investments patterns. *BRI* is a dichotomous measure denoting countries that have signed a memorandum of understanding (MOU) on the BRI with China (coded "1," and "0" otherwise). *CIDCA* is another binary measure that stands for countries that have signed agreements with China's International Development Cooperation Agency (CIDCA) in 2018–2019.

To examine the extent to which China's assistance is responsive to the needs of the countries fraught with the health crisis, we used the total number of deaths due to COVID-19 as a measure of the severity of the pandemic's effects.[77] Socioeconomic background and countries' "absorbing" capacity that condition decisions about the aid allocations are measured by a country's GDP and population.

To test whether China follows the principle of political non-interference in aid allocations, we controlled for the recipient countries' political regime. We also included several control variables, which can potentially influence Beijing's decisions concerning the selection of aid recipients and volumes of aid allocated to them. To test whether the Chinese government rewards countries that adhere to its "One China" policy with aid, we created an ordinal scale with countries recognizing Taiwan coded "3"; countries that have non-diplomatic relations with Taiwan short of official recognition were coded "2", and "1" otherwise. We also created an additional variable – Xinjiang2019 – that denotes countries' support for or opposition to the UN Human Rights Council's condemnation of Chinese practices in Xinjiang. Among other control variables was a measure of the membership in an alliance in China (including nonaggression pacts or a treaty containing a stipulation of nonaggression).[78] Proximity of recipient states was measured by distance from the donor's capital to the country's capital (in km).[79] Table 3 contains a full list of independent and control variables

---

77   The scholarship on humanitarian assistance typically measures the "need" for aid by the number of fatalities or the number of people affected by a disaster. The half-year total deaths estimate due to COVID-19 (as of 1 July 2020) was used in the study.

78   Brett Ashely Leeds, Jeffrey M. Ritter, Sara McLaughlin Mitchell, and Andrew G. Long, "Alliance Treaty Obligations and Provisions, 1815–1944," *International Interactions* 28 (2002): 237–260. http://www.atopdata.org/data.html.

79   Kristian S. Gleditsch and Michael D. Ward, "Measuring Space: A Minimum-Distance Database and Applications to International Studies," *Journal of Peace Research* 38, no. 6 (2001): 739–758.

4.1   *Humanitarian Donations Follow the Development Trail*

Table 4 contains the results of two separate models testing China's motivations for choosing the recipients of its COVID-19 aid as well as decisions about the volume of aid allocations.[80] Models 1 and 2 use "One China" variable among predictors of China's COVID-19 aid allocations, while Models 3 and 4 integrate the "Xinjiang2019" variable as an alternative measure China's foreign policy.

TABLE 4   China's COVID-19 aid allocations

	(1) Selection stage	(2) Outcome stage	(3) Selection stage	(4) Outcome stage
BRI	1.45**	3.38**	1.19*	2.59*
	(0.66)	(1.547)	(0.663)	(1.49)
CIDCA	1.102*	3.075	0.800	2.27
	(0.616)	(1.924)	(0.697)	(1.88)
Trade Balance (logged)	-0.015	0.0012	-0.007	0.0001
	(0.035)	(0.11)	(0.037)	(0.111)
Development Assistance	-0.052	-0.928	-0.033	-0.041
	(0.037)	(0.105)	(0.036)	(0.099)
Hospital Beds (per thousand)	0.384**	0.982***	0.237	0.689**
	(0.167)	(0.294)	(0.155)	(0.307)
Recognition of Taiwan	-1.042*	-1.77		
	(0.581)	(1.30)		
Xinjiang Issue			-1.005	-2.966**
			(0.649)	(0.110)
COVID-19 Deaths (per million)	0.004**	0.015***	0.0039**	0.137***
	(0.0017)	(0.005)	(0.0018)	(0.005)
Membership in Alliances	0.261	0.927	0.078	0.728
	(0.402)	(1.27)	(0.408)	(1.19)
Distance to Capital	-0.0005	-0.0002	-0.0001*	-0.004
	(0.00007)	(0.0002)	(0.0000)	(0.0002)

80   We opted for a separate logistic regression for the first "selection" stage, and ordinary least squares with robust standard errors for the second "outcome" stage instead of the better theoretically suited Heckman's (1979) two-step estimator, which allows for correlation of the error terms of the two decisions at hand. The Heckman model generates a Wald test statistic. When significant, it indicates that the two models are not independent and must be solved together. In our case, the Wald test statistic was insignificant.

TABLE 4   China's COVID-19 aid allocations (*cont.*)

	(1) Selection stage	(2) Outcome stage	(3) Selection stage	(4) Outcome stage
Liberal Democracy	1.718	2.95	2.553	6.59*
	(1.22)	(3.3)	(1.607)	(3.86)
GDP, PPP in 2019 (logged)	-0.123	-0.293	0.245	0.645*
	(0.113)	(0.423)	(0.161)	(0.371)
Total Population (logged)	0.75***	1.72***	0.403**	0.965**
	(0.216)	(0.502)	(0.201)	(0.461)
US COVID-19 Assistance	1.23*	2.963	1.74**	3.59*
	(0.746)	(1.815)	(0.821)	(1.89)
Constant	-12.95***	-23.029**	-10.254***	-16.859*
	(3.9)	(10.294)	(3.345)	(9.196)
N	140	140	134	134
LRchi2(9) / F(13)	41.67	11.74	40.07	13.84
Prob > chi2 / Prob > F	0.00	0.00	0.00	0.00
[Pseudo] R-squared	0.29	0.34	0.31	0.37

Note: Robust errors in parentheses

* $p < 0.1$, ** $p < 0.05$, *** $p < 0.01$

The strongest relationship that emerged from the statistical analysis of China's COVID-19 assistance is between Beijing's signature development projects and its humanitarian aid. Countries that are part of Beijing's BRI and which signed economic partnership agreements with China's International Development Cooperation Agency were significantly more likely to be selected as recipients of COVID-19 aid. Those same countries received significantly higher volumes of the COVID-19 assistance, although only the BRI coefficient reached a conventional level of statistical significance ($p < 0.05$).[81]

Chinese authorities have stressed that foreign aid, including humanitarian assistance, was an integral part of development and BRI cooperation. Health has been on the BRI agenda since 2015 when Chinese leadership added international cooperation in preventing and containing epidemics among the main

---

81   This conclusion is consistent with the findings of Gong's study (Gong, "The Belt and Road Initiative: Vehicle for China's Humanitarian Action").

objectives of the BRI.[82] It is not surprising, therefore, that Chinese officials portrayed their fight against COVID-19 through the provision of aid as an effort to build the "Health Silk Road," an offshoot of the BRI. This idea was succinctly expressed by China's Foreign Minister Wang Yi who affirmed Beijing's stalwart commitment to strengthening "solidarity with countries along the Belt and Road" and jointly marching "on the 'Health Silk Road' through concerted efforts to combat the epidemic."[83] The approach comports with Beijing's intellectual underpinnings of humanitarian aid, whose goal is to shore up investments in development. Together with development assistance, humanitarian aid is designed to foster an environment conducive to China's economic interests and its pursuit of global ambitions.[84]

The ties of China's COVID-19 aid to its development assistance are stronger than Beijing's trade relations with its recipient states. The balance of trade between China and recipient countries returned statistically insignificant coefficients in our models. One of the reasons for this finding might have to do with the nature of Chinese development assistance, which bundles trade and joint ventures with concessional loans, investments, and aid. The BRI and CIDCA measures capture these bundles of "aid-trade-investments" implemented based on these agreements better than the more refined measures of imports, exports, and total trade.

It could also be that the relationship between aid and trade is reverse, i.e., aid may serve as a tool for opening new foreign markets to Chinese products and businesses. Some scholars noted that the "aid for trade" model was piloted in the 1990s in China.[85] Beijing's largest companies – China Railway Engineering Corporation, China Railway Construction, CRBC, CCECC, CNPC, and others – were able to enter developing countries' markets in great measure

---

82   Moritz Rudolf, "China's Health Diplomacy during Covid-19: the Belt and Road Initiative (BRI) in Action," SWP Comment, no. 9 (2021), https://www.swp-berlin.org/publications/products/comments/2021C09_ChinaHealthDiplomacy.pdf.

83   Stella Chen, "Community of Common Destiny for Mankind," China Media Project (August 25, 2021), https://chinamediaproject.org/the_ccp_dictionary/community-of-common-destiny-for-mankind/.

84   China's COVID-19 assistance has also allowed it to emphasize friendly ties and gloss over negative perceptions of BRI by the recipient states (Jacob Kurtzer, "China's Humanitarian Aid: Cooperation Amid Competition," Center for Strategic and International Studies (2020), https://www.csis.org/analysis/chinas-humanitarian-aid-cooperation-amidst-competition).

85   Fuchs and Rudyak, "The Motives of China's Foreign Aid"; Yasutami Shimomura and Wang Ping, "The Evolution of 'Aid, Investment, Trade Synthesis' in China and Japan," in *The Rise of Asian Donors: Japan's Impact on the Evolution of Emerging Donors*, edited by Jin Sato and Yasutami Shimomura (Abington, UK: Routledge, 2012), pp. 114–132.

due to foreign aid.[86] Some preliminary data have emerged showing that Beijing has successfully bolstered its economic and diplomatic influence in countries, which received its medical assistance.[87] However, many of the countries, which signed new investment and trade deals with Beijing, had already had substantial or strong relationships with China even before the pandemic. Whether China's provision of COVID-19 aid allowed it to make significant inroads in countries where it did not already have significant influence is yet to be seen.

4.2 *Sending Assistance to Countries Where It Promises Highest Return*

Another strong relationship that emerged from our analysis of the data on Chinese COVID-19 aid allocations is that between the number of hospital beds per 1,000 people, which we proxied for a recipient states' capacity to absorb and successfully deploy COVID-19 assistance, and COVID-19 assistance. The Chinese government has justified its decision on aid volumes by the principle of "aid within capacity" or "aid within means." With lesser humanitarian aid at its disposal, China has always sought to invest the scarce resources into the highest-yield projects. The relationship that we found between the hospital beds and mostly in-kind assistance in medical supplies and materials is largely consistent with the described trend. Countries with the greatest capacity to utilize the medical assistance have received the largest volumes of Chinese COVID-19 aid.

A variant of the "highest yield on aid" explanation may have to do with the fact that long before the COVID-19 pandemic, China had sent medical personnel to many countries, especially in Africa but also in Asia and Latin America.[88] According to the Chinese Ministry of Foreign Affairs, over the last 60 years, Beijing had sent a total of 23,000 medical team members to Africa alone. In 2021, there were nearly 1,000 Chinese medical workers in 45 African countries.[89] Chinese medics have treated the general public but also political leaders and their family members, which helped Beijing to project its "soft power" and attain desired foreign policy objectives.[90] How do hospital beds fit into this narrative? Countries with the greater number of hospital beds per

---

86   Fuchs and Rudyak, "The Motives of China's Foreign Aid."

87   China Power, "Is China's COVID-19 Diplomacy Succeeding?" (2021), https://chinapower
      .csis.org/china-covid-medical-vaccine-diplomacy/.

88   Yanzhong Huang, "Pursuing Health as Foreign Policy: the Case of China," *Indiana Journal
      of Global Legal Studies* 17, no. 1 (2010): 105–146.

89   Ministry of Foreign Affairs of the People's Republic of China, "China and Africa in the
      New Era: A Partnership of Equals," 2021, https://www.fmprc.gov.cn/mfa_eng/wjdt_665385
      /2649_665393/202111/t20211126_10453904.html.

90   Huang, "Pursuing Health as Foreign Policy."

capita are more likely to have Chinese personnel working in those medical facilities. Beijing have always had a strong preference for its own laborers – workers, technicians, and medics – working on the projects funded through development and humanitarian aid. The same preference for Chinese medical personnel in the country may explain higher volumes of COVID-19 aid in the countries with higher number of hospital beds.

4.3 *COVID-19 Aid to Reward Supporters of China's Politics*

We have also looked separately at two prominent issues in China's foreign policy, namely, "One-China" policy and human rights of the Uyghur minority in the Xinjiang province. The Chinese government has used aid to goad states with diplomatic relations with Taiwan to recognize the PRC, while other countries have used the Taiwan issue as a bargaining chip for getting more aid from both Beijing and Taipei.[91] In recent years, the inhumane treatment of Uyghurs in the Xinjiang province – what some governments called "the Uyghur genocide" – has caused a huge consternation for China's image and broader foreign policy. Throughout 2020, the Trump administration debated whether it should formally label China's brutal repression of the Uyghurs' rights, including through the use of internment camps and forced labor, a "genocide."[92] The State Department's declaration accusing the Chinese government in crimes against humanity and genocide against a Muslim minority in Xinjiang was made on President Trump's final day in office and was followed by a series of sanctions imposed on China by the Biden cabinet.[93]

The "One China" variable that measures other countries' support for the One-China policy is both negative and significant in the selection model. This means that Beijing was less likely to choose countries recognizing Taiwan or having diplomatic relations with Taiwan as recipients of its COVID-19 assistance. Although in the expected direction, the One-China variable is insignificant in the outcome model, meaning that it played lesser, if any role, in

---

91 Fergus Hanson, *The Dragon Looks South* (Sydney: Lowy Institute for International Policy, 2008); Kevin D. Stringer, "Pacific Island Microstates: Pawns or Players in Pacific Rim Diplomacy?" *Diplomacy and Statecraft* 17, no. 3 (2006): 547–577; Jian Yang, "China in the South Pacific: Hegemon on the Horizon?" *The Pacific Review* 22, no. 2 (2009): 139–158.

92 Daniel Lippman and Nahal Toosi, "Trump Administration Weighs Accusing China of 'Genocide' Over Uighurs," *Politico* (August 15, 2020), https://www.politico.com/news/2020/08/25/trump-administration-china-genocide-uighurs-401581.

93 Humeyra Pamuk and David Brunnstrom, "In Parting Shot, Trump Administration Accuses China of 'Genocide' Against Uighurs," *Reuters*, January 19, 2021, https://www.reuters.com/article/us-usa-china-genocide/in-parting-shot-trump-administration-accuses-china-of-genocide-against-uighurs-idUSKBN29O25F.

China's decision-making about the volume of aid. This finding is not overall surprising. In the past, Beijing had shown its willingness to depart from the strict adherence to the "One China" policy by extending assistance to Haiti, which recognizes Taiwan as a sovereign state. Haiti is one of the recipients of China's COVID-19 assistance as is Paraguay, the only South American country that has diplomatic relations with Taiwan.[94] In 2014, China passed a new regulation that legalized humanitarian aid to countries, with which China does not have diplomatic relations. Article 3 of the "Foreign Aid Management Method" document states, "Recipients of overseas development mainly include developing countries that have already established diplomatic relations with the People's Republic of China [...] In emergency and exceptional circumstances such as humanitarian assistance, developed countries or developing countries without diplomatic relations with the People's Republic of China can also be a recipient."[95] Although, Beijing has extended its humanitarian (but not development) assistance[96] to countries with diplomatic relations with Taiwan, in terms of the volume of COVID-19 aid, these countries received the smallest amounts of assistance.

In July 2019, a group of United Nations member-states submitted a letter addressed to the president of the UN Human Rights Council and the UN High Commissioner for Human Rights condemning China for inhuman practices in Xinjiang and calling on Beijing to halt its detention program for Uyghurs.[97] We have coded all signatories and re-run our models substituting the Xinjiang variable for "One China" measure (see Models 3 and 4 in Table 4). As expected, countries that condemned China's policies in Xinjiang received smaller volumes of coronavirus assistance, if selected to receive any COVID-19 aid from Beijing. It appears that China has used its foreign aid to reward countries, which supported its domestic politics and foreign relations.

---

94   Interestingly though, the announcement of Chinese donations came from Paraguay's political party Frente Guasu, which supports the idea of switching its diplomatic recognition to China (Telias and Urdínez, "China's Foreign Aid Determinants").

95   Shangwubu Tiaoyue Falusi 2014 as cited in Hirono, "Exploring the Links between Chinese Foreign Policy and Humanitarian Action", p. 12.

96   The studies of China's development aid confirm that countries that recognize Taiwan receive virtually no aid (see, for example, Axel Dreher and Andreas Fuchs, "Rogue Aid? The Determinants of China's Aid Allocation," Courant Research Centre Discussion Paper 93, September 6, 2011.

97   Catherine Putz, "Which Countries Are for or Against China's Xinjiang Policies," The Diplomat, June 15, 2019. https://thediplomat.com/2019/07/which-countries-are-for-or-against -chinas-xinjiang-policies/.

4.4   *Great Power Competition*

As we discussed earlier, China's foreign assistance has always had geopolitical undertones. When it began providing aid in the 1950s, it was in the context of political isolation and sanctions by the US. The newly founded PRC sought to broaden its sphere of influence by means of development assistance. At the height of the Sino-Soviet split and ongoing effort by the US to disrupt, destabilize and weaken communist governments, China's aid amounted to 64.7 percent of all aid given by communist countries.[98] China's foreign aid contributions dropped sharply in the late 1970s partly due to Beijing's reproachment with Washington. Still, these experiences set in a pattern of China's deployment of foreign aid as a reaction to US activities perceived as damaging to China's interests or responding to the opportunities in the areas where the US action has faltered.

China's COVID-19 assistance has followed the trend. Our statistical analysis shows that countries-recipients of the US COVID-19 assistance were more likely to receive COVID-19 aid from Beijing. To put it differently, Washington's assistance featured prominently in Beijing's decisions about the allocations of its coronavirus aid. There has also been a marked difference in the ways in which the two governments have framed their COVID-19 assistance. China's framing had an explicit geopolitical coloring. Beijing shrouded its coronavirus assistance in the language of new political principles, most notably the "community of common destiny" linking the concept to the advancement of global health goals. Beijing has applied the principles of a "community of common destiny" in rendering COVID-19 assistance to the world inculcating the world community in a set of new and alternative ideas to those of liberal governance.[99]

Many observers have noted that these trends of seeking to supplant US leadership and dominance of liberal international norms extend to the multilateral institutions where China has been seeking to fill the niche opened with the American retrenchment. One way in which it has done so is by placing Chinese official at the top of multinational organizations. China's influence in the World Bank, International Monetary Fund, and UN agencies which tie financial contributions and voting prerogatives to the member-states' economic

98   John F Copper, *China's Foreign Aid and Investment Diplomacy. Vol. II: History and Practice in Asia, 1950-Present* (New York, NY: Palgrave Macmillan, 2016), p. 152.

99   Chen, "Community of Common Destiny for Mankind"; Naoko Eto, "China's Propaganda Maneuvers in Response to COVID-19: The Unified Front Work that Contributes to 'the Community of Common Destiny for Mankind' Promotion," SPF China Observer, No. 31 (May 20, 2020), https://www.spf.org/spf-china-observer/en/document-detail031.html.

size have grown.[100] Beijing has managed to thrust its diplomats to lead some key UN institutions. Out of the UN's 15 specialized agencies, Chinese representative head four responsible for global standards for air travel, telecommunications, and agriculture. Only a concerted campaign by the US and its partners halted China's effort to claim chairmanship of another UN body, the World Intellectual Property Organization.[101] Facing a rivalry from the US, China has used all tools at its disposal – from humanitarian assistance to leadership in international institutions – to sway the global order in the direction favorable to Beijing.

4.5   *Other Determinants of China's COVID-19 Assistance*
The principle of political non-interference has also transpired in our assessment of the determinants of China's COVID-19 aid. Political regime has played negligible role in Beijing's determination of aid recipients or volumes. In fact, it appears that China was more likely to select countries, which score higher on the liberal democracy scale in the outcome model, which included the Xinjiang measure ($p<0.1$).

We also found a strong and consistent relationship between the magnitude of COVID-19 outbreak, as measured by the total number of people who died due to the COVID-19 pandemic, and China's coronavirus assistance. Beijing has prioritized countries gravely affected by the spread of the virus and channeled more assistance to counties experiencing higher levels of deaths due to COVID-19. Neither the countries' capacity to deal with the consequences of COVID-19 (measured by GDP) nor their proximity to China seemed to matter for Beijing's decisions about the COVID-19 assistance.

100   Scott Morris, Rowan Rockafellow and Sarah Rose, "Mapping China's Participation in Multilateral Development Institutions and Funds," Center for Global Development (November 28, 2021), https://www.cgdev.org/publication/mapping-chinas-participation-multilateral-development-institutions-and-funds.
101   Yaroslav Trofimov, Drew Hinshaw and Kate O'Keeffe, "How China is Taking Over International Organizations, One Vote at a Time." *Wall Street Journal* (September 29, 2020).

CHAPTER 3

Russia's COVID-19 Aid Opportunism

Academic and policy communities began taking interest in Russia's role as an international donor following Moscow's highly publicized and controversial involvement in the humanitarian crises in Syria and Venezuela. Yet, the history of Russia's aid programs goes back to the post-World War II period when the Soviet regime invested lavishly in various infrastructure projects in South Asia and the Middle East. The levels of aid, which fluctuated during the Soviet period, declined precipitously in the years preceding the Soviet Union's dissolution. In the 1990s, Russia curtailed its aid activities but reemerged in the donor circles in the 2000s following a decade-long economic growth stimulated by the booming oil markets.

This chapter begins with an overview of Russia's resurgence in the global development and humanitarian fields. It traces the roots of the Russian logic for humanitarian action to its leadership's geopolitical vision of international relations and their beliefs about Russia's own role in global politics. This discussion illuminates the primacy of national interests in Russia's aid distribution, linkages of aid-based decisions with the great power image, and the Cold War legacy of looking at foreign aid through the lens of great power competition. The remainder of the chapter reviews patterns and dynamics of Russia's COVID-19 aid and details the findings of the statistical analysis of Russian coronavirus assistance. While some of Russia's aid has been tied to humanitarian objectives, it has also been an integral part of Moscow's strategy for projecting power on the global stage. Countries in Russia's neighborhood as well as those supporting Russia's foreign policy goals were more likely to secure Moscow's COVID-19 aid.

1   Historical Background on Russia's Humanitarian Aid

Frequently tacked under the "new donor" rubric, Russia is anything but new to the business of foreign aid. Some trace the roots of Russia's foreign assistance to the post-1917 revolutionary period when the young Bolshevik government inspired by its own success sought to exploit class contradictions and anti-imperial sentiments around the world. In the Middle East, Soviet Russia provided political support, medical supplies, and discounted Soviet

© MARIYA Y. OMELICHEVA AND BRITTNEE CARTER, 2024 | DOI:10.1163/9789004692671_005

merchandise to Saudi Arabia and Yemen.[1] The newly created People's Commissariat for Foreign Affairs offered economic aid for the anti-imperialist national liberation movements in Russia's southern neighbors - Turkey, Iran, China, and Afghanistan. While some of this aid had highly ideological underpinnings, other assistance was premised on a belief that support for foreign economies could help in the development of the Soviet domestic economy.[2]

The levels of Soviet foreign assistance peaked after the Second World War reaching roughly US$1 billion in 1960 and approaching the levels of Washington's aid in terms of the share of the country's gross domestic product.[3] With a knack for the spectacular, the Soviet Union built India's first plant at Bhilai that became the main producer of steel rails in the country.[4] Famously, the Soviet Union won the bid for the Aswan Dam in Egypt, which had a water storage capacity double that of the combined resources of the Grand Coulee Dam in Washington and the Kuibyshev Dam in the USSR.[5] The USSR built hospitals, stadiums, hotels, and universities in developing countries in order to project its power, build global image, counter the influence of the Western states, and gain new allies. In the 1960s, Afghanistan, Egypt, Iran, Turkey, Guinea, Ghana, Syria, and Somalia were among the largest per capita recipients of Soviet assistance. Many of these aid projects had a commercial aspect to them, but the transfer of Soviet technology and funding of projects on preferential and subsidized terms put them into the foreign aid category.[6]

Although the Soviet Union shunned the global institutions established in the wake of World War II and did not rejoin the World Health Organization until 1955, it was willing to engage in international collaboration around

1   John Baldry, "Soviet Relations with Saudi Arabia and the Yemen 1917–1938," *Middle Eastern Studies* 20, no. 1 (1984): 53–80; see also Mariya Y. Omelicheva, "'Good' Samaritan? The Geopolitics of Russia's Covid-19 Assistance," *Canadian Journal of European and Russian Studies* 16, no. 1 (2020): 1–25.

2   Norihiro Naganawa, "'The Red Sea Becoming Red? The Bolsheviks' Commercial Enterprise in the Hijaz and Yemen, 1924–1938," Unpublished paper, 2013, https://www.academia.edu/23791104/The_Red_Sea_Becoming_Red_The_Bolsheviks_Commercial_Enterprise_in_the_Hijaz_and_Yemen_1924_1938.

3   Marshal I. Goldman, "A Balance Sheet of Soviet Foreign Aid," *Foreign Affairs* 43, no. 2 (1965): 349–360; Kul B. Rai, "Foreign Aid and Voting in the UN General Assembly, 1967–1976." *Journal of Peace Research* 17, no. 3 (1980): 269–277.

4   Bernard D'Mello, "Soviet Collaboration in Indian Steel Industry, 1954–84," *Economic and Political Weekly* (1988): 473–486.

5   Goldman, "A Balance Sheet of Soviet Foreign Aid."

6   Orah Cooper and Carol Fogarty, "Soviet Economic and Military Aid to the Less Developed Countries, 1954–78," *Soviet and Eastern European Foreign Trade* 21, no. 1/2/3 (Spring-Fall 1985): 54–73.

disease control and prevention. The Soviet Union highly valued prophylactic health measures and embraced coercive vaccination to eradicate deadly viral diseases at home. It also sought to spread mass vaccination practices to other countries. Profoundly ideological, the Soviet Union global vaccination campaign against poliomyelitis, a deadly and disabling disease caused by the poliovirus, is still touted as the most significant health event of the postwar period.[7] Although the first polio vaccine was developed by an American virologist and biomedical scientist Jonas Salk in 1953, the Cutter Incident involving the contraction of polio by hundreds of vaccinated American children, set back US effort to vaccinate the world.[8] Openly critical of the capitalist medicine, the Soviet government, nevertheless, endorsed collaboration between another American microbiologist, Albert Sabin, and Soviet scientists that resulted in the production of oral polio vaccine, which was successfully tested on millions of Soviet citizens.[9] On the heels of large trials, Soviet scientists invented a procedure for preserving the polio vaccine in harsh environments. With the US funding, the Soviet Union produced millions of doses of the freeze-dried vaccine, which became the basis for elimination of smallpox from East Europe, China, India, and dozens of countries in Africa, East Asia, and Latin America.[10]

Another unique aspect of Soviet (and post-Soviet) humanitarian assistance has to do with a considerably broader meaning that is imbued in the notion of humanitarianism. In Russian, the adjective "humanitarian" (*gymanitarnyi*) comes closest to the English term "humanities," which is widely used to describe the study of arts, history, philosophy, languages, and literatures. "Humanitarian," in Russian, usually denotes cooperation in the realm of culture, education, science, and sports.[11] Subsequently, Soviet and Russian humanitarian activities abroad have included initiatives in the sphere of education, sports, and science, efforts to preserve Russia's historical heritage, and outreach to the Russian diaspora abroad. As discussed in greater detail below,

7   Erez Manela, "A Pox on Your Narrative: Writing Disease Control into Cold War History," *Diplomatic History* 34, no. 2 (April 2010), pp. 299–323.

8   Manela, "A Pox on Your Narrative"; Boram Shin, "The East-West Collaboration across the Iron Curtain against Polio Epidemics: Soviet Engagement with Global Health and Poliomyelitis Vaccine Development in 1956–1964," *Journal of Eurasian Studies* 14, no. 1 (2023): 19–29.

9   Manela, "A Pox on Your Narrative".

10   Shin, "The East-West Collaboration across the Iron Curtain against Polio Epidemics."

11   Yevgenii Primakov, "Russia's Humanitarian Mission," *Pathways to Peace and Security* 54, no. 1 Special Issue: Humanitarian Challenges, Humanitarian Support and Human Protection in Armed Conflicts (2018): 182–196; Anna A. Velikaya, "The Russian Approach to Public Diplomacy and Humanitarian Cooperation," *Rising Powers Quarterly* 3, no. 3 (2018): 39–61.

this broad understanding of humanitarianism served as a conceptual bridge to embracing humanitarian activities in a narrow sense as an element of Russia's "soft power" and a great power image.

At the beginning of the Cold War era, the Soviet Union expressed clear preference for developing countries pursuing a non-capitalist path of development in its aid allocations. By the 1970s, pragmatic interests in asserting Soviet influence in the areas of strategic importance and filling in vacuum left by the colonial powers' withdrawal from the Third World supplanted Moscow's ideological concerns. The Soviet leadership discovered that military aid was a more direct and faster route to influence in the countries, which could not secure financial and military benefits from the West. Military sales of weapon systems and arms to states that could afford to buy them also meant an influx of revenue into the Soviet budget. Because of this shift, the ratio of military to economic aid of the Soviet Union grew 3 to 1 in the 1970s–80s.[12] Concurrently, the Soviet Union experienced a dramatic shift in its economic growth patterns. The high growth rates of the post-World War II period gave way to the economic stagnation of the late Brezhnev era. Productivity growth rates fell due to the growing structural imbalances of the Soviet economy and the depletion of readily available raw materials. Economic slowdown entailed a precipitous decline in the levels of economic support provided by the Soviet Union to other countries.

The dissolution of the Soviet Union ushered in a period of complete economic breakdown in Russia. Moscow curtailed its foreign aid activities and became a net recipient of Western assistance.[13] Formally, the international financial institutions, most notably the International Monetary Fund and the World Bank, became the main channels of financial and technical assistance to Russia.[14] Between 1992 and 2006, Russia also received over $US3.3 billion in US assistance authorized by the FREEDOM Support Act (FSA) of 1992

---

12   Cooper and Fogarty, "Soviet Economic and Military Aid to the Less Developed Countries;
      Primakov, "Russia's Humanitarian Mission."

13   Russia's aid activities did not stop completely during the 1990s. Moscow continued issuing loans to a handful of countries, most notably Belarus, Armenia, and Yugoslavia. It sustained post-disaster reconstruction funding to Armenia in the wake of the destructive 1998 Armenian earthquake. It also offered loans to Cuba and Georgia for repaying debt for Russian goods and services.

14   The IMF, for example, issued US$16.2 billion loans to Moscow to stabilize its economy and support macroeconomic stabilization reforms. The World Bank portfolio contained 47 stabilization loans for Russia in the 1990s (John Odling-Smee, "The IMF and Russia in the 1990s," IMF Working Paper, WP/04/155," IMF, 2004, https://www.imf.org/external/pubs/ft/wp/2004/wp04155.pdf.

(P.L. 102–511). The assistance went toward diverse foreign policy goals, but it also prioritized three objectives of democracy promotion, development of free market economy, and non-proliferation of nuclear, chemical, and biological weapons.[15]

The levels of international support to Russia declined in the 2000s on the backdrop of its economic recovery stimulated by the boom in global oil markets. Between 2000 and 2008, the average price of oil, Russia's main export commodity, grew nearly fivefold to over US$100 per barrel of crude oil, and the Russian economy saw average GDP growth of seven percent.[16] This period coincided with Russia's resurgence as an international donor. In 2007, Moscow adopted its first official policy on development assistance reflecting the United Nations Millennium Development Goals.[17] The document was updated in 2014 with a presidential decree that approved a new concept for international development assistance.[18]

Like China, Russia lacks transparency in data reporting. There is no comprehensive information on the levels of Russia's development and humanitarian aid. As part of the accession process to the OECD, Russia began reporting its official development assistance to OECD's DAC in 2011. Moscow's annexation of Crimea led to a suspension of Russia's accession process, which was terminated following its invasion of Ukraine in 2022. The lack of a single federal agency responsible for implementation of assistance policies further complicates the task of collecting and analyzing Russia's data on foreign assistance. The responsibilities for humanitarian aid in Russia are divided among the Ministry of Foreign Affairs,[19] the Ministry of Finance, the Ministry for Civil Defense, Emergencies, and the Elimination of Consequences of Natural

---

15   Curt Tarnoff, "US Assistance to the Former Soviet Union," Congressional Research Service, 2007, https://sgp.fas.org/crs/row/RL32866.pdf.

16   Martin Russell, "Seven Economic Challenges for Russia: Breaking out of Stagnation?" European Parliamentary Research Service, July 2018, https://www.europarl.europa.eu /thinktank/en/document/EPRS_IDA(2018)625138.

17   Mark Rakhmangulov, "Establishing International Development Assistance Strategy in Russia," *International Organizations Research Journal* 31, no. 5 (2010): 50–67, https://iorj.hse .ru/data/2011/03/15/1211461715/9.pdf.

18   The President of the Russian Federation, "Concept of the Russian Federation's State Policy in the Area of International Development Assistance," (Unofficial Translation), approved by Decree No, 259 of the President of the Russian Federation of April 20, 2014, https:// www.mid.ru/en/foreign_policy/official_documents/-/asset_publisher/cptickb6bz29 /content/id/64542/.

19   Russia's Ministry of Foreign Affairs coordinates a substantial part of humanitarian cooperation but does not make decisions on humanitarian aid.

Disasters,[20] Defense Ministry, and the Federal Agency for Commonwealth of Independent States Affairs, and Compatriots Living Abroad, and International Humanitarian Cooperation (Rossotrudnichestvo).[21] A number of public foundations and state-sponsored NGOs are also engaged in the field of humanitarian aid administration.[22]

Until 2022, Russia continued reporting its ODA statistics to the OECD and the UN Office for the Coordination of Humanitarian Affairs (OCHA) through the Financial Tracking Service. This makes Russia's aid allocations more transparent than assistance by other non-DAC donors, even if its data is incomplete[23] and only available at the recipient country's level, not at the project-level. Despite these limitations, several important trends about Russia's humanitarian aid can be discerned. First, the share of Russia's humanitarian aid in its total foreign assistance is minuscular. Based on the OCHA data, Russia's humanitarian aid constitutes, on average, 2 percent of its total assistance and only about 0.002 percent of its GDP (see Figure 3). These levels of humanitarian aid are far below the levels of "traditional" and some "emerging" donors' assistance, both in absolute terms and as a percentage of GDP. If Russia's development assistance more than quadrupled between 2011 and 2015 (from US\$136.7 million in 2011 to US\$1,022.1 million in 2015), its humanitarian aid did not increase much during the same timeframe and saw a greater decline following the imposition of Western sanctions on Russia's economy, which was further battered by the fall of global oil prices.

Second, it has been widely assumed that Russia's aid giving has been slanted toward the former Soviet republics, but this pattern held until 2014 when two Central Asian republics – Kyrgyzstan and Tajikistan – accounted for a significant

---

20   The Agency for Support and Coordination of Russian Participation in International Humanitarian Operations within this Ministry supports and coordinates Russia's participation in humanitarian emergencies with UN agencies and other international organizations. The Agency is a technical partner of the UN World Food Programme (Velikaya, "The Russian Approach to Public Diplomacy and Humanitarian Cooperation").

21   Rossotrudnichestvo is under the umbrella of Russia's Ministry of Foreign Affairs. It coordinates humanitarian and development assistance toward Russia's neighbors through the Russian – UNDP Trust Fund for Development.

22   Velikaya, "The Russian Approach to Public Diplomacy and Humanitarian Cooperation."

23   The OCHA data is far from being comprehensive and do not include, for example, Russia's transfers to several humanitarian agencies, such as Switzerland-based International Civil Defense Organization and Russian-Serbian Humanitarian Centre. Russia's official ODA does not include measures of public debt forgiveness. On several occasions, Moscow has cancelled debt to Kyrgyzstan and North Korea (Martin Russell, "At a Glance – Russia's Humanitarian Aid Policy," European Parliamentary Research Service, May 2016, https://www.europarl.europa.eu/RegData/etudes/ATAG/2016/582039/EPRS_ATA(2016)582039_EN.pdf).

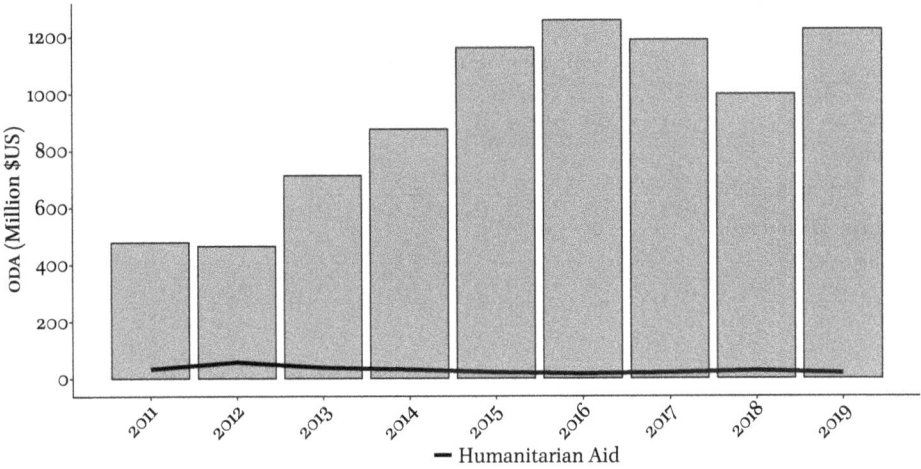

FIGURE 3   Russia's Official Development (ODA) and humanitarian assistance
SOURCE: OECD DATA (HTTPS://DATA.OECD.ORG)

percentage of Moscow's assistance. While Russia continues directing some of its aid toward its neighbors, it has increased aid allocations to countries in the Middle East, Africa, and East Asia. Syria, North Korea, Yemen, and the Palestinian territories have been among the top recipients of Russia's aid (Table 5). World Food Organization and World Health Organization have received the vast majority of Russia's multilateral assistance.

Third, Russian humanitarian aid has been very heterogeneous but primarily in-kind. Moscow has delivered processed foods, grains, wheat and flour to the famine-stricken areas or countries with food insecurity. It has also sent experts, equipment, and training to assist in clearing landmines. It supplied search and rescue teams in the wake of natural disasters and provided medical supplies in health crises.[24] Fourth, until recently, the vast majority of Russian assistance had been implemented through multilateral organizations rather than bilaterally. Between 2010 and 2020, less than 10 percent of Russia's overall humanitarian assistance was channeled bilaterally. The preference for working through multilateral venues could be due to the weaknesses of Russia's own aid infrastructure and the lack of capacity to administer large volumes of in-kind humanitarian aid.[25]

24   Russell, "At a Glance – Russia's Humanitarian Aid Policy."
25   Anna Brezhneva and Daria Ukhova, *Russia as a Humanitarian Aid Donor*, OXFAM Discussion Paper, July 15, 2013, https://www-cdn.oxfam.org/s3fs-public/file_attachments /dp-russia-humanitarian-donor-150713-en_0.pdf.

TABLE 5   Top recipients of Global (G) and Russian (R) humanitarian assistance

	2010	2011	2012	2013	2014	2015	2016	2017	2018	2019	2020
Afghanistan	G/R	G	G	G	G		G		G/R	G	G/R
Bangladesh								G	G	G	G
Central African Republic					G						
Congo, The Democratic Republic	G	G	G	G	G	G		G	G	G	G
Ethiopia	G	G	G	G	G	G	G	G	G	G	G
Haiti	G/R										
Iraq						G	G	G	G	G	G
Japan		G					G				
Jordan				G/R	G	G		G	G	G	G
Kenya			G								
Kyrgyzstan	R	R	R	R							
Lebanon				G/R	G	G	G	G	G	G	G/R
Liberia					G						
Nepal						G					
Nigeria								G	G	G	G
North Korea			R				R	R	R	R	R
Pakistan	G/R	G									
Palestinian territories		R	G		G	G/R	G/R	R	R		R
Philippines				R	G						
Serbia		R									
Sierra Leone					G						
Somalia		G	R	G	G	G	G	G/R		G	G
South Sudan		G		G	G	G	G	G	G	G	G
Sudan	G	G		G	G/R	G	G	G	G	G	G
Syria			G/R	G/R	G/R	G/R	G/R	G/R	G/R	G/R	G/R
Tajikistan		R									
Turkey							G	G	G	G	G
Ukraine (occupied territories)						R					
Yemen		R				G/R		R	G	G	G/R

Note: Top recipients of global assistances are the countries (and territories) which received over $500 million USD in total assistance during the year. Top recipients of the Russian humanitarian assistance are the countries (and territories), which cumulatively account for more than 50 percent of Russia's total humanitarian aid for the year.

SOURCE: FINANCIAL TRACKING SERVICE OF THE UN OFFICE FOR COORDINATION OF HUMANITARIAN AFFAIRS (HTTPS://FTS.UNOCHA.ORG/HOME/2023/DONORS/VIEW).

Finally, Russia has been reluctant to work with non-governmental organizations (NGOs) in aid delivery and administration. This is to be expected given that the Kremlin has been wary of civil society's role in political transitions abroad and has placed restrictions on the operations of NGOs at home. Something of a break with this tradition, Russia cooperated with the International Committee of the Red Cross in Ecuador and Syria and channeled about one-fifth of its humanitarian assistance to Damask through Russian civil society groups. Many of the non-state entities, nevertheless, are informally accountable to the Kremlin through the senior leadership within these organizations and funding streams.[26]

At first glance, Moscow's humanitarian aid has not consistently followed any clear pattern. On the one hand, Russia has supplied aid to some of the same countries – Afghanistan, Yemen, Lebanon, and the Palestinian territories - that have been the top recipients of global humanitarian aid. Russia's search and rescue teams were sent to Nepal after the disastrous 2015 earthquake and to Serbia after the 2014 floods. On the other hand, Syria has been the single largest recipient of Moscow's humanitarian aid since 2012, while Serbia and North Korea have been prioritized for disaster relief in certain years (see Table 5). Russia's own policies on humanitarian assistance exhibit a mix of objectives ranging from poverty eradication and elimination of natural disasters' consequences to influence on global processes, image building, and fostering new friendships and partnerships abroad.[27] This reflects a tension between Russia's desire to be viewed as a responsible member of the exclusive club of Western donors committed to helping the peoples in need and its penchant for acting in self-interest consistent with Moscow's great power aspirations. These tensions are evident in Russia's logic for humanitarian assistance rooted in a distinct geopolitical imagery of the Russian state and its place in the world that are discussed next.

---

26   Russia's non-state humanitarian deliveries to Syria were carried out by at least thirteen organizations, such as the Russian Humanitarian Mission and the Center for Reconciliation of Conflicting Sides in Syria. All these organizations have direct ties to the Russian state or indirect ties to the Kremlin through the Russian Orthodox Church (Jonathan Robinson, "Five Years of Russian Aid in Syria Proves Moscow is an Unreliable Partner," The Atlantic Council, June 8, 2021, https://www.atlanticcouncil.org/blogs/menasource /five-years-of-russian-aid-in-syria-proves-moscow-is-an-unreliable-partner/).

27   The President of the Russian Federation, "Concept of the Russian Federation's State Policy."

2   The Elements of Russia's Geopolitical Logic for Humanitarian Aid

Despite the long history of aid-giving, Russia does not have a well-developed intellectual foundation for its humanitarianism. It has a small corpus of written works on the subject of Russia's foreign assistance and is the only mid-size donor that lacks a legal and institutional backbone for foreign aid. There is not a federal law that defines humanitarian aid and its purpose, nor is there a separate and independent state agency for providing direction and administering Russia's foreign aid.[28] At the same time, Russia's position on humanitarian and development assistance has been inseparable from the key elements of Moscow's foreign policy. By engaging with the conceptual architecture of Russia's foreign policy, informed by the narratives on Russia's identity and its leadership's geopolitical thinking, we can infer Moscow's views on and beliefs about humanitarian aid.[29]

Russia's military, economic, and diplomatic rise in international politics under the leadership of Vladimir Putin has reinforced a set of geospatial assumptions about Russia's identity and Moscow's place in the world. Arguably, the key objective of the Kremlin since the Soviet Union's dissolution has been Russia's great power status restoration. Neither the Russian leadership nor the Russian public can imagine their country in any other terms than as one of the leading players in the world. Boris Yeltsin's famous expression that Russia is "a great power by virtue of history, of its place in the world, and of its material and spiritual potential" strongly reverberates with the Russian elites and population.[30] The self-image of great power has endowed Russia with certain "special rights and duties,"[31] which include a "privileged sphere of influence" in the "near abroad" and a set of responsibilities with regard to peace and security in the international system. According to the Russian government, to be a great power in the 21st century it is not enough to have advanced military, nuclear weapons, and largest territory in the world. A modern great power must enjoy domestic stability and economic growth, lead in technological innovation, and be able to deploy different forms and instruments of power.[32] Furthermore, a

28   Brezhneva and Ukhova, *Russia as a Humanitarian Aid Donor.*

29   Derek Averre and Lance Davies, "Russia, Humanitarian Intervention and the Responsibility to Protect: the Case of Syria," *International Affairs* 91, no. 4 (2015): 813–834.

30   As cited in John Erickson, "'Russia will Not be Trifled with': Geopolitical Facts and Fantasies," *Journal of Strategic Studies* 22 no. 2–3 (1999), p. 255.

31   Hedley Bull, *The Anarchical Society,* 3rd edition (Basingstoke: Palgrave, 2002), p. 196.

32   Bobo Lo, *Russia and the New World Disorder* (The Brookings Institution Press, 2015), p. 47.

great power should flaunt an attractive model of political and economic development and parade moral greatness.[33]

Russian decision-makers have frequently opined that Russia needs to learn to effectively deploy "soft power" if it wants to firmly establish itself in the ranks of the world's most powerful nations.[34] In addition to the Kremlin's own grant-making schemes and the use of traditional and electronic media in support of Russia's global image and its foreign policy positions, Russia's Foreign Minister Sergei Lavrov has specifically alluded to his country's participation in international aid programs as one of Russia's "soft power" tools.[35] Subsequently, humanitarian aid has been embraced as a prerequisite for Russia's status as a great power nation. It has also been conceived as a tool for defending Russia's interests and great power ambitions abroad. This juxtaposition of identity-based and pragmatic considerations in aid allocation has become a staple of Russia's approach to humanitarian aid.

2.1   Humanitarian Assistance as a Great Power's Responsibility

Despite the significant deterioration of the relationship between Russia, on one side, and the US and European countries, on the other, during Vladimir Putin's third term in the office, Moscow has traditionally looked up to the West as an important symbolic referent for its self-identification.[36] In the 1990s, for example, Russia aspired to achieve the main characteristics of the West and become industrially developed, prosperous, and democratic. In the 2000s, Russia continued to view the West as an epitome of progress, modernity, and leadership, but it began expressing serious disagreements with Washington and Brussels on certain value dimensions and security policies. Nevertheless,

33   Charles E. Ziegler, "Conceptualizing Sovereignty in Russian Foreign Policy: Realist and Constructivist Perspectives," *International Politics* 49 (2012): 400–417

34   Konstantin Kosachev, "Rossotrudnichestvo Kak Instrument 'Myagkoi Sily'," [Rossotrudnichestvo as a Tool of "Soft Power"], Bel'giyskaya Federatsiya Russkoyazychnykh Organizatsiy, 2012, https://www.bfro.be/%2oru/k.kosachev.-rossotrudnichestvo-kak-instrument-mjagkoj-sily.html?cmp_id=108&news_id=5334; Konstantin Kosachev, "Rossotrudnichestvo: Pervye Itogi Deyatelnosti i Perspektivy Razvitiya," [Rossotrudnichestvo: Initial Outcomes and Perspectives for Future Development], *Mezhdunarodnaya Zhizn*," 2012, https://interaffairs.ru/author.php?n=arpg&pg=691; Yulia Kiseleva, "Russia's Soft Power Discourse: Identity, Status and the Attraction of Power," *Politics* 35, no. 3–4 (2015): 316–329.

35   Kiseleva, "Russia's Soft Power Discourse: Identity, Status and the Attraction of Power;" Sergey Lavrov, "Intervyu Ministra Inostrannykh Del Rossii Gazete 'Kommersant'," [Interview of the Minister of Foreign Affairs to Russian Newspaper 'Kommersant'], October 3, 2012, https://www.mid.ru/en/press_service/minister_speeches/1631545/?lang=ru.

36   Mariya Y. Omelicheva, "Critical Geopolitics on Russian Foreign Policy: Uncovering the Imagery of Moscow's International Relations," *International Politics* 53 (2016): 708–726.

the willingness of economically advanced countries, particularly the US, to invest their national wealth for assisting less developed states and countries in crises[37] has led to a strong association between great power status and the provision of aid. Russia's desire to reassert itself as a great power state after years of being an aid recipient had a decisive impact on its decision to become an international donor.[38] Russian decision makers and general population began viewing the position of a country as a recipient of aid as a sign of weakness, whereas an ability to provide assistance has been regarded a mark of strength.

By adopting its first Concept on Participation in International Development Assistance in 2007, Russia officially signaled its intent to reverse the directionality of aid from being a recipient to donor of international assistance.[39] The impetus for this change came after the 32nd G8 summit hosted by Russia, which confirmed its status as a full member of the "Group of Eight." For Russian officials, membership in G8 was a matter of international prestige. Addressing the participants of the G8 forum, Vladimir Putin highlighted the spread of infectious diseases and conflict between Israel and Lebanon among the pressing issues for world leaders' attention.[40] Yet, following the G8 summit, the Russian press taunted the country as the only "Group of Eight" member that did not have a strategy for development assistance.[41]

By adopting its first official strategy for international assistance and announcing commitments to deliver foreign aid, Russia showed that it, too, was capable of pursuing a more active policy in the field of development consistent with its great power aspirations.[42] By declaring its adherence to the principles

---

37   Russia received significant international assistance in its two Chechen wars. The US was the largest single provider of humanitarian aid to the North Caucasus, but various UN agencies, the International Committee of the Red Cross, and non-governmental organizations also provided much need emergency health care, water, sanitation projects, education, shelter, and more (Steven Pifer, "U.S. Policy on Chechnya," US Department of State Archive, 2002, https://2001-2009.state.gov/p/eur/rls/rm/2002/10034.htm).

38   Brezhneva and Ukhova, *Russia as a Humanitarian Aid Donor*.

39   Patty A. Gray, "Looking 'The Gift' in the Mouth: Russia as Donor," (2011), https://mural .maynoothuniversity.ie/3028/1/PG_Gift.pdf.

40   Vladimir Putin, "Address by Russian President Vladimir Putin to visitors to the official site of Russia's G8 Presidency in 2006," Official site of Russia's G8 Presidency in 2006, https:// web.archive.org/web/20060214023902/http:/en.g8russia.ru/agenda/.

41   Gray, "Looking 'The Gift' in the Mouth."

42   The Ministry of Finance of the Russia Federation, "Concept of Russia's Participation in International Development Assistance," 2007, https://minfin.gov.ru/common/upload /library/2007/06/concept_eng.pdf; See also Claire Provost, "The Rebirth of Russian Foreign Aid," *The Guardian* (May 22, 2011), https://www.theguardian.com/global-development /2011/may/25/russia-foreign-aid-report-influence-image.

of the Paris Declaration on Aid Effectiveness (2005)[43] and the Accra Agenda for Action (2008)[44] seeking to improve the quality and effectiveness of foreign aid, Russia accepted an obligation to make its donations more transparent and accountable.[45] In 2008, Russia's Ministry of Finance organized a workshop on development aid statistics sponsored by the World Bank, the OECD, USAID, and the United Nations Development Programme. The goal of the meeting was to help Russia with the establishment of a new accounting and reporting system for foreign aid and to signal Moscow's compliance with the OECD DAC principles for reporting assistance. Following these engagements, Russia's famous Higher School of Economics published the first Russian textbook on international development and aid, which concluded that Moscow's participation in the OECD and DAC was critical for integrating the country's economy into the global market and raising its influence and prestige in global affairs.[46]

The six years that preceded Russia's illegal annexation of Crimea in 2014 were the heyday of its humanitarian activities. Moscow supported the UN Security Council resolutions authorizing UN peacekeeping operations with a significant humanitarian element in Mali, Central African Republic,[47] and South Sudan. It provided direct, if limited, humanitarian aid in various conflict and post-conflict settings.[48] As a long-standing partner of the World Food Programme, Russia worked with the WFP and other international partners to provide food and medical supplies to Yemen and countries of sub-Saharan Africa (Somalia, Sudan, the Democratic Republic of Congo, etc.).[49] Moscow responded to natural disasters and health emergency crises in South-East Asia and sent medical teams to assist with the Ebola outbreak in Guinea, Liberia,

---

43   OECD, *Paris Declaration on Aid Effectiveness* (Paris: OECD Publishing, 2005).

44   OECD, *Accra Agenda for Action* (Paris: OECD Publishing, 2008).

45   Gray, "Looking 'The Gift' in the Mouth"; The Ministry of Finance of the Russian Federation, "Assessing Action and Results Against Development-Related G8 Commitments: The Russian Federation Contribution," June 21, 2010, https://minfin.gov.ru/common /gen_html/?id=10050&fld=FILE_MAIN.

46   Y.K., O.V. Perfil'eva, I.A. Rakhmangulov, and Y.A. Shvets, *Mezhdunarodnye Instituty v Global'noi Arkhitekture Sodeistviia Razvitiiu* [International Institutions in the Global Architecture of Development Assistance] (Moscow: Izdatel'skii Dom Gosudarstvennogo Universiteta Vysshei Shkoly Ekonomiki, 2010).

47   United Nations Security Council, Resolution 2149 (2014), adopted by the Security Council at its 7153rd meeting, on 10 April 2014, https://digitallibrary.un.org/record/768393?ln=en.

48   In 2006, for example, Russia deployed over 300 military engineers and equipment on a humanitarian mission to Lebanon to build bridges destroyed during the conflict with Israel (Center for Security Studies, "Russia's 'Humanitarian Aid', or What the Russian Military Personnel are Doing in Europe," May 5, 2020, https://censs.org/russias-humanitarian -aid-or-what-the-russian-military-personnel-are-doing-in-europe/?lang=en#_edn1).

49   Brezhneva and Ukhova, *Russia as a Humanitarian Aid Donor.*

and Sierra Leone. While Russia pursued humanitarian purposes in many humanitarian emergencies, it also viewed its foreign aid as inextricably linked to its global reputation. To put it differently, Russia's approach to foreign aid has embodied the ongoing effort by the Russian leadership to renegotiate and defend Russia's great power identity vis-à-vis its significant others.

The Russian leadership has often expressed chagrin over what they have perceived as a refusal of the West to recognize Russia as a great power state and respect its legitimate national interests. To elevate and defend Russia's great power image, the Russian leadership has resorted to a tactic of disparaging and rejecting the norms and values that they deem inconsistent with the Russian national identity centered in Russian language, culture, religion, and traditional values, and drawing on its purportedly eternal and transcendental qualities of being a great power state. The anti-Western and anti-American rhetoric has been central to this approach. Washington and other Western countries have been presented as ignorant and intolerant of Russia's way of life and, therefore, threatening its national identity, which had to be defended by the state by all available means.[50] Humanitarian and development assistance and Russia's engagement in global crises became one of the many tools deployed by the Kremlin to counter the perceived threats of the US to Russia. This dimension of foreign assistance has become more pronounced in Russia's approach to humanitarian aid since 2014.

2.2   *Humanitarian Aid as a Tool for Defending Russia's Great Power Identity and Its Geopolitical Space*

Historically and in modern Russia, foreign aid has been viewed as a tool for achieving Russian national interests and defending its great power ambitions. Aptly described by a Russian aid scholar, the purpose of humanitarian aid is to create a global system favorable to Russia's interests.[51] According to the Russian leadership, for reasons of history, geography, and patterns of relations with other great powers, Russia has been bound to a quintessentially pragmatic approach to foreign aid. Moscow's influence and global reach, including by means of foreign assistance, have been regarded as prerequisites for state security and economic well-being.[52]

The primacy of state interests over the interests and welfare of humans has been an enduring philosophical tradition of Russian statism that has been appropriated and embraced by the Kremlin as one of the defining elements

---

50   Omelicheva, "Critical Geopolitics on Russian Foreign Policy."
51   Primakov, "Russia's Humanitarian Mission."
52   Primakov, "Russia's Humanitarian Mission."

of Russia's great power image.[53] The commitment to the state and to its power, strength, and prestige are among the chief statist beliefs. This tradition also holds individuals subordinate to the state and gives priority to state interests over individuals' interests and considerations. While criticized by some, this pattern of subduing individual autonomy to state authority has been discursively transformed into a key source of Russia's vitality by prominent Russian pandits and the Kremlin ideologues.[54]

Vladimir Putin, himself, has always propagated the idea of a strong Russian state[55] and defended its public veneration as an inalienable feature of Russia's tradition and culture: "For us, the state and its institutions and structures have always played an exceptionally important role in the life of the country and the people. For Russians, a strong state is not an anomaly to fight against. Quite the contrary, it is the source and guarantor of order, the initiator and the main driving force of any change ...".[56] During the 2000s, statist beliefs were part of an eclectic mixture of ideas that the Russian government deployed in justification of its policies. This has changed in 2012 when Vladimir Putin assumed Russian presidency for the third term. Faced with large-scale anti-regime protests, Putin and the Kremlin ideologues elevated statist ideas in public discourse emphasizing Russia's civilizational identity folded in conservative values. The official "national idea," centered in the notion of Russia as a unique "civilization-state," endowed the country with a special mission that the Russian president was called for to defend using any means, including by the force arms, but also using the tools of development and humanitarian assistance.[57]

The shift from using nationalist and statist ideas as rhetorical devices to deploying them as the kinds of "ontological truths" about Russia's identity and its place in the world marked an important change in Russia's thinking and practices of humanitarian assistance. First, linkages between Russia's national interests and humanitarian aid solidified. In 2014, the Russian government

---

53   Andrei P. Tsygankov has identified it as one of three "distinct traditions, or schools, of foreign policy thinking" with its own specific preferences and priorities (Andrei P. Tsygankov, *Russia's Foreign Policy: Change and Continuity in National Identity.* Rowman & Littlefield, 2013), p. 4.

54   Ivan Fomin, "Sixty Shades of Statism: Mapping the Ideological Divergences in Russian Elite Discourse, *Democratizatsiya: The Journal of Post-Soviet Democratization* 30, no. 3 (2022): 305–332.

55   Vladimir Putin, "Rossiia na Rubezhe Tysiacheletii," [Russia at the Turn of the Millennium]. *Nezavisimaia Gazeta,* December 30, 1999, http://www.ng.ru/politics/1999-12-30/4_millenium.html.

56   Fiona Hill and Clifford Gaddy, "Putin and the Uses of History," *The National Interest* (January 4, 2012), https://nationalinterest.org/article/putin-the-uses-history-6276?page=0%2C1.

57   Omelicheva, "Critical Geopolitics on Russian Foreign Policy."

published a Concept on Cooperation in International Development, which maintains that Russia's foreign aid is designed to further its national interests as defined in national security strategy and foreign policy concept.[58] Russia's Ministry of Foreign Affairs became more direct about Moscow's intentions for humanitarian aid. For example, the agency declared that Russia's humanitarian assistance to Syria was integral to the Kremlin's effort in achieving Russia's foreign policy objectives in the Middle East.[59]

Institutionally, development and humanitarian assistance were permanently housed under the umbrella of Russia's Ministry of Foreign Affairs. In the early 2010s, the Russian government discussed a possibility of instituting a separate agency of international development tasked with the design and implementation of Russia's aid programs. At the time, a separate agency was viewed as necessary for greater policy coherence, coordination, monitoring, reporting, and analysis of the programs' implementation. The plans for creating such an agency were scrapped in favor of empowering an existing state organization – Rossotrudnichestvo – to play a more active role in aid. Created in 2008 for fostering relations between Russia and its neighbors, Rossotrudnichestvo resides in the structure of the Ministry of Foreign Affairs. This institutional makeup subordinates Russia's humanitarian assistance policy to its objectives in foreign affairs.[60] It also signals the special place of Russia's neighborhood in its geopolitical views.

The second consequence of a shift toward greater pragmatism in Russia's aid allocations was an increased deployment of aid for countering threats to Russia's national interests. Moscow has inherited a rich tapestry of Soviet-era military and political thinking about threats. For example, Russia's geography, experiences of multiple defensive wars, and its own expansionist tendencies resulted in a persistent feeling of vulnerability. Moscow has sought to establish a forward security zone in the face of growing external pressure, such as NATO's advancement to the Russian borders. It, therefore, has always guarded its influence in countries in the "near abroad" (for the stated security reasons and identity-based claims to the spheres of "privileged interests" that ought

---

58   The President of the Russian Federation, "Concept of the Russian Federation's State Policy."

59   Jonathan Robinson, "Five Years of Russian Aid in Syria Proves Moscow Is an Unreliable Partner," The Atlantic Council, June 8, 2021, https://www.atlanticcouncil.org/blogs/menasource/five-years-of-russian-aid-in-syria-proves-moscow-is-an-unreliable-partner/.

60   Mikhail O. Yermolov, "Rossiiski Mehanism Mezhdunarodnoi Pomoschi: Nezavershennyi Proekt," [The Russian Mechanism of Foreign Assistance: An Incomplete Project], Vestnik Mezhdunarodnyh Organizatsii: Obrazovaniye, Nauka, Novaya Ekonomika 10, no. 3 (2015): 134–155.

to be recognized by other great power nations). Subsequently, Moscow has reacted vigorously to the perceived encroachment of the NATO and EU on its "buffer zones."[61]

These ideas and threat perceptions have been further informed by Russia's contemporary experiences, which have led the Russian government to believe that a unipolar state-centric international order with the United States at its helm was fundamentally incompatible with and threatening to Russia's interests. According to the Kremlin, the US has exploited global power asymmetries to attain its special interests under the guise of liberal humanitarianism. From the Russian standpoint, a history of American support to political opposition through various tools of democracy promotion and funding to civil society groups has resulted in the destabilization of countries and regions. Russia's own regional and international interests have been systematically undermined by the US seeking to replace pro-Russian governments with the leadership pliable to Washington.[62] Overtime, the Kremlin's views of the world have been narrowed down to its geopolitical competition with the US. Moscow has deployed all instruments and elements of its national power to counter and undermine American influence around the world. Like the Soviet Union's foreign assistance that had a highly geopolitical character, the types and volumes of Russia's aid have become determined through the lens of competition with the US. At a minimum, Russia's aid has been designed to raise its image; at a maximum, to subvert and counter the "soft" influence of the US.

To summarize, Russia's thinking about foreign aid has been influenced by its beliefs about rights, responsibilities, and privileges associated with great power status. For Russia, humanitarian aid is an indicator of strength. As a great power, Moscow is expected to partake in assisting countries afflicted by natural disasters and conflict-related crises. Until 2014, Moscow had viewed its humanitarian activities as consistent with the image of a responsible great power and constructive actor of global politics in addition to using foreign aid

---

61   See, for example, Yury Nikolayevich Baluyevsky, "Regional and Global Threat Assessment; Nature of Future War; Future Force Structure of the Russian Armed Forces," *Vestnik of the Academy of Military Sciences*, no. 1 (2008); Yury Nikolayevich Baluyevsky, "Theoretical and Methodological Bases for the Military Doctrine of the Russian Federation." *Vestnik of the Academy of Military Sciences*, no. 1 (2007); Olga Oliker, C. Chivvis, Keith Crane, Olesya Tkacheva, and Scott Boston, *Russian Foreign Policy in Historical and Current Context. A Reassessment*, (Santa Monica, California: RAND Corporation, 2018).

62   For further discussion, see Bruce McClintock, Jeffrey W. Hornung, and Katherine Costello, *Russia's Global Interests and Actions: Growing Reach to Match Rejuvenated Capabilities* (Santa Monica, CA: RAND Corporation, 2021), https://www.rand.org/pubs/perspectives /PE327.html.

as an instrument of foreign policy for attaining national interests. The balance of identity-based and interest-based considerations in allocations of aid has tipped toward greater pragmatism in the post-2014 context. The Kremlin has begun more often to deploy foreign aid in support of its foreign policy priorities, such as countering American influence and fostering economic interests, especially in the Eurasian region, which has been a top priority for Moscow. Russia's COVID-19 assistance has followed this trend. While not entirely heedless of human suffering due to the ravaging consequences of the pandemic, Moscow has favored countries in Russia's periphery for aid allocations as well as Russia's allies, trade partners, and supporters of Moscow's foreign policy. The Kremlin has also used COVID-19 aid to countervail the "soft power" influence of the US.

3   Analysis of Russia's COVID-19 Allocations

During the first year of the pandemic, Russia allocated between $66.5 million (lowest estimate) and $842 million (highest estimate)[63] of COVID-19 assistance to at least 36 countries in all parts of the world. More than 40 percent of the total COVID-19 aid went to Russia's neighbors in Central Asia, Belarus, Moldova, and Armenia. However, it was Italy, Serbia, and Bosnia and Herzegovina that were the single largest recipients of Moscow's assistance. Moscow also sent medical aid to its statelets in South Caucasus (Abkhazia and South Ossetia), to the occupied territories of eastern Ukraine, and to the Palestinian territories (see Map 2).

In addition to bilateral assistance, Russia allocated funding for fighting the COVID-19 pandemic through several multilateral mechanisms. The Russian Federation – UNDP Trust Fund for Development established in 2015 for implementing Russia's assistance to countries of the Commonwealth of Independent States and low-income countries in other regions received between $6 million and $10 million in support of health initiatives aimed at limiting the consequences of COVID-19.[64] The Russian government decreed a one-time voluntary donation in the amount of 500,000 Swiss francs to the International

---

63   The lowest and highest estimates are based on the lowest and highest market prices for various types of medical supplies, equipment, and PPE provided by Russia to the recipient countries.

64   Experts for Development, "Russia Allocates $30 Million to the Russia-UNDP Trust Fund for Development, Including to Tackling the Pandemic," May 7, 2020, https://experts fordevelopment.ru/news/project-news/rossiya-vydelila-30-millionov-dollarov-trastovomu -fondu-rossiya-proon-v-tselyakh-razvitiya-v-tom-chi.html; TASS, "Russia to Allocate up to

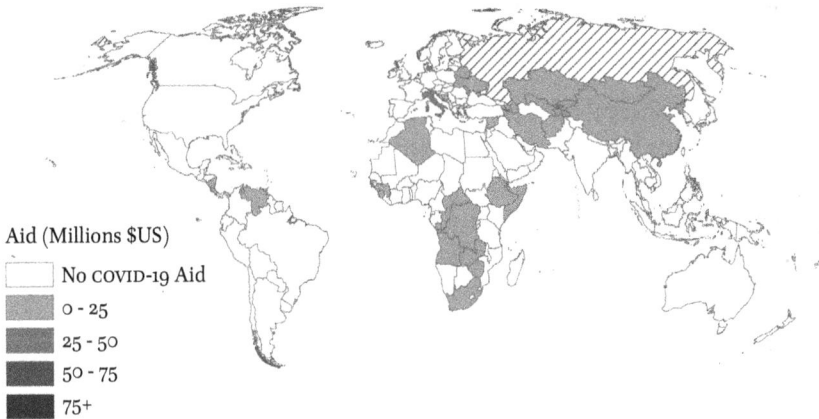

MAP 2   Russia's COVID-19 aid allocations

Committee of the Red Cross[65] and $1,000,000 to the World Health Organization[66] for fighting the spread of the novel coronavirus. This bilateral and multilateral COVID-19 assistance was approved on top of nearly $62.1 million that Russia allocated to various international organizations based on the consolidated appeals process by aid agencies.[67]

The combined bilateral and multilateral allocations by Russia toward the health crisis pale in comparison to COVID-19 assistance by China and the US reflecting limits to Moscow's capacity as an international donor. The Kremlin's poor management of the pandemic that involved misleading messaging about ways to mitigate the spread of infectious disease and inadequate allocation of health resources resulted in a health crisis in Russia. By the start of the

---

$10 Million to the UN Development Program by the End of the Year," TASS, December 21, 2020, https://n.tass.ru/politika/10313993.

65   The Government of the Russian Federation, "Decree of the Government of the Russian Federation dated 28 May 2020 No.1415-p," [in Russian] Official Internet portal of legal information, 2020, http://publication.pravo.gov.ru/Document/View/0001202006010009.

66   The Government of the Russian Federation, "Decree of the Government of the Russian Federation dated 3 April 2020 No.863-p, [in Russian]," Official Internet portal of legal information, 2020 http://publication.pravo.gov.ru/Document/View/0001202004060017.

67   More than 70 percent of the pledged funds went to World Food Organization in support of food security programs in Syria, Yemen, and Palestine (Financial Tracking Service, "Russia: Government Donor Snapshot, 2020, https://fts.unocha.org/donors/3006 /summary/2020).

pandemic, the Russian economy had already been battered by sanctions and low crude oil prices. The pandemic-induced global economic slump had further delayed Russia's economic recovery curtailing its ambitions in supporting other countries' fights against COVID-19. Still, Moscow's COVID-19 aid had acceded significantly its annual financial pledges to international aid organizations[68] and its bilateral humanitarian support to individual states.

Russia's multilateral COVID-19 assistance was in currency, but its bilateral allocations were in-kind. The transfers of COVID-19 test systems and kits produced by the State Research Center of Virology and Biotechnology "Vector" along with the personal protective equipment were among the most common types of aid supplied by Moscow. It also sent ventilators, contactless thermometers, disinfectants, and medicine to coronavirus-hit states. At least 11 countries received Russian medical personnel and other infectious disease and biohazard specialists. Most of the aid transfers were one-off deliveries of medical supplies and equipment with unknown impact.

The government of the Russian Federation (the Cabinet of Ministers) authorized nearly 80 percent of aid transfers, which were delivered through various state agencies. A federal service overseeing consumer rights[69] and the Federal Medical-Biological Agency under the Ministry of Health were involved in the implementation of aid deliveries involving test kits, medical equipment, and PPE. The actual transport of assistance was carried out on the planes of the Ministry of Defense and the Ministry of Emergency Situations (EMERCOM),[70] on which medical personnel and experts in biological, chemical, and radioactive hazards were also sent to a handful of states, including Italy and

---

68   Russia's annual assessed contributions to the World Health Organization, for example, were about $6 million (World Health Organization, "Assessed Contributions Payable by Member States and Associate Members 2020–2021," 2021, https://cdn.who.int/media /docs/default-source/documents/about-us/accountability/assessed-contributions-payable -summary-2020-2021.pdf?sfvrsn=2e62a9c1_3&download=true). Its annual allocations to the International Red Cross were about 1 million Swiss Francs (The Government of the Russian Federation, "Decree of the Government of the Russian Federation dated 9 March 2019 No.406-r" [in Russian], Official Internet portal of legal information, 2018, http://publication .pravo.gov.ru/Document/View/0001201803120011) and to the United Nations Development Program – about $9 million (The Government of the Russian Federation, "Decree of the Government of the Russian Federation of 18 March 2016 N 456-r On the implementation, starting from 2016, of the payment of the annual voluntary contribution of the Russian Federation to the budget of the United Nations Development Program," 2016, https://base .garant.ru/71356744/#friends).

69   The name of the service is The Federal Service for Surveillance on Consumer Rights Protection and Human Wellbeing or Rospotrebnadzor.

70   The full name of the agency is the Ministry of the Russian Federation for Civil Defense, Emergency Situations and Elimination of Consequences of Natural Disasters.

Serbia. A small percentage of the total COVID-19 assistance came from non-government agencies – commercial banks, financial institutions and corporation, NGOs, and the Russian church. However, the links of these organizations to the Russian state and the opacity of their funding mechanisms renders their independence from the government invalid.

The participation of the Russian Ministry of Defense (MOD) and the MOD-linked security contractors in COVID-19 assistance administration has been the most controversial Russia's aid delivery channels. Russia's security contractors delivered personal protective equipment, test kits, and ventilators in Syria and Sudan under the cover of shell companies. In April 2020, Meroe Gold, a subsidiary of Russian M Invest that serves as a cover for Wagner Group, was seen delivering medicine and personal protective equipment in Sudan.[71] Another security contractor with links to the Wagner Group delivered PPE, test kits, and ventilators in Syria.[72] Russia's private military companies (PMC) have been accused of gruesome violence on the frontlines, election interference, and the suppression of demonstrators. Their involvement in COVID-19 aid distribution has been seen as a public relations stint designed to clean the tarnished image of Russia's security contractors.

Russia's COVID-19 aid continued a trend in establishing an aid ecosystem that is non-transparent, increasingly government-to-government, and free from outside influence. As explained by the Head of Rossotrudniche-stvo, Konstantin Kosachev, an increasing share of bilateral "government-to-government" aid allocations followed a shift in the approach to humanitarian assistance in the post-2014 context. Russia's aid became "more strategic," serving Russia's national interests and working for building its global image. "As it often happens with assistance provided via trust funds and multilateral channels, nobody in partner countries knows that it comes from Russia."[73] To increase the visibility of Russia's COVID-19 aid, the largest Russian aid deliveries followed a similar pattern. Either the Russian president or the foreign minister had a phone conversation with a counterpart in a recipient state, thus partially circumventing traditional diplomatic channels. Once the offer of assistance was made and accepted, details were coordinated by lower-level

---

71   M Invest is on the US Treasury Department's sanctions list for its meddling in Sudanese politics (Erin Sindle, "COVID-19 Assistance to Africa: From Russia With Love," *Institute for Defense Analysis Africa Watch* 25, 2021, https://www.jstor.org/stable/pdf/resrep29557.5.pdf).

72   Sindle, "COVID-19 Assistance to Africa."

73   Lorenzo Piccio, "Konstantin Kosachev: A Change of Course for Russian Foreign Aid," *Devex* (December 4, 2014), https://www.devex.com/news/konstantin-kosachev-a-change-of-course-for-russian-foreign-aid-85005.

officials and the aid delivery was promptly made and broadcasted on official social media accounts and media channels. The close involvement of Russia's top politicians in humanitarian aid blurred the line of neutrality and independence, the two key humanitarian principles that inform aid administration by the Western donors. By delivering aid outside the UN-led humanitarian coordination channels, Russia eschewed strict rules applied to traditional donors, such as registration with recipient governments and partnering up with local NGOs for distributing aid.

To examine the patterns of Russia's COVID-19 aid allocations, we continue conceptualizing aid decision-making in two stages. In the "selection" stage a donor decides which countries will receive aid. In the "outcome" stage, a donor decides on the amount and types of aid distributed to states identified as recipients of humanitarian assistance. The dependent variable for the first decision-making stage is a binary (yes/no) measure with "1" assigned to those countries, which received any amount of COVID-19 aid, and "0" otherwise. The dependent variable for the second state is the total amount of aid allocated by Russia to a recipient states during 2020, assessed in US dollars.

Table 6 contains a complete list of independent variables used in the statistical analysis of Russia's coronavirus aid allocations. The humanitarian "need" is measured by the total number of deaths due to COVID-19.[74] To measure recipient countries' support for Russia's foreign policy, we used roll call votes on the United Nations General Assembly Resolution 74/17 on the militarization of Crimea adopted on December 9, 2019. The resolution condemned Russia's temporary occupation of the Crimean Peninsula.[75] We also used an alternative measure based on the voting pattern for the United Nations General Assembly Resolution 68/262 adopted on March 27, 2014, in response to the Russian illegal annexation of Crimea. It was a non-binding resolution that called on states not to recognize changes in status of the Crimea region, affirmed the territorial integrity of Ukraine, and invalidated the 2014 Crimean referendum. All votes in favor of these resolutions were coded "1", non-votes were coded "2", abstentions – "3" and votes against the resolution – "4." To measure the extent to which Russia's aid favored its neighbors, we used distance

---

74   The half-year total deaths estimate as of 1 July 2020 were used in the study.

75   United Nations General Assembly, Resolution A/Res/74/17 "Problem of the militarization of the Autonomous Republic of Crimea and the City of Sevastopol, Ukraine, as well as parts of the Black Sea and the Sea of Azov," (December 13, 2019), https://documents-dds-ny.un.org/doc/UNDOC/GEN/N19/400/94/PDF/N1940094.pdf?OpenElement.

TABLE 6   Independent and control variables used in the models of Russia's COVID-19 assistance

Independent variables	Definition	Source
Total COVID-19 Deaths	The number of reported deaths in a country as of June 30, 2020, per million population	The Center for Systems Science and Engineering at Johns Hopkins University 2020.
UN Resolution A74/17	An ordinal measure denoting whether a country voted to condemn Russia's militarization of Crimea in 2019	United Nations General Assembly 2019.
Distance to Capital	A measure of distance from the donor capital to the capital of the recipient country (in km)	Gleditsch and Ward 2001.
Membership in Alliances	A binary measure of whether a country was a member of the alliance with Russia (yes = 1, no=0)	Leeds et al. 2002.
US Development Assistance	The total amount of aid obligated from all US government agencies to a recipient country in 2019	USAID 2022.
Trade	Average trade turnover for 2016–2019	United Nations Statistics Division 2020.
GDP per Capita	Per capita values for gross domestic product (GDP) expressed in millions of current international dollars (for 2019) converted by purchasing power	World Bank 2019.
Population	Total population	United Nations Statistics Division 2020.
Liberal Democracy	A composite index that measures the extent to what an ideal liberal democracy is achieved in the country (0–1 scale)	Coppedge et. al. 2021.
Arms Transfers	A binary measure with 1=a country received arms from Russia between 2014 and 2019 and 0 otherwise	SIPRI 2020.

from the donor's capital to the country's capital (in km)[76] and membership in alliances.[77] Finally, we used the total volume of US development assistance received by a country before the pandemic (in 2019)[78] as a measure of Russia's geopolitical competition with the United States. The expectation is that countries which received higher amounts of US development assistance will have a greater chance of being selected for Russia's COVID-19 aid.

We also included a battery of control variables, such as the total volume of a recipient country's trade with Russia, its Gross Domestic Product,[79] population,[80] and regime type.[81] Finally, we included a binary variable denoting whether a country was a recipient of arms sales from Russia since 2014 ("yes" = 1; and "no" = 0).[82]

We used both separate logistic and OLS regression for the selection and outcome stages, respectively, and the Heckman's (1979) two-step estimator,[83] but only report findings from the separate models based on the Wald statistic suggesting that the two models are independent and can be tested separately. Our sample includes all states in the year of 2020 (but excludes unrecognized territories – Abkhazia, Transnistria, South Ossetia, in addition to Palestine – to which Moscow also provided assistance).[84]

The Russian media and official social media platforms framed Moscow's aid as a goodwill gesture in support of people in extremely difficult situations

---

76   Kristian S. Gleditsch and Michael D. Ward, "Measuring Space: A Minimum-Distance Database and Applications to International Studies," *Journal of Peace Research* 38, no. 6 (2001): 739–758.

77   Brett Ashley Leeds, Jeffrey M. Ritter, Sara McLaughlin Mitchell, and Andrew G. Long, "Alliance Treaty Obligations and Provisions, 1815–1944." *International Interactions* 28 (2002): 237–260. http://www.atopdata.org/data.html.

78   Source: https://explorer.usaid.gov/data.

79   GDP 2019, PPP (in millions of international dollars) (World Bank 2019).

80   World Bank. *World Development Indicators Database* (2019).

81   Coppedge, Michael, et al. "V-Dem Codebook v.10" Varieties of Democracy (V-Dem) Project. 2020, https://www.v-dem.net/en/. The aid literature often uses Polity IV scores or Freedom House scores that are highly correlated with the V-Dem measures of democracy. The choice of the Liberal Democracy index is premised on the assumption that Russia is less concerned with the institutional makeup of other countries and more with its ideological underpinnings. Liberal ideas and principles have been perceived to be threatening the stability of the Russian regime.

82   SIPRI Arms Transfers Database, https://www.sipri.org/databases/armstransfers.

83   James J. Heckman, "Sample Selection Bias as a Specification Error," *Econometrica: Journal of the econometric society* (1979): 153–161.

84   The Heckman model generates a Wald test statistic. When significant, it indicates that the two models are not independent and must be solved together. In our case, the Wald test statistic was significant suggesting that a null hypothesis of the two models' independence could be rejected.

hinting that humanitarian concerns defined by the severity of the health crisis played a decisive role in Russia's decisions about the COVID-19 aid. Yet, there is considerable evidence indicating that the dominant motives for Russia's COVID-19 assistance were political and pragmatic, rather than humanitarian (see Table 7). In fact, only the choice of the recipients of aid was affected by the level of mortality due to COVID-19 in the recipient states. The relationship was born out in practice in that Russia's assistance appeared to be tracing the spread of the infectious disease around the globe. In March 2020, the epicenter of the COVID-19 outbreak shifted to Europe with Italy experiencing higher daily deaths tolls than China. In late spring-early summer of 2020, Central Asian republics had the peak of the first wave of the pandemic. African countries experienced the outbreak later. Russia's assistance roughly followed the same pattern with the first aid packages going to Europe, then Central Asian and African states. Yet, Russia's aid was not conditional on the levels of countries' development (as measured by their GDP) nor on their population suggesting that state capacity to deal with the health crisis was not a consideration in the decisions about the allocations of Russia's COVID-19 aid.

Consistent with the expectations, Russia prioritized its "near abroad" in aid allocations. The members of Russian-led organizations were more likely to be selected as recipients of Moscow's coronavirus assistance and receive higher volumes of COVID-19 aid (the relationship is statistically significant in both the selection and outcome models at $p < 0.001$). Furthermore, the distance between the capitals of Russia and recipient states was also negatively associated with its COVID-19 assistce suggesting that Russia's preference for aid lied with the countries in proximity to its capital ($p < 0.1$). In the highly publicized conversations between Russia's leadership with counterparts in the recipient states, the Russian government often linked coronavirus support to the imperatives of deeper cooperation with Moscow. Referring to Kyrgyzstan as Russia's "strategic ally and partner," Russia's Prime Minister, Mikhail Mishustin, expressed hope that Bishkek would continue promoting joint actions in the Eurasian Economic Union and creating favorable conditions for the operation of Russia's investors.[85] Similar sentiments have been expressed in the conversations between the Russian and Armenian presidents[86] as well in conversations with the Kazakh counterparts.

---

85   The Government of the Russian Federation, "Mikhail Mishustin's Meeting with Prime Minister and Chief of Staff of the Presidential Executive Office of Kyrgyzstan Akylbek Japarov," (November 22, 2021), http://government.ru/en/news/43876/.

86   Radio Free Europe/Radio Liberty, "Russia Offers to Help Armenia Fight COVID-19 Pandemic," (2020), https://www.azatutyun.am/a/30646563.html.

TABLE 7   Russia's COVID-19 aid allocations

	(1) Selection stage	(2) Outcome stage
COVID-19 Deaths (per million)	0.006*	0.0044
	(0.003)	(0.004)
Membership in Alliances	1.579***	2.979***
	(0.555)	(1.123)
Distance to Capital	-0.0001*	-0.00006
	(0.00007)	(0.0001)
UNGA A/74/PV.41	0.515**	-0.928
	(0.2340	(0.105)
Liberal Democracy	-3.658**	-5.943***
	(1.69)	(2.148)
Trade (logged)	0.037	0.255*
	(0.871)	(0.148)
US Assistance (logged)	0.271**	0.06
	(0.128)	(0.083)
Arms Sales	0.00009	0.0003
	(0.0001)	(0.0006)
GDP, PPP in 2019 (logged)	-0.063	-0.191
	(0.09)	(0.211)
Total Population (logged)	-0.29	-0.425
	(0.224)	(0.331)
Constant	-0.439	7.99**
	(2.879)	(3.91)
N	153	153
LRchi2(11)	18.86	3.62
Prob > chi2	0.06	0.000
R-squared	0.25	0.23

Note: Robust errors in parentheses

$*\ p < 0.1, **p < 0.05, ***p < 0.01$

Political affinity, as measured by countries' votes in the United Nations General Assembly, was also a significant determinant of Russia's decision about the recipients of its coronavirus aid. Moscow appeared to reward countries supporting its foreign policies by resorting to the "checkbook" diplomacy of humanitarian assistance. The odds of being chosen for Russia's COVID-19 assistance were higher for those states who voted against or abstained from voting for the United Nations General Assembly Resolution A/74/PV.41 condemning Russia's temporary occupation and militarization of the Crimean Peninsula. Most of the countries that voted against the resolution and many among those that abstained from voting became the recipients of Russia's COVID-19 assistance in 2020 (Table 8). A similar result was attained when an alternative measure – roll call votes for the UN General Assembly Resolution of 2014 calling on states not to recognize changes in status of the Crimea region was plugged into the equation. States that voted against the resolution had higher chances of receiving the COVID-19 aid from Russia.

The nature of political regime of the affected countries has been highly relevant to Russia's decisions about COVID-19 aid. Countries that scored higher on the liberal democracy index were less likely to be chosen as recipients of Russia's coronavirus assistance, and they were also less likely to receive higher volume of the COVID-19 aid. Finally, trade relations also conditioned Russia's decisions about the COVID-19 aid. Countries with higher volumes of trade turnover with Russia received higher volumes of coronavirus assistance from Moscow.

Finally, our statistical analysis shows that countries-recipients of the US development assistance were more likely to be selected as recipients of Russia's COVID-19 aid. This is consistent with our expectation that Russia's foreign policy, including its aid allocations, has geopolitical undertones in that it reflects Moscow's competition with the US. This pattern of Russia using its humanitarian aid for a geopolitical purpose was on full display following Moscow's announcement of COVID-19 assistance to Washington. On 1 April 2020, a Russian military cargo plane landed in a New York City airport. The Russian media went into the overdrive discussing how the tables were turned in the US–Russia relations with "a gift from the Kremlin to its coronavirus-stricken rival."[87] The State Department quickly published a press release stating that the US government paid for the Russian shipment of PPE and ventilators.

Russia's offer of support to the US had both image-making and strategic purposes. It was used to present Moscow as a responsible power on the international scene while simultaneously depicting Washington as a global player in decline struggling with a health crisis at home. Russia's state-controlled international television network, Russia Today (RT) derided the US as a global powerhouse, which doctors worked in garbage bags lacking appropriate PPE. Other Russian media sources poked fun at the world's hegemon forced to

---

87   Russia Today 2020. The info campaign included the Facebook and Twitter accounts of Russia's Ministry of Foreign Affairs, as well as the accounts of Russian diplomatic missions and embassies abroad.

TABLE 8　United Nations voting patterns and Russia's COVID-19 aid

"Against" UN GA RES 68/262	Aid recipient	"Against" UN GA RES A/74/PV.41	Aid recipient
Armenia	X	Armenia	X
Belarus	X	Belarus	X
Bolivia		Burundi	X
		Cambodia	X
		China	X
Cuba	X	Cuba	X
North Korea	X	North Korea	X
		Iran	X
		Kyrgyzstan	X
		Laos	
		Myanmar	
Nicaragua	X	Nicaragua	X
		Philippines	
		Serbia	X
Sudan	X	Sudan	X
Syria	X	Syria	X
Venezuela	X	Venezuela	X
Zimbabwe	X	Zimbabwe	X

ask for aid from its geopolitical rivals.[88] In addition, both the company that shipped medical supplies and the one participating in their production were on a US Treasury sanctions list. Moscow's decision to involve companies under US sanctions in the supply of humanitarian assistance to Washington might have been an attempt to undermine the American sanctions' regime.[89] Due to the controversy surrounding Russia's shipment of medical supplies and equipment to the US, this event was excluded from the statistical analysis of Russia's humanitarian assistance.

88　Gigitashvili 2020.
89　Osborn and Marrow 2020.

CHAPTER 4

Geopolitical, Geoeconomic, and Humanitarian Considerations for COVID-19 Assistance by the United States

The US has been the top donor of humanitarian assistance during most of the years in the post-Cold War period. It has also provided highest levels of humanitarian aid in response to COVID-19. This chapter discusses the growth and institutionalization of US role in the field of humanitarian aid. It illuminates a perennial tension between geopolitical and geoeconomic discourses foregrounding American security and economic interests and a universalizing discourse prioritizing moral obligations toward all humans in its aid allocation decisions. The Office of the US Foreign Disaster Assistance (OFDA) and its parent agency – the United States Agency for International Development (USAID) – have become the sites of integration, cultivation, and transposition of these discourses into practice of aid administration consistent with US foreign policy objectives and its liberal internationalist vision of the global order.

The chapter traces the dynamic interplay of geopolitical, geoeconomic, and universalizing discourses about US foreign aid to the post-World War II period. During this time, the practitioners and pandits of foreign aid in the US framed American assistance as a response to the communist danger coupled with the need to foster global development via market reforms and democratization in the recipient nations. The tension between geopolitical narrative stressing the strategic necessity of sending aid to failing states and geoeconomic considerations favoring the creation of a liberal economic order featuring interdependence of capitalist economies persisted in the post-Cold War era. Yet, critical shifts in global power distribution and the appearance of novel threats expanded Washington's military and development footprint in more world corners.

To adapt its humanitarian response to the rapidly changing conflict and development dynamics, the US government instituted changes to its aid architecture. Due to these administrative reforms, humanitarian aid has become tethered to development assistance. These institutional changes happened on the backdrop of the growing involvement of the US military, development, and humanitarian agencies in complex emergencies. The integration of the various state functions, actors, and roles at the operational and institutional levels have contributed to the fusion of geopolitical and

© MARIYA Y. OMELICHEVA AND BRITTNEE CARTER, 2024 | DOI:10.1163/9789004692671_006

neoliberal economic logics with humanitarian imperatives in US foreign policy. As in other sectors of the disaster relief aid, the US government has relied on its development assistance infrastructure to distribute COVID-19 aid. Subsequently, the recipients of US development assistance benefited more from its COVID-19 allocations. In addition, the US government has favored its allies as well as those countries supporting US foreign policy in the United Nations. In this way, the new cartography of humanitarian aid has become to resemble the map of development assistance reflecting the neoliberal vision of the world populated by capitalist nation-states participating in free economic interchanges and capable of guaranteeing security and delivering political freedoms at home.

1   Background on American Humanitarian Assistance

The United States is one of the oldest state-donors, which engagement in disaster relief aid can be traced to the beginning of the American republic.[1] Prior to the 20th century, American disaster relief was mostly ad hoc, infrequent, and often internally focused. Whether during 19th century cholera outbreaks or the 1918 Spanish flu pandemic, the US response was persistently local and dependent on collaborations between public health authorities and voluntary organizations, a feature that colors a US approach to humanitarian aid to this date.[2] In the wake of the first World War, the US supplanted the UK as a global economic superpower and developed a considerable economic advantage over the European economies. With an expanding diplomatic presence and military footprint globally, the US government became more actively involved in international disaster response by itself and through partnerships with American voluntary humanitarian organizations.[3] However, it was after

---

1   The beginnings of the US involvement in humanitarian assistance can be traced to the early American republic. In 1812 for example, US Congress allocated $50,000 in disaster relief to Venezuela in the wake of a devastating earthquake in the city of Caracas. However, this was a rare instance of the US government's involvement in humanitarianism at the time. Until the mid-20th century, American private citizens and voluntary associations carried out the bulk of humanitarian effort (Julia F. Irwin, "The Origins of U.S. Foreign Disaster Assistance," *The American Historian*, 2018, https://www.oah.org/tah/issues/2018/february/the-origins-of-u.s-foreign-disaster-assistance/).

2   Marian Moser Jones, "The American Red Cross and Local Response to the 1918 Influenza Pandemic: A Four-City Case Study," *Public Health Rep*, 125, Suppl 3 (2010): 92–104.

3   Notably, this period marks the beginning of the US military involvement in the provision of aid. In the 1920s-30s, the War and Naval Departments donated food, medicine, and other

the conclusion of World War II that the US government assumed a more prominent and institutionalized role in the financing and delivery of humanitarian aid.

Even before President Truman signed the Marshall Plan of economic assistance to Europe (officially, the European Recovery Program) into law in 1948, the US government spent billions of dollars to restore European infrastructure and help refugees.[4] George Kennan, who Secretary of State Marshall appointed to head a planning group tasked with assessing the risk of Soviet expansion into Europe, envisioned this massive economic aid package as more than humanitarian aid, but as a tool to fight communism in Europe. The massive aid package was designed to bring the continent on a path to prosperity through economic integration and industrial modernization, and to prevent another Great Recession at home.[5] Although economic and security considerations were at the heart of the Marshall Plan, its concept embraced humanitarian spirit in that it sought, among other things, to feed, employ, and house the survivors of the Second World War. Concerns with the wellbeing of survivors of natural disasters and wars were further reflected in the Agricultural Trade Development and Assistance Act adopted by President Eisenhower's administration in 1954. Known as PL – 480 or "Food for Peace" law, this act established a broad basis for the US distribution of food as part of its foreign aid programs.[6]

America's vaccine diplomacy followed on the heels of the Marshall Plan. In the 1950s – 1960s, American and Soviet virologists worked together to create a life-saving oral polio vaccine and develop technologies for scaling up its production and distribution around the world. It is believed that the scare that poliomyelitis inflicted in the American and Soviet citizens encouraged their governments to set ideological differences aside and collaborate on solving the public health crisis.[7] This partnership set an important precedent for international collaboration in vaccine development, and it also highlighted

---

supplies to countries in Latin America and Southeast Asia (Irwin, "The Origins of U.S. Foreign Disaster Assistance").

4 U.S. Bureau of the Census, "Statistical Abstract of the United States: 1949" (Washington, D.C., 1949), p. 846, https://www2.census.gov/library/publications/1949/compendia/statab/70ed/1949-01.pdf.

5 Michael J. Hogan, *The Marshall Plan: America, Britain, and the Reconstruction of Western Europe, 1947–1952* (Cambridge University Press, 1987), p. 27.

6 US Department of State Office of the Historian, "USAID and PL-480, 1961–1969," https://history.state.gov/milestones/1961-1968/pl-480.

7 Peter J. Hotez, "Vaccines as Instruments of Foreign Policy: The New Vaccines for Tropic Infectious Diseases May Have Unanticipated Uses Beyond Fighting Diseases," EMBO Rep. 2, no. 10 (October 2001): 862–868; Peter J. Hotez and K.M. Venkat Narayan, "Restoring Vaccine Diplomacy," JAMA 325, no. 23 (June 2021): 2337–2338, https://pubmed.ncbi.nlm.nih.gov/34047758/.

how technical and scientific resources could be used in great powers' foreign policy.

The experiences and successes of the Marshall Plan and vaccine diplomacy shaped the debates over US foreign assistance in the 1950s and early 1960s. The Kennedy administration that resolved to improve management of American assistance set the Marshall Plan as a template for subsequent development strategy and institutions.[8] The passing of the landmark Foreign Assistance Act of 1961[9] not only defined what constituted foreign aid and its different types,[10] but also required the establishment of a single government agency for coordinating foreign assistance. The Agency for International Development (USAID) was established by Kennedy's executive order to oversee and coordinate the disbursement of US resources and technical assistance to developing nations.[11] Born at the height of the Cold War, the USAID was also charged with geopolitical and geoeconomic objectives. Among its goals were the promotion of US national interests while simultaneously assisting the Third World countries in their development. While the Cold War objectives foregrounded geopolitical logic of assistance, USAID also devised and implemented strategies and projects tied to the liberal internationalist vision of the world.[12] The USAID's geoeconomic logic was articulated in its own documents and statements

---

8   Jamey Essex, *Development, Security, and Aid: Geopolitics and Geoeconomics at the U.S. Agency for International Development*. Geographies of Justice and Social Transformation Series, Athens, GA: University of Georgia Press, 2013).

9   The 1961 Foreign Assistance Act with subsequent amendments serves as the legal basis for the US government's current foreign aid strategy, administration, and planning.

10   The Foreign Assistance Act classifies US aid into two broad categories. The first is economic aid, which subsumes both humanitarian and development assistance. The second category is military aid, which refers to peace and security programs aimed at building countries' law enforcement, counterterrorism, and anti-narcotics capacity. In practice, however, this distinction can be blurred when, for example, economic assistance during a complex emergency is used to build infrastructure projects serving military goals (Salvador Santino F. Regilme, Jr. and Obert Hodzi, "Comparing US and Chinese Foreign Aid in the Era of Rising Powers," *The International Spectator* 56, no. 2 (2021): 114–131; Marian L. Lawson and Emily M. Morgenstern, "Foreign Assistance: An Introduction to US Programs and Policy," Congressional Research Service Report 40213, 2020, https://crsreports.congress .gov/product/pdf/R/R40213.

11   Richard Stuart Olson, "The Office of US Foreign Disaster Assistance (OFDA) of the United States Agency for International Development (USAID): A Critical Juncture Analysis, 1964–2003," *Macfadden & Associates* (2005): 1–52.

12   Essex, *Development, Security, and Aid.*

suggesting that economic and political development was not an end but a means for advancing US trade and other economic interests.[13]

Although, the creation of USAID consolidated multiple separate streams of foreign assistance, it did not immediately result in better coordination of the disaster relief aid. In fact, in 1963, the US government botched its response to the devastating earthquake in Skopje, Yugoslavia, that killed more than 1,100 people and left 170,000 homeless.[14] Responding to the Skopje event showed considerable delays in mobilizing the disaster relief aid and serious coordination challenges internal to the US government. Four months after a heated and incriminatory hearing on Skopje held by the House Subcommittee on Foreign Agricultural Operations, the US government determined that disaster relief assistance needed a central and distinct coordinating authority. A year later, the Foreign Disaster Relief Coordinator's Office (a predecessor of the Office of US Foreign Disaster Assistance) was established within USAID.[15] The clear expectation was that the new office would be agile, quick, and creative in its response to disasters and crises.

The institutional apparatus of US humanitarian assistance that is in place today was consolidated in the 1970s–80s. The US government expanded its disaster relief commitments providing millions of dollars' worth of food, cash, and other aid to scores of disaster-stricken countries. In fact, with the exception of several years between 1989 and 2001, during which Washington conceded its first place as a top foreign donor to other countries, it has led the developed countries in net disbursements of not only humanitarian, but also development assistance (see Figure 4).[16] The worldwide focus on development in the early 21st century along with the post-9/11 recognition of the link between development, democratization, and national security has led to substantial increases in the US budget for foreign aid. Adjusted for inflation, annual foreign assistance funding in the post-9/11 context has been the highest in American history reflecting the growing number of large-scale humanitarian crises and complex emergencies, like those in Syria, South Sudan, Iraq, and Afghanistan (see Figure 5).[17]

---

13   USAID, "The Aid Story," USAID Document PN – ABT – 249 (Washington, D.C., 1966) as cited in Essex, *Development, Security, and Aid*, p. 39.

14   Alex Whitemire, "How the 1963 Skopje Earthquake Brought the World a Little Bit Closer," United Macedonian Diaspora, July 25, 2021, https://umdiaspora.org/2021/07/26/how-the -1963-skopje-earthquake-brought-the-world-a-little-bit-closer/.

15   Olson, "The Office of US Foreign Disaster Assistance (OFDA) of the United States Agency for International Development (USAID)".

16   Lawson and Morgenstern, "Foreign Assistance."

17   Lawson and Morgenstern, "Foreign Assistance."

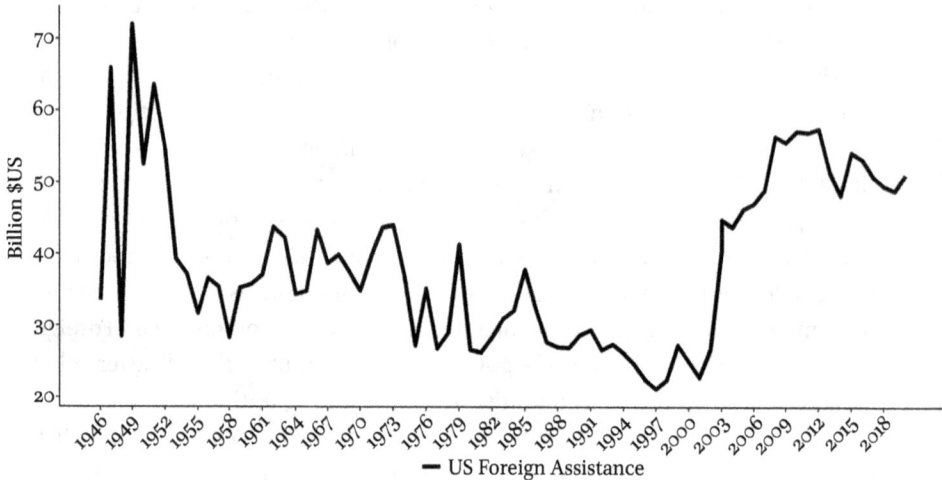

FIGURE 4   US foreign assistance (1946–2020)
SOURCE: U.S. AGENCY FOR INTERNATIONAL DEVELOPMENT (USAID) AND U.S.
DEPARTMENT OF STATE, FOREIGNASSISTANCE.GOV

Even as Washington continues leading the world in terms of the dollar amounts of aid flows, it ranks low when aid is calculated as a percentage of gross national income (GNI) (0.17 percent of GNI in 2019).[18] The best-known international target in the foreign assistance field sets a suggested level of official development assistance at 0.7 percent of the donor's national income.[19] Humanitarian assistance, which constitutes about 15–18 percent of the total foreign aid budget in the US, is a tiny fraction of the American national income.

Consistent with its long-standing tradition of cooperating with the American voluntary sector and decades of multilateralism, the US has relied on a pluralistic approach to aid administration. Only about one-fifth of US foreign assistance is delivered via state-to-state channels, while more than a half of its aid is distributed through multilateral agencies and non-governmental organizations. This reflects an important shift in the development assistance paradigm in the 1980s from a belief that the state is the most effective agent of development to the emphasis on free market forces, private sector, and private

18   OECD, "United States," in *Development Co-operation Profiles* (Paris: OECD Publishing, 2021).

19   OECD, "History of the 0.7% Oda Target," https://www.oecd.org/dac/financing-sustainable -development/development-finance-standards/ODA-history-of-the-0-7-target.pdf.

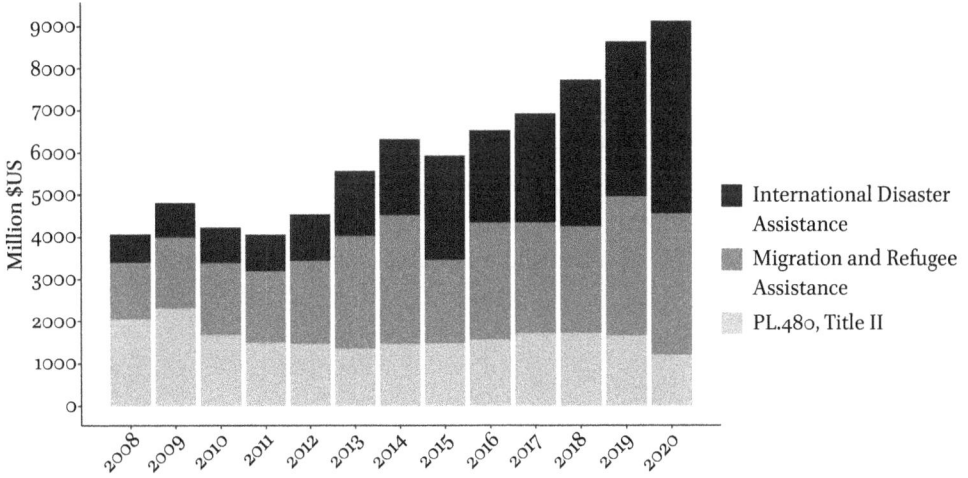

FIGURE 5   US humanitarian assistance
Note: The US foreign assistance comes from different accounts and is administered by different agencies. The International Disaster Assistance (IDA) account is the largest source of funding for responding to disasters and complex emergencies. The IDA funds are used by the USAID's Office of Foreign Disaster Assistance (OFDA). USAID uses a portion of IDA for the Emergency Food Security Program. Food assistance is also provided from the Title II funding of the Food for Peace Act, which is administered by US Department of Agriculture. The State Department's Bureau of Population, Refugees, and Migration receives funds for the migration and refugee assistance. Other agencies, such as the National Institute of Health and the Center for Disease Control and Prevention, can also use their budgets for administering humanitarian initiatives.[20] USAID also uses Economic Support Funds for certain humanitarian missions. All these funding streams were used in obligating COVID-19 assistance for foreign countries. Disbursements are reported in the graph, which include an outlay of funds placed at the disposal of a recipient government or organization.
SOURCE: U.S. AGENCY FOR INTERNATIONAL DEVELOPMENT AND U.S. DEPARTMENT OF STATE, FOREIGNASSISTANCE.GOV.

capital in solving development problems.[21] Furthermore, the US rarely supplies bilateral aid in American dollars. Most foreign aid involves the financing of US-made goods and services for specific development and security activities

---

20   Lawson and Morgenstern, "Foreign Assistance"; Rhoda Margesson, "International Crises and Disasters: US Humanitarian Assistance Response Mechanisms," Library of Congress, (Washington D.C.: Congressional Research Service, 2015).

21   Regilme and Hodzi, "Comparing US and Chinese Foreign Aid in the Era of Rising Powers." See also USAID, "Blueprint for Development: The Strategic Plan of the Agency for International Development," USAID Document PN – AAS – 485 (1985), p. 4.

and projects, which constitute another reflection of the geoeconomic thinking that underpins American foreign aid.[22]

Although NGOs administer a sizable portion of US humanitarian assistance, the US government has a robust disaster relief infrastructure consisting of not only the USAID representatives in nearly every US embassy around the world, but also multiple countries with full humanitarian response staff, USAID regional offices, several emergency stockpiles, and advisor officers at the US combatant commands and missions of international organizations.[23]

2   The Universalizing Logic of the US Humanitarian Assistance

The US government has unparalleled resources and capabilities that it has deployed in response to overseas disasters and conflicts when it has chosen to do so. Since the post-World War II, American rising economic and political stature has only been matched by growing demand for humanitarian assistance and expanding objectives that the US government has pursued with its foreign aid. The US policymakers have never achieved total consensus on the role of humanitarian aid in US foreign affairs. Discursively, Washington has embraced humanitarian principles for providing foreign disaster relief assistance. It has also made a concerted effort to translate these principles into its practice and policies regulating the administration of humanitarian aid. On the other hand, housed in the USAID, a site of the American geopolitical and geoeconomic discourses, the US humanitarian aid agencies could not stay completely immune to non-humanitarian dimensions of US foreign policy. The novel challenges of the post-Cold War context and fundamental shifts in the global distribution of power convinced the US government in the political and economic importance of the disaster relief aid.

2.1   *Neutrality and Impartiality of US Assistance*
The US government has consistently maintained that humanitarian aid should not be dictated by self-interested foreign policy imperatives.[24] American legislation and doctrine enshrines humanitarian principles of need, impartiality, and neutrality reflecting the beliefs in the preeminence of individuals above

---

22   Essex, *Development, Security, and Aid.*

23   USAID, "USAID Humanitarian Assistance Fact Sheet," 2021, https://www.usaid.gov /humanitarian-assistance/bha-fact-sheet.

24   Rob Kevlihan, Karl DeRouen Jr. and Glen Biglaiser, "Is US Humanitarian Aid Based Primarily on Need or Self-Interest?" *International Studies Quarterly* 58, no. 4 (2014): 839–854.

all else. These principles underpin the universalizing logic depicting the world of common humanity transcending the physical and political boundaries of individual countries. The Bush administration's National Security Strategy published in 2002, for example, explicitly states that the US government will provide humanitarian aid "based on needs alone."[25] The 2010 National Security Strategy of the Obama administration similarly states that the US will maintain its commitment to responding to humanitarian needs.[26] While the 2017 National Security Strategy of the Trump White House shifts emphasis on national interests and domestic politics, it still adheres to the humanitarian imperative of the previous administrations by committing the US to the goal of reducing human suffering globally.[27] The policies and procedures that guide USAID/OFDA and the State Department's humanitarian operations and programs explicitly state that humanitarian concerns are the "overriding principle" in developing and managing disaster relief aid. The latter is designed to provide life-saving assistance and alleviate suffering by ensuring that vulnerable and crisis-affected individuals receive protection and aid.[28]

A smart institutional design for American disaster relief has allowed the US government to translate these humanitarian principles into disaster assistance, which has been shielded from the domestic politics and unwieldy bureaucratic machine to the greater extent than development and security assistance. Until the USAID reform of 2020, the Office of US Foreign Disaster Assistance was a leading agency that coordinated US government's humanitarian assistance efforts overseas. The OFDA was housed in the United States Agency for International Development, a federal government agency responsible for economic, development and humanitarian assistance around the world. While the USAID has emerged as an important catalyst, transmitter, and purveyor of the development ideas and projects tied to American geopolitical concerns and economic interests linked to its liberal internationalist vision of world order (which at times placed this agency in the grind of American

---

25 The White House, *The National Security Strategy of the United States of America* (Washington, DC: The White House, 2002).

26 The White House, *The National Security Strategy of the United States of America* (Washington, DC: The White House, 2010).

27 The White House, *The National Security Strategy of the United States of America* (Washington, DC: The White House, 2017).

28 USAID, "ADS Chapter 251 International Disaster Assistance," 2020, https://2017-2020.usaid .gov/sites/default/files/documents/1866/251.pdf; US Department of State, "Refugee and Humanitarian Assistance," 2021, https://www.state.gov/policy-issues/refugee-and -humanitarian-assistance/.

foreign policy making[29]), the OFDA with its much smaller staff and inconspic-
uous location in the USAID headquarters had rarely shared a functional space
and duties with other federal agencies. Placing the OFDA within USAID, rather
than nesting it within the large bureaucracies of the Department of State or
Department of Defense responsible for the US foreign and defense policy, gave
the agency just enough independence to send aid based on the assessment
of need rather than political expediency.[30] At the same time, the OFDA could
leverage the USAID's extensive field presence and diplomatic support of the
State Department to remove political and logistical difficulties with accessing
the crisis-stricken territories in a timely manner.

The OFDA was unique and different from other government agencies in, yet,
another way. Not only could it respond immediately (generally within 24 hours)
with cash, personnel, relief materials, or grants up to US$50,000 released to
the USAID mission or the US embassy in the affected country,[31] but it could
also send its assistance anywhere in the world, including to countries that were
precluded from receiving other forms of American assistance. The so-called
"notwithstanding clause" added to the Foreign Assistance Act in 1975 means
that no other "statutory or regulatory requirements," like those restricting US
foreign aid to regimes implicated in human rights violations and engaging in
civil strife, can block the OFDA's ability to transfer aid to disaster or crisis victims in a timely fashion.[32] This "notwithstanding clause" allowed the delivery
of humanitarian assistance to Communist China in the wake of devastating
floods in the 1970s. It was also used to provide disaster relief to the victims on

---

29   It is not uncommon for USAID regional bureaus work side-by-side with their parallel
      regional bureaus in the US Department of State, which gives USAID staff a direct seat at
      the foreign policy table but also make them subject to US national interests and priorities.

30   When the Foreign Assistance Act was still deliberated, the Department of Defense was
      considered as the central coordinating authority for the US disaster relief. Even after
      this role was vested in the OFDA/USAID, proposals have been made to transfer this pri-
      mary responsibility for humanitarian aid to the Department of State. These institutional
      changes would have endangered the neutrality and impartiality of the OFDA and led
      to further politicization of humanitarian assistance (Olson, "The Office of US Foreign
      Disaster Assistance (OFDA) of the United States Agency for International Development
      (USAID)").

31   A response to a disaster generally begins with a US ambassador or chief of mission
      responding to a request from an affected country's government for assistance (Margesson,
      "International Crises and Disasters").

32   Office of the U.S. Disaster Assistance, "OFDA Annual Report for Fiscal Year 1995: BHR/
      OFDA," (1996), pp. 8–9, https://reliefweb.int/report/world/ofda-annual-report-fiscal-year
      -1995. See also Olson, "The Office of US Foreign Disaster Assistance (OFDA) of the United
      States Agency for International Development (USAID)", p. 15.

both sides of conflicts in Angola, Ethiopia, Libera, and Sudan, or in the aftermath of the collapse of authoritarian regimes in Panama and Romania.[33]

Furthermore, in 1981, the US Congress granted the USAID/OFDA the so-called "borrowing authority" that allows the agency to respond to the growing disaster needs that exceed the annual IDA appropriations (up to $50 million per year). Since disasters and conflicts cannot be predicted, this "borrowing authority" was intended to afford USAID/OFDA greater administrative flexibility to increase funds for disaster assistance by reallocating resources from other accounts. For example, in 1988, the OFDA "borrowed" $2.8 million from the Africa Bureau development account to respond to the civil strife disaster in Mozambique. The borrowed money may be repaid, but it is not a requirement for funds' reallocation. While the "borrowing authority" has been a source of contention within the USAID because it reduces other development accounts and alters budget priorities,[34] it gave the OFDA the fiscal prowess to respond to disasters promptly based on the considerations of need.

The OFDA was envisioned as a coordinating agency with a slender staff. In 2019, for example, it had approximately 525 personnel worldwide, working from Washington, D.C. headquarters, five regional offices and more than 20 field offices. To be able to respond efficiently to 50 or more crises in any given year, the OFDA relied on other US government agencies, foreign governments, international organizations, non-governmental organizations, and private or religious voluntary organizations.[35] The USAID/OFDA, however, developed sufficient capabilities for crisis response. USAID maintains strategically located warehouses stocked with essential emergency materials and relief supplies. It also possesses a response capability called the Disaster Assistance Response Team (DART) of humanitarian experts and technical advisers deployable within hours of an emergency to identify the most urgent needs and coordinate a prompt and effective US government response to the crisis.[36] The unprecedented flexibility in financial commitment and contracting, coupled

---

33   These types of assistance are often controversial especially when the disasters and crises are the result of the policies of the host government itself (Office of the U.S. Disaster Assistance, "OFDA Annual Report for Fiscal Year 1995", p. 7).

34   United States General Accounting Office, "Foreign Disaster Assistance: AID Has Been Responsive but Improvements Can Be Made," (Washington, DC, United States General Accounting Office (GAO), 1992), https://www.gao.gov/assets/nsiad-93-21.pdf.

35   USAID, "USAID's Office of U.S. Foreign Disaster Assistance," 2019, https://2017-2020.usaid .gov/sites/default/files/documents/1866/OFDA_Fact_Sheet_02-25-2019.pdf.

36   USAID, "Field Operations Guide for Disaster Assessment and Response, Version 4.0," (September 2005), p. IV-3, https://2012-2017.usaid.gov/sites/default/files/documents/1866 /fog_v4_0.pdf.

with a degree of institutional independence, made the OFDA agile and prompt in responding to humanitarian imperatives, rather than subject to political whims and bureaucratic impasse.

2.2 *The Merger of Geopolitical, Geoeconomic and Universalizing Logics in Humanitarian Assistance*

The neutrality and impartiality of humanitarian assistance distinguishes it, in theory, from other types of foreign aid, most notably, development and security assistance. The latter are often used as the main tools of foreign policy to advance American interests, such as helping to stabilize and democratize US allies and build market economies. The Marshall Plan, for example, was used to jumpstart Western European economies and turn Europe into a key market for American goods. Of the top fifteen American partners, eleven "were once recipients of US aid, and some of the faster-growing markets are former aid recipients."[37] The Western economies rebuilt with American assistance were envisioned as the cornerstone of its defense against the communist threat looming in Europe. At the same time, by focusing its investments on restoring and increasing the industrial potential and military capabilities of the European allies the US government sought to build loyalty of the Western capitals to Washington against the Soviet Union in global and regional affairs. Thus, from the beginning, US thinking about its development assistance interlaced beliefs in capitalist economic growth with geopolitical reasoning focused on attaining mutual security under the hegemonic leadership of the United States.[38]

Even at the height of the Cold War, when the US deployed its foreign assistance with the goals of curbing the expansion of communism around the world and opening foreign markets to its commercial interests, the OFDA was persistent in its humanitarian advocacy. As illuminated in the 1992 Government Accountability Office (GAO) report, "OFDA often provides assistance in politically charged environments (countries experiencing conflict or civil strife), and the agency occasionally receives pressure or instructions from Congress or higher executive branch authorities, including the Department of State and the National Security Council, regarding the timing and extent of assistance. In general, OFDA officials have advocated nonpolitical humanitarian assistance

---

37   USAID, "USAID Key Accomplishments," 2017, https://www.usaid.gov/reports-and-data/key-accomplishments.
38   Essex, *Development, Security, and Aid.*

and made a good-faith effort to ensure that assistance is provided equitably."[39] Departures from the humanitarian principles, however, happened when, for example, the relief aid provided in the form of food commodities was designed to not only help the developing countries in need but to also benefit American farmers and food exporters.[40]

As discussed above, the 1980s saw a significant reorientation from geopolitical to geoeconomic (and fully neoliberal) logic within the US foreign aid and development assistance infrastructure. This shift entailed greater reliance of the USAID on market mechanisms and involvement of the private sector in aid administration. The goal of this shift was to stimulate "international trade by opening markets, both within and among countries" while seeking to improve the political environment and the "climate for private investments and the transfer of technology accompanying such investment."[41] Without fully supplanting the geopolitical logic of foreign assistance, this geoeconomic approach envisioned foreign aid as a tool for stimulating global economic activity, growth, and connectivity through the liberalization of trade relations.[42]

Several developments in the post-Cold War era have infused the universalizing logic of humanitarian assistance with the prevailing geoeconomic and geopolitical narratives embraced by the USAID in its approach to development and foreign aid. First, the collapse of the Warsaw Pact in Eastern Europe and the Soviet Union's dissolution set off multiple ethnic and sub-national conflicts. Although, the OFDA was involved in complex humanitarian emergences before, its participation in humanitarian operations on the sidelines of conflict dwarfed its involvement in disaster response. A corollary of the OFDA's entanglement into US foreign policy has been the occasional subordination of disaster response to "the geopolitical focus of American foreign policy."[43] To improve the coordination of humanitarian assistance with US defense plans and programs and to better leverage the capabilities of the Department of Defense, the Office of Civilian-Military Cooperation (CMC) was established within USAID[44]

39   United States General Accounting Office, "Foreign Disaster Assistance: AID Has Been Responsive but Improvements Can Be Made," p. 5.

40   Essex, *Development, Security, and Aid.*

41   USAID, "Agency for International Development: Congressional Presentation, Fiscal Year 1983, Main Volume," USAID Document PD – ACE – 292 (Washington, D.C., 1982), as cited in Essex, *Development, Security, and Aid*, p. 51.

42   Essex, *Development, Security, and Aid.*

43   Andrew S. Natsios, "The Politics of United States Disaster Response." *Mediterranean Quarterly* 6, no. 2 (Spring 1995):46–59.

44   The CMC was established in 2011 in USAID's Bureau for Democracy, Conflict, and Humanitarian Assistance (DCHA), the same bureau where the OFHA was placed in 2001.

and senior USAID personnel was assigned to the geographic Combatant Commands. At the operational level, these changes worked to increase inter-agency knowledge, cooperation, and capacity. Yet, at the level of policy and strategy, military-security and political considerations began getting in the way of the humanitarian assistance imperative.

Second, a series of administrative changes motivated by the desire to link humanitarian assistance with development have broadened considerations for disaster relief beyond those involving the assessment of need. The Clinton and Bush administrations directed "effectiveness reviews" of US foreign assistance, which found that humanitarian aid was poorly coordinated with development and other post-conflict programs.[45] This, in turn, "impaired" American foreign assistance, especially in complex emergencies.[46] Before 1992, OFDA reported directly to the head of USAID, also known as the AID Administrator. This chain of authority was advantageous to OFDA allowing the agency to remain outside the USAID sprawling bureaucracy and remain quick and agile in its response to disasters and crises. In 1992, OFDA was moved under the newly created Bureau for Humanitarian Response, which was reconfigured into the USAID's Bureau for Democracy, Conflict, and Humanitarian Assistance (DCHA) in 2001. With this significant institutional change, not only OFDA became more bureaucratized, but it lost some of its autonomy and became "more AID-like."[47]

This bureaucratic restructuring took place on the backdrop of the increasingly ambitious US foreign policy. During the 1990s, democracy promotion and development became the core objectives of US foreign assistance. Infectious diseases, on the other hand, were named among the chief threats to political stability and economic growth and, therefore, elevated to the strategic level. The US National Intelligence Council published a report in January 2000 claiming that "persistent infectious disease burden is likely to aggravate and, in some cases, may even provoke economic decay, social fragmentation and political destabilization in the hardest hit countries in the developing and former communist worlds" in this way intensifying "the struggle for political power to control scarce state resources."[48] This trend of linking the matters of

---

45   Morton H. Halperin and James Michel, "Interagency Review of US Government Civilian Humanitarian and Transition Programs (Washington: US Department of State, 2000).

46   Halperin and Michel, "Interagency Review of US Government Civilian Humanitarian and Transition Programs", p. 9.

47   Olson, "The Office of US Foreign Disaster Assistance (OFDA) of the United States Agency for International Development (USAID)".

48   Alan Ingram, "The New Geopolitics of Disease: Between Global Health and Global Security," *Geopolitics* 10, no. 3 (2005): 522–545.

public health to national and international security threats only accelerated in the post-9/11 context.

Shaken by the horrors of the 9/11 attacks on the World Trade Center and the Pentagon, the US government augmented its aid programs with the goals of security and stabilization. As a result, the two decades following the Soviet Union's dissolution saw a solidification of the linkages between economic interdependence and national security in the American thinking about foreign aid and, with that, a merger of the geopolitical and geoeconomic logics for foreign assistance. This marriage of the geopolitical and geoeconomic narratives found expression in the US government's 2002 National Security Strategy. The document explicitly linked US national security to a "strong world economy" fostered through "free trade and free markets."[49] The strategic document also illuminated the risks posed by underdevelopment calling on the US government to increase development assistance to "countries that have met the challenge of national reform" in promoting democratization and trade liberalization.[50] The geopolitical construct informing US thinking about foreign assistance directed aid toward countries displaying what Washington considered to be acceptable signs and promises of neoliberal and democratic reforms and toward "weak states" regarded as potential hotbeds of instability, organized crime, and terrorism. From this point on, a US approach to foreign policy and national security has been firmly seated on a three-legged stool of "development, defense, and diplomacy."[51]

The weaving of foreign aid into the very fabric of national security tied to neoliberal globalization led to a proliferation of programs and initiatives in US foreign policy seeking to help developing countries strengthen the rule of law, investments, open societies, and trade liberalization. The creation of new programs and authorities contributed to the dispersion of coordination and control over aid across various agencies within the structure of the US government. And, when the government tried to instill greater policy consistency, the new coordinating and fiscal authority was placed in the Department of State making AID hostage to the tussle of bureaucratic power and political expediency in Washington.[52] For example, the FREEDOM Support Act, enacted in 1992 to support free market and democratic reforms in the

---

49   The White House, "The National Security Strategy of the United States of America" (2002), p. 17.

50   Essex, *Development, Security, and Aid*, p. 91.

51   Essex, *Development, Security, and Aid*, p. 107.

52   Olson, "The Office of US Foreign Disaster Assistance (OFDA) of the United States Agency for International Development (USAID)".

countries of the former Soviet Union, assigned coordination authority and, with that, authority to allocate budget for various programs in the Department of State.[53] In 1998, the State Department acquired another authority over AID – a formal review of the USAID budget. With the establishment of the State Department's Office of Foreign Assistance, this formal review of the USAID budget has extended into an unproductive micromanagement of the agency's policy and programs.[54]

The creation of the Millennium Challenge Corporation (MCC) in 2004 not only reaffirmed "the relationship between neoliberal economic growth, poverty reduction and security,"[55] but it has also resulted in further dispersion of control and authority over development assistance programs. Pledging to increase American foreign assistance, the Bush administration sought to ramp up the funding level for MCC to $5 billion per year. The proposal met with funding resistance from the Congress, which appropriated $1.5 billion in FY 2005 and $1.77 billion in FY 2006 for the MCC.[56] While the new Millennium Challenge Account managed by the MCC increased the level of American foreign aid, it also tethered assistance to the recipient countries' compliance with certain performance indicators adapted from measures and data provided by international financial and development institutions, such as the World Bank. These criteria in the categories of governance, economic freedom, and investment in people used by the MCC left a strong imprint on the subsequent foreign assistance frameworks adopted by the USAID.[57] With this fusion of the neoliberal criteria into the USAID decisions about foreign aid, many of the same considerations began coloring American humanitarian assistance.

China's rapid economic advances across Africa, Eurasia, and Latin America set off alarm bells in Washington putting the US government on the defensive. The Donald Trump administration adopted a coordinated policy framework

---

53   George H.W. Bush, "Statement on Signing the FREEDOM Support Act," The American Presidency Project, October 24, 1992, https://www.presidency.ucsb.edu/documents/statement-signing-the-freedom-support-act.

54   George Ingram, "Making USAID a Premier Development Agency," The Brookings Institution, February 27, 2021, https://www.brookings.edu/research/making-usaid-a-premier-development-agency/.

55   Emma Mawdsley, "The Millennium Challenge Account: Neo-Liberalism, Poverty and Security," Review of International Political Economy 14 (2007): 487–509.

56   James W. Fox and Lex Rieffel, "Strengthening the Millennium Challenge Corporation: Better Results are Possible," The Brookings Institution, December 10, 2008, https://www.brookings.edu/research/strengthen-the-millennium-challenge-corporation-better-results-are-possible/.

57   Essex, Development, Security, and Aid.

designed "to compel Beijing to cease or reduce actions harmful to the United States' vital national interests and those of [its] allies and partners."[58] As part of Washington's geostrategic competition with China, the US adopted a host of bilateral and multilateral economic and security initiatives with governments around the world and commenced a "trade war" with China. To counter Beijing's Belt and Road Initiative, the Trump administration instituted the US International Development Finance Corporation (DFC) in 2018. A type of global development bank overseen by the US government, the DFC "invests across sectors including energy, healthcare, critical infrastructure, and technology."[59] With the capacity to disburse annually 60 billion dollars' worth of loans, insurance, and financial guarantees to American companies engaged in commercial activities and infrastructure projects in the developing countries, the DFC held more than 15 billion dollars in assets in 2021.[60] The DFC explicitly invokes respect for human rights as a condition for loans abroad. The establishment of a new federal agency has, once again, scattered authority and control over development assistance away from the USAID.

The bipartisan support for the China challenge-centric US foreign policy remained intact in Washington with the arrival of the Biden administration, which added an ideological dimension to its competition with Beijing. Marshalling the world's liberal democracies to confront the challenges posed by authoritarian political systems has become a pillar of the Biden administration's National Security Strategy of 2022.[61] Building on the Trump era Blue Dot Network initiative, partly funded by the DFC, the Biden administration spearheaded the G7 Build Back Better World undertaking. Designed to provide a global alternative to China's BRI, the Build Back Better World program seeks to catalyze private funding for building roads, bridges, power plants, and airports in developing countries on the principles of climate stewardship, recognition of health considerations, as well as gender equity and

58   The White House, "United States Strategic Approach to the People's Republic of China," 2020, https://trumpwhitehouse.archives.gov/wp-content/uploads/2020/05/U.S.-Strategic -Approach-to-The-Peoples-Republic-of-China-Report-5.24v1.pdf.

59   US International Development Finance Corporation, "Who We Are," 2020, https://www .dfc.gov/who-we-are.

60   US International Development Finance Corporation, "Annual Management Report Fiscal Year 2021," 2021, https://www.dfc.gov/sites/default/files/media/documents/DFC%20 Annual%20Management%20Report%20FY%202021.pdf; See also Regilme and Hodzi, "Comparing US and Chinese Foreign Aid in the Era of Rising Powers."

61   The White House, National Security Strategy 2022 (Washington, D.C., 2022).

equality.[62] By reinforcing neoliberal conditionality of development assistance and insisting on coordination of development and humanitarian aid in this and other projects, the US government has allowed geoeconomic and geopolitical considerations to creep in to its decisions about disaster relief aid. To put it differently, considerations for development and security assistance have begun affecting humanitarian decisions premised on the assessment of need. The disaster relief aid has become an integral part of American development and security strategies housed in the newly instituted Bureau for Humanitarian Assistance that integrated the USAID's offices of disaster assistance (OFDA) and Food for Peace (FFP) in 2020.

To sum up, the moral imperative of alleviating individual suffering due to disasters and crises has served as an ethical foundation for the US humanitarian aid and a key pillar of its universalizing logic for humanitarian assistance. However, the post-Cold War institutional changes have anchored Washington's humanitarian practices in its development assistance infrastructure. The US reasoning about its development and security assistance has always featured a blend of geopolitical and geoeconomic considerations. While the reform of the American aid infrastructure has allowed the US government to adapt its humanitarian practices to the rapidly changing global environment, it has also entailed some distortion in its original humanitarian mission. More recently, policymakers have begun viewing foreign assistance as a tool to counter the global influence of nations that may threaten US interests, particularly, China. The institutional changes that brought the office of humanitarian assistance under the purview of development, conflict, and democracy agency certainly impaired the OFDA independence. Yet, they did not turn humanitarian aid into Washington's political instrument. The talented and hard-working staff at each level of AID administration embrace development as a goal in and of itself. Responding to people's basic health needs and expanding their opportunities for education and employment is not only in US security and economic interests, but it is also a moral imperative.

3   US COVID-19 Assistance

The United States' response to the coronavirus pandemic was slow, inconsistent, heavily politicized, and marred in geopolitical squabbles. At home, the

---

62   The White House, "Fact Sheet: President Biden and G7 Leaders Launch Build Back Better World (B3W) Partnership," 2021, https://www.whitehouse.gov/briefing-room/statements -releases/2021/06/12/fact-sheet-president-biden-and-g7-leaders-launch-build-back -better-world-b3w-partnership/.

Trump Administration was reluctant to institute appropriate public health and testing measures and sought to silence the nation's top infectious disease experts.[63] The President and some of the top officials actively spread misinformation about the efficacy of masks, downplayed the seriousness of the disease, and suggested unproven treatments that left the public more vulnerable to contracting the novel coronavirus.[64] In 2019, the Trump administration quietly shut down PREDICT, a USAID program established to track and research zoonic diseases and to serve as an early warning mechanism and a platform for assembling and disseminating good practices in combating infectious diseases. While the program enjoyed significant support under the Bush, Jr. and Obama administrations and was highly praised for identifying and studying over 1,000 novel viruses, it was discontinued under President Trump. This signaled a notable shift in the White House's attitudes toward the threat of pandemics and corresponding requirements for investing in research and building capacity for dealing with spread of infectious diseases.[65] With the dismantling of the PREDICT project, the related efforts at pandemic preparedness and dissemination of the expertise and best practice nationally and globally were considerably downscaled.

Lacking testing capacity and experiencing shortages of medical supplies and equipment,[66] the US nevertheless authorized a shipment of 17.8 tons of PPE and other medical materials to China's Wuhan province in early February 2020. With this first act of generosity, the State Department faced a harsh blowback from American politicians and media commentators criticizing the Trump administration for endangering the lives of American nurses, doctors, and other first responders by transferring critical medical supplies to other

---

63   US Subcommittee on the Coronavirus Crisis, "More Effective, More Efficient, More Equitable, Year-End Staff Report: Overseeing an Improving & Ongoing Pandemic Response," 2021, https://coronavirus.house.gov/sites/democrats.coronavirus.house.gov/files/SSCCInterim ReportDec2021V1.pdf.

64   Sarah Evanega, Mark Lynas, Jordan Adams, Karinne Smolenyak, and Cision Global Insights, "Coronavirus Misinformation: Quantifying Sources and Themes in the COVID-19 'Infodemic'," *JMIR Preprints* 19, no. 10 (2020), https://allianceforscience.org/wp-content /uploads/2020/10/Evanega-et-al-Coronavirus-misinformation-submitted_07_23_20.pdf.

65   Kesley Piper, "A Crucial Federal Program Tracking Dangerous Diseases is Shutting Down," *Vox*, 29 October, 2019, https://www.vox.com/future-perfect/2019/10/29/20936921 /usaid-predict-pandemic-preparedness.

66   Of interest to note is that the lack of PPE and other medical supplies to meet US domestic demands was itself a consequences of the earlier American administrations' political choices linked to neoliberal premises of efficiency and market-based principles of demand and supply.

countries.[67] To preserve critical pandemic-related materials in short supply at home from being transferred abroad, the Federal Emergency Management Agency (FEMA) issued a temporary order in April 2020 prohibiting the exports of a wide range of medical equipment.[68]

The row over medical resources happened on the backdrop of the heated exchanges between the highest-ranking members of the Trump administration and leadership in Beijing about the origin of the novel coronavirus and responsibility for its spread around the world. The geopolitical blame-game hindered early efforts to coordinate a global response to the pandemic and continued shaping Washington's foreign policy, including its demonstrative pullout from the WHO. The withdrawal of the US from WHO, which the Trump Administration accused in favoritism of China, would have threatened myriad programs administered by the organization and created uncertainty in global health governance. The impact of this decision and the cessation of financial contributions to WHO was amplified by a political dispute and a suspension of assessed contributions to Pan-American Health Organization over its role in Mais Médicos, a program that placed Cuban doctors in underserved communities in Brazil.[69]

Washington's policies and rhetoric concerning the novel coronavirus generated a strong public impression that the United States detested international cooperation and was letting the rest of the world go it alone. Even though in practical terms the US provided more COVID-19 assistance than any other country to help other nations cope with the health crisis. In 2020, the US Congress enacted five emergency supplemental funding bills to address the COVID-19 pandemic. Another bill – the American Rescue Plan Act – was enacted in 2021. While most of the funding in these bills was designated for the domestic response, approximately $19 billion was appropriated for global efforts through the Coronavirus Preparedness and Response Supplemental,[70] the Coronavirus Aid, Relief, and Economic Security (CARES) Act,[71] the Coronavirus Response

---

67   Annie Pforzheimer, "Pandemic Help to Latin America and the Caribbean: The Roles of USAID and the Department of State," The Wilson Center Latin American Program, 2021, https://www.wilsoncenter.org/publication/pandemic-help-latin-america-and-caribbean-roles-usaid-and-department-state.

68   Federal Emergency Management Agency 2020.

69   The United States had paid its PAHO assessment in full by the end of 2020, even though its overall funding to the organization fell considerably (Pforzheimer, "Pandemic Help to Latin America and the Caribbean").

70   US Congress, "Coronavirus Preparedness and Response Supplemental Appropriations Act HR 6074," Public Law 116–123, 116 Congress, March 6, 2020, https://www.congress.gov/116/plaws/publ123/PLAW-116publ123.pdf.

71   US Congress, "An Act to Amend the Internal Revenue Code of 1986 to Repeal the Excise Tax on High Cost Employer-Sponsored Health Coverage," Public Law 116–136, 27 116

and Relief Supplemental Appropriations Act,[72] and the American Rescue Plan Act.[73] Only \$3.2 billion of these designated funds were distributed in 2020.[74] Of this amount, about \$2.4 billion (75%) was designated for country, regional, and worldwide programming efforts through the USAID, Department of State, and CDC. The remainder of the 2020 COVID-19 package (and significant portion of the 2021 aid package) was for operating expenses, including for repatriation of US personnel.[75] The US has also increased spending on other humanitarian programs, including emergency food security assistance and migration and refugee assistance.[76]

Compared to China and Russia, US coronavirus assistance has been allocated mostly in dollars. This has been consistent with the American practice of foreign aid and shaped by the export control order[77] that prohibited the transfer of PPE and medical equipment abroad. This order was applied broadly to not only ban donations of certain kinds of medical supplies and equipment to foreign countries but also to limit the recipients of US aid from buying PPE using US government funding. This led to bad publicity for the US despite the overall high levels of the monetary donations.[78]

Most COVID-19 funding allocated in 2020 went to the Middle East (30%), closely followed by Africa (29%). East and South Asia was allocated 18% of the total funding, Europe – 12%, and Latin America – 10%. Yemen, Ethiopia, Cambodia, Italy, and Colombia were the largest recipient of US assistance in their respective regions (Table 9). Urged to act promptly in face of the

---

       Congress, March 27, 2020, https://www.congress.gov/116/plaws/publ136/PLAW-116publ136
       .pdf.

72   US Congress, "Rules Committee Print 116–68. Text of the House Amendment to the Sen-
       ate Amendment to H.R. 144," 2020, https://docs.house.gov/billsthisweek/20201221/BILLS
       -116HR133SA-RCP-116-68.pdf.

73   US Congress, "American Rescue Plan Act of 2021," 117th Congress, 2021, https://www.congress
       .gov/117/plaws/publ2/PLAW-117publ2.pdf.

74   Kellie Moss, Stephanie Oum and Jennifer Kates, "U.S. Global Funding for COVID-19 by
       Country and Region," KF, October 23, 2020, https://www.kff.org/global-health-policy
       /issue-brief/u-s-global-funding-for-covid-19-by-country-and-region/.

75   Moss, Oum and Kates, "U.S. Global Funding for COVID-19 by Country and Region."

76   Erin Collinson and Jocilyn Estes, "A Global Pandemic Needs a Global Response: US Con-
       tributions to COVID Relief," Center for Global Development, April 2, 2021, https://www
       .cgdev.org/blog/global-pandemic-needs-global-response-us-contributions-covid-relief.

77   Federal Emergency Management Agency, "Prioritization and Allocation of Certain
       Scarce and Critical Health and Medical Resources for Domestic Use," Federal Register
       44 CFR Part 328, updated December 31, 2020, https://www.federalregister.gov/documents
       /2020/12/31/2020-29060/prioritization-and-allocation-of-certain-scarce-and-critical
       -health-and-medical-resources-for.

78   Pforzheimer, "Pandemic Help to Latin America and the Caribbean".

TABLE 9   Top countries receiving US COVID-19 assistance (2020)

Region	Estimated regional total funding	Largest recipient within the region	Estimated country total funding
The Middle East	$452,862,494	Yemen	$225,600,000
Africa	$440,780,507	Ethiopia	$62,568,459
East and South Asia	$272,560,442	Cambogia	$49,330,934
Europe	$174,798,335	Italy	$99,712,747
Latin America	$144,049,020	Colombia	$22,595,954

sprawling infections, the US channeled most of its assistance through international organizations with active field operations. The UN High Commissioner for Refugees, UNICEF, and the UN's Food and Agriculture Organization were among the top international partners of Washington.[79] USAID also oversaw several US foreign assistance agencies, most notable US African Development Foundation and Inter-American Foundation. While neither foundation received additional COVID-19 funds, they adapted their activities in response to challenges posed by the coronavirus pandemic.[80]

4   Analysis of US COVID-19 Assistance

What follows from the discussion of US logic of humanitarian assistance is that the American government has been committed to humanitarian principles but has increasingly used aid for development and security imperatives, and as a tool in geopolitical competition with China. In allocating its COVID-19 aid, the US government has been motivated by the need-based considerations of the affected countries, but its decisions have also been shaped by the patterns of development assistance and other foreign policy initiatives. To test the determinants of US COVID-19 aid, we followed the same design used in the analyses of Chinese and Russian coronavirus assistance. We tested the impact of a range of independent and control variables in two separate equations

79   Collinson and Jocilyn Estes, "A Global Pandemic Needs a Global Response."
80   USAID Office of Inspector General, "Information Brief USAID Covid-19 Activity Update," 2020, https://oig.usaid.gov/sites/default/files/2020-10/COVID-19%20Information%20Brief%2009.21.20.pdf.

corresponding to two decision-making stages: the first stage, where the donor selects recipients for assistance, and the second stage where decisions about the volume of assistance are made. In the first (selection) stage, the dependent variable is the binary (yes/no) measure of whether the COVID-afflicted country received any coronavirus aid at all. In the second stage, the dependent variable is the total volume of coronavirus aid allocated by Washington (in US dollars).[81]

Table 10 contains a complete list of independent variables. We used the total number of deaths due to COVID-19 as a measure of the severity of the

TABLE 10   Independent and control variables used in the analysis of US COVID-19 assistance

Independent and control variables	Definition	Source
Development Assistance	The total volume of development assistance disbursed by USAID in 2019	USAID and State Department at https://foreignassistance.gov.
Aid Recipients' "Political Proximity" to the US	The average of the ideal distance points (between the US and its aid recipient) based on the roll-call votes during the five UNGA sessions preceding the COVID-19 pandemic	Bailey, Strezhnev and Voeten 2017.
Trade Balance (2014–2019)	An average trade balance (exports minus imports) for 2014–2019	United Nations Statistics Division 2020.
Membership in Alliances	The recorded number of alliances that a country has with China Countries with no recorded alliances are coded "0"	Leeds et al. 2002.
Total COVID-19 Deaths	The number of reported deaths in a country as of June 30, 2020, per million population	The Center for Systems Science and Engineering at Johns Hopkins University 2020.

---

81   COVID health aid is aid data from the US foreign aid explorer and is defined as COVID specific funding based on DAC sector purpose in the US foreign aid explorer (Source: https://explorer.usaid.gov/cd).

TABLE 10   Independent and control variables used in the analysis of US COVID-19 assistance (*cont.*)

Independent and control variables	Definition	Source
Distance to Capital	A measure of distance from the donor capital to the capital of the recipient country (in km)	Gleditsch and Ward 2001.
Liberal Democracy	A composite index that measures the extent to what an ideal liberal democracy is achieved in the country (0–1 scale)	Coppedge et. al., 2021.
GDP per Capita	Per capita values for gross domestic product (GDP) expressed in millions of current international dollars (for 2019) converted by purchasing power	World Bank 2019.
Population	Total population	United Nations Population Division 2019.

COVID-19 crisis.[82] To measure the impact of development assistance trends on US COVID-19 aid, we used the total volume of development assistance disbursed by USAID in 2019.[83] To proxy US security and other foreign policy interests, we used a measure of countries "political proximity" to the US, as well as membership in alliances with the US. "Political proximity" to the US was operationalized through countries' voting alignment in the United Nations General Assembly (UNGA) and measured by the "ideal point estimates" derived from the roll-call votes during the five UNGA sessions preceding the COVID-19 pandemic onset.[84] The average of the ideal distance points (between a donor and a recipient) was calculated. The "longer" the distance (i.e., the greater the disagreement between the donor and another country over issues voted on in the UNGA), the less likely that the donor will provide assistance to that

---

82   Esteban Ortiz-Ospina, Joe Hasell, Bobbie Macdonald, Diana Beltekian and Max Roser, "Coronavirus Pandemic (COVID-19)," 2020, https://ourworldindata.org/coronavirus.

83   Source: https://explorer.usaid.gov/data.

84   For further discussion of the estimation strategy and data, see Michael A. Bailey, Anton Strezhnev, and Erik Voeten, "Estimating Dynamic State Preferences from United Nations Voting Data." *Journal of Conflict Resolution* 61, no. 2 (2017): 430–456.

state. A variable measuring membership in an alliance (including nonaggression pacts or a treaty containing a stipulation of nonaggression) was used for alliance ties between the US and other countries.[85]

We also included a battery of controls, such as a country's GDP and population, a total volume of trade turnover with the US in 2019 (in US dollars, thousands), proximity of recipient states (measured by distance from the donor's capital to the country's capital (in km), and regime type (measured with the V-Dem's interval-scale index for Liberal Democracy for 2019).[86]

Humanitarian (need-based) considerations played a role in US decisions about the recipients of COVID-19 aid in the first (selection) stage of the decision-making process (see Table 11). Countries with higher levels of deaths from the novel coronavirus were more likely to be chosen as recipients of

TABLE 11   US COVID-19 aid allocations

	(1) Selection stage	(2) Outcome stage
COVID-19 Deaths	0.0001*	-0.00003
	(0.00005)	(0.00007)
Membership in Alliances	3.682***	3.274***
	(0.984)	(1.032)
Political Proximity	2.327***	2.868***
	(0.605)	(0.786)
Distance to Capital	0.0003**	0.0001
	(0.00016)	(0.00016)
Liberal Democracy	3.082*	2.125
	(1.639)	(2.419)
Trade Balance (logged)	0.0199	0.042
	(0.047)	(0.061)
US Development Assistance (2019)	0.00***	0.822***
	(0.183)	(0.157)
China's Aid	-0.331	-0.207
	(0.697)	(0.943)

85   For coding rules, see Brett Ashley Leeds, Jeffrey M. Ritter, Sara McLaughlin Mitchell, and Andrew G. Long. "Alliance Treaty Obligations and Provisions, 1815–1944." *International Interactions* 28 (2002): 237–260. http://www.atopdata.org/data.html.

86   Micahel Coppedge, et al. "V-Dem Codebook v10" Varieties of Democracy (V-Dem) Project 2020, https://www.v-dem.net/en/.

TABLE 11   US COVID-19 aid allocations (*cont.*)

	(1) Selection stage	(2) Outcome stage
GDP, PPP in 2019 (logged)	-0.328	-0.652**
	(0.206)	(0.273)
Total Population (logged)	0.433	1.206***
	(0.327)	(0.423)
Constant	-31.228***	-27.408***
	(6.465)	(6.77)
N	144	144
LRchi2(11)	39.15	15.38
Prob > chi2	0.00	0.000
R-squared	0.61	0.55

Note: Robust errors in parentheses

* $p < 0.1$, ** $p < 0.05$, *** $p < 0.01$

Washington's bilateral humanitarian assistance. However, this was less of a factor in the second stage of decision-making concerning the volume of humanitarian aid. We found no statistically significant difference in the volume of COVID-19 assistance allocated to countries with different levels of deaths due to COVID-19 pandemic. However, the levels of US coronavirus aid have been somewhat calibrated by recipients' capacity. When deciding on the volume of aid (the "outcome" stage), the US prioritized countries with the lower levels of GDP and higher population. The less developed recipients of US aid (as measured by GPD) and more populous countries received higher volumes of the coronavirus aid from the US.

In practical terms, when the WHO declared COVID-19 a global pandemic, multiple US agencies responsible for administering and overseeing development and humanitarian assistance launched various initiatives – trackers, survey questionnaires, etc. – to collect updates about the ways that the COVID-19 pandemic was affecting communities and programs. This information was used to revise the programs to better address operational needs.[87] At the level of the USAID, COVID-19 Task Force was created to coordinate

---

87   USAID Office of Inspector General, "Information Brief USAID COVID-19 Activity Update."

inter-agency international COVID-19 response.[88] The Task Force was responsible for distributing COVID-19 supplemental funds based on the assessment of need of the recipient countries, but the push and pull of various agencies with different priorities and excessive focus on coordinating response to mitigate the pandemic's impact on the US own personnel, travel, and facilities affected the US government's responsiveness to needs. Furthermore, following the Trump administration's announcement of the US withdrawal from the WHO, Washington paused all new funding to the organization. During the pandemic, the WHO continued playing a unique coordinating role with the local and national authorities. While the US identified alternative partners to work with in the implementation of its wide-ranging COVID-19 programs, there was no other implementer whose capacity level, an ability to identify countries' needs, and match those needs with the health programming options raised to that of the WHO.[89]

Given the desire to get money to the affected countries quickly amid the virus' spread, a large share of US COVID-19 bilateral assistance was transmitted through established channels involving active field operations. In March 2020, the USAID issued an authorization that allowed its officers to eschew "full-and-open competition" in rewarding new or modifying the existing contracts and programs. This authorization, justified by the need for flexibility and speed in implementing activities in response to the COVID-19 outbreak, allowed the USAID to rely on the existing programs and field operations for administering the increased funding levels. It comes to no surprise, therefore, that the strongest relationship that emerged from the analysis of the US data is that between the volumes of USAID development assistance in the year prior to the pandemic and US COVID-19 aid. USAID and State Department relied on existing contracts, programs, and field operations that were often extended beyond their initial scope of work to bridge gaps between the ongoing activities and new tasks, including those that involved efforts to contain and mitigate the outbreak of the COVID-19 infections.[90]

---

88   According to the 2020 report prepared by the USAID Office of Inspector General, USAID coronavirus response was administered through a task force that existed from March through September 2020. When the Task Force was disbanded, USAID's Global Health Bureau took over coordinating responsibilities in US Government foreign health assistance efforts (USAID Office of Inspector General, "Information Brief USAID Covid-19 Activity Update").

89   USAID Office of Inspector General, "Information Brief USAID Covid-19 Activity Update."

90   United States Government Accountability Office, "COVID 19: Better USAID Documentation and More-Frequent Reporting Could Enhance Monitoring of Humanitarian Efforts," 2022, https://www.gao.gov/assets/gao-22-104431.pdf.

Because the US government has tried to coordinate its disaster relief efforts with development assistance, and the latter has been tethered to the various metrics of the recipient countries' governance and relations with the US, these considerations have also colored Washington's decisions about humanitarian aid. These trends have been reflected in the patterns of the US COVID-19 assistance. Thus, the US slightly privileged countries that scored higher on the democracy index as the recipients of its COVID-19 aid. It also systematically preferred and gave more COVID-19 aid to countries, which are US allies. Furthermore, countries which have expressed support for US foreign policy priorities, as reflected in their voting patterns in the United Nations General Assembly, were also favored by Washington as the recipients of its coronavirus assistance.

Global Geopolitics of Vaccine Distribution

If 2020 was the year of the raging pandemic with many countries scrambling for resources and supplies to cope with it, 2021 was the year of vaccine politics. The race to develop a vaccine to curb the spread of novel coronavirus gave way to the vaccination marathon that took place on the backdrop of the battle of narratives about the superiority of diverging responses to COVID-19. Both China and Russia have framed their COVID-19 vaccine donations as part of their humanitarian effort at a time when major donors in Europe and North America prioritized their own populations for vaccination to the disappointment of the rest of the world. Washington and its allies countered these narratives by accusing Beijing and Moscow of using vaccine diplomacy for expanding their influence throughout the world.

For over a century, vaccine geopolitics have been characterized by the efforts of vaccine producing states to exercise influence and dominate discourse surrounding their humanitarian efforts. This chapter looks at the motives for Chinese, Russian, and American bi-lateral vaccine allocations and the rhetoric that accompanied their vaccine donations. We find that the patterns of these states' vaccine allocations largely followed their geopolitical logics that informed their approaches to humanitarian aid. Thus, China's vaccine assistance has become another foreign policy tool for achieving Beijing's interest in prosperity at home. Facing considerable challenges of mass production and distribution of the Sputnik V vaccine, Russia chose to provide assistance to its neighbors in the "near abroad," states of geopolitical importance, and other countries neglected for vaccine assistance by Western nations. Much like its decisions on COVID-19 aid, the US focused on maintaining a commitment to humanitarian principles, which it combined with development priorities and strategic ambitions. The geopolitical rivalry has also affected COVID-19 vaccine research, development, and distribution as the three nations competed to be the first in bringing vaccines to market, outpacing the others in terms of sales and donations, and securing contracts with recipient countries. The goal of outpacing the competitor has become another driving force in these donors' decisions about the allocations of COVID-19 vaccines.

© MARIYA Y. OMELICHEVA AND BRITTNEE CARTER, 2024 | DOI:10.1163/9789004692671_007

1   Vaccine Humanitarianism

Vaccinations have been an integral part of the humanitarian work of state and non-state actors as well as international humanitarian organizations. Long before vaccines became a cornerstone of global public health initiatives, they have been part of health campaigns to make life-saving vaccines available to vulnerable populations to decrease morbidity from preventable and curable diseases. Vaccination efforts have also been important in humanitarian emergencies, including conflict zones, where refugees and internally displaced persons have been particularly susceptive to outbreaks of communicable diseases. The UN member-states established the World Health Organization to directly address crises of disease and illness. In addition, there are other international organizations, private-public partnerships and international NGOs that engage in global vaccine campaigns, examples of which include UNICEF, GAVI, and the Bill and Melinda Gates foundation.

States themselves and state-run organizations are also critical cogs in global vaccine assistance. Vaccine donors, such as the United States and United Kingdom, leaned into their moral commitments to protecting the sanctity of human life, and ethical action to prevent human suffering, while also integrating development assistance priorities in order to afford states future capacity to combat crises, including pandemic and epidemic outbreaks. Meanwhile, China and Russia sought to consolidate their image of great power states and emphasized strengthening of governing regimes. Beijing has also viewed bilateral assistance as mutually beneficial exchanges that would put it in a better position to deliver more aid.

Donor states have also used vaccine assistance, both in donations and sales, toward their strategic objectives, such as strengthening relations with regional neighbors and allies, increasing their ability to influence domestic politics and foreign policies of the recipient states, deriving economic benefit, and promoting the donors' image.[1] Responding to the urgency of a global pandemic is both a lesson in health security, but also in understanding the international political

---

1   Mao Suzuki, and Shiming Yang, "Political Economy of Vaccine Diplomacy: Explaining Varying Strategies of China, India, and Russia's COVID-19 Vaccine Diplomacy," *Review of International Political Economy* (2022): 1–26; Bawa Singh, Sandeep Singh, Balinder Singh, and Vijay Kumar Chattu, "India's Neighbourhood Vaccine Diplomacy During COVID-19 Pandemic: Humanitarian and Geopolitical Perspectives," *Journal of Asian and African Studies* (2022); David P. Fidler, "Vaccine Nationalism's Politics," *Science* 369, no. 6505 (2020): 749–749, https://www.science.org/doi/10.1126/science.abe2275; Rajani Mol, Bawa Singh, Vijay Kumar Chattu, Jaspal Kaur, and Balinder Singh, "India's Health Diplomacy as A Soft Power Tool Towards Africa: Humanitarian and Geopolitical Analysis," *Journal of Asian and African Studies* (2021);

order and power configurations among powerful states. For some donors, vaccine assistance has been a way to project power and attain international prestige, as well as to "cash in" on geopolitical opportunity, ultimately "emphasizing power politics over humanitarian relief."[2]

Donor states' strategic interests have left some countries neglected in times of need. Humanitarian campaigns, such as vaccine assistance, provide states with opportunities to "spatialize" their understanding of the international system.[3] This geopolitical orientation can potentially shift foreign policy priorities from moral frameworks that center concerns for humanity toward policies that reflect long standing "historical particulars" and the "political sociology" of the donor state, as well as dynamic power configurations in the international system.[4] As a result some countries have been neglected in times of need, while donor states prioritized their own interests.

The development and distribution of the COVID-19 vaccine is no exception. It has been marred by geopolitical competition and conflicting logics about humanitarian aid. According to Dr. Scott Gottlieb, former commissioner of the Food and Drug Administration (FDA), "the first country to the finish line will be the first to restore its economy and global influence."[5] This vaccine "race" set forth the mindset of "winner take all" for states participating in vaccine development.[6] These high stakes conditions led to rifts in inter-state relations and a "fierce geopolitical race" between international donors. [7] Similarly, recipient countries were faced with differing political and ideological influences from donor countries, including the US, Russia, and China. Recipient states were put into positions where they had to choose from the geopolitical logic of the US, which promoted public service and human-centered vaccine assistance, and the foreign aid rationality of China, which emphasized development and economic performance.

Peng Lin, "China's Evolving Humanitarian Diplomacy: Evidence From China's Disaster-Related Aid to Nepal," *Asian Journal of Comparative Politics* 6, no. 3 (2021): 221–237.

2 Rachel Lambart, Carisa Shah, Josh Wiener, "The Distribution of COVID-19 Vaccines: A Geopolitical and Strategic Analysis of Southeast Asia," UPENN (Spring 2021): https://global.upenn.edu/sites/default/files/perry-world-house/Vaccines.pdf.

3 Thomas Moore, "Saving Friends or Saving Strangers? Critical Humanitarianism and the Geopolitics of International Law," *Review of International Studies* 39, no. 4 (2013): 940.

4 Moore, "Saving Friends," 925.

5 John Xie, "In Coronavirus Vaccine Hunt, a Race to Be First," VOA, May 8, 2020, https://www.voanews.com/a/covid-19-pandemic_coronavirus-vaccine-hunt-race-be-first/6188984.html.

6 Xie, "In Coronavirus."

7 Yanqiu Rachel Zhou, "Vaccine Nationalism: Contested Relationships Between COVID-19 and Globalization," *Globalizations* 19, no. 3 (2022): 450–465.

Early in the pandemic China called COVID-19 vaccines a "global public good," and later committed to "facilitating equitable vaccine distribution globally" with an initial pledge of $100 million toward equitable access in developing countries.[8] Russia, a self-professed global leader in pandemic assistance, quickly committed to prioritizing low-income nations that it felt were left out by other large donors and in which it felt Western nations were withdrawing.[9] To facilitate global cooperation on COVID-19 testing and on a vaccine campaign aimed at ensuring equitable access, the GAVI vaccine alliance, the WHO, and the Coalition for Epidemic Preparedness Innovation instituted COVID-19 Vaccines Global Access (COVAX), a global organization comprised of 30 donor countries aiming to vaccinate the world against COVID-19.[10] Dozens of nations quickly joined COVAX, and Western nations vowed to become major donors to the program. Consistent with their respective historical political positionings on foreign aid, China and Russia, while still maintaining a commitment to equitable access, preferred to provide vaccines through bilateral channels.

When the first COVID-19 vaccines were made available to the public through emergency use authorization, a commitment to equitable vaccine distribution was quickly brushed aside as the wealthy donors, themselves, saw vaccination of their populations as the only solution to the tight grip of the pandemic.[11] Traditional donors, including the US, quickly engaged in "vaccine nationalism," seeking preferential access to buy vaccine doses for inoculating their populations. By October 2021, traditional donors had pre-ordered and secured more than 60 percent of the total COVID-19 vaccine global supply, despite the fact that their populations make up only 16 percent of the world's population.[12] Many nations, including the US and Australia, ordered vaccines in amounts that

8   National Health Commission of the People's Republic of China, "China Committed to Facilitating Equitable Vaccine Distribution Globally," June 24, 2021, http://en.nhc.gov.cn/2021 -06/24/c_83960.htm; OCHA, "China Pledges US$ 100 Million Towards Equitable Access to COVID-19 Vaccines for Lower-Income Countries," August 5, 2021, https://reliefweb.int/report /world/china-pledges-us-100-million-towards-equitable-access-covid-19-vaccines-lower -income.

9   Sam Meredith, "As Russia and China Seek to Boost Their Global Influence, Analysts Warn Vaccine Diplomacy is Here to Stay," CNBC, February 17, 2021, https://www.cnbc.com /2021/02/17/covid-vaccine-diplomacy-russia-china-seek-to-boost-global-influence.html.

10   Bridge, "China COVID-19 Vaccine Tracker," accessed June 30, 2022, https://bridgebeijing .com/our-publications/our-publications-1/china-covid-19-vaccines-tracker/.

11   Zhou, "Vaccine Nationalism," 455.

12   Khan Sharun, and Kuldeep Dhama, "COVID-19 Vaccine Diplomacy and Equitable Access to Vaccines Amid Ongoing Pandemic," Archives of Medical Research 52, no. 7 (2021): 761–763.

went "well beyond their domestic requirements," with Canada ordering enough doses for vaccinating nine times its population.[13]

In the early days of the pandemic, China was already attempting to solidify itself as a "global health leader" through a major COVID-19 assistance campaign. Vaccine distributions became an additional element of Beijing's ostentatious global health diplomacy. In 2021 alone, China singularly exported more vaccine doses than the whole of COVID-19 Vaccines Global Access (COVAX). China declared to the WHO its commitment to making Chinese vaccines a global public good and followed through on this commitment by joining the COVAX in fall 2020. However, many were skeptical of China's purportedly humanitarian commitment to COVAX and speculated that its joining was merely an "insurance policy" for Beijing to be able to obtain vaccines, should any of its own vaccine development efforts fail. It has been argued that China's membership in COVAX gives the Chinese Communist Party (CCP) an element of influence and control over a major international apparatus and serves not only as an extension of Beijing's soft power efforts, but has the potential to bleed into its hard power efforts in other areas.[14] Additionally, onlookers saw China's COVID-19 vaccine allocations as one more play in China's "self-serving politics of generosity."[15]

In August 2020, the Russian government lauded the launch of Sputnik V COVID-19 vaccine in a show of "technological prowess and national pride" of the Russian Federation.[16] Although, the Kremlin touted the vaccine as a key part of the global solution to the pandemic, Moscow has made negligible contributions to the COVAX programs and offered limited vaccine donations abroad. The following sections detail each of China's, Russia's, and the US' endeavors in COVID-19 global vaccine aid, including statistical analysis, which illustrates the selection of recipients and volumes of vaccines' allocations.

2   China's COVID-19 Vaccine Assistance

CanSino, owned by the Chinese government, was among the first companies to produce a COVID-19 vaccine and to begin testing it on a pool of tens of

---

13   Sharun and Dhama, "COVID-19 Vaccine."

14   Jon Cohen, "China's Vaccine Gambit." *Science*, 370, no. 6552 (2020): 1263–1267.

15   Khairulanwar Zaini, "China's Vaccine Diplomacy in Southeast Asia - A Mixed Record," *Research Institute at ISEAS,* June 24, 2021, https://www.iseas.edu.sg/wp-content/uploads /2021/06/ISEAS_Perspective_2021_86.pdf.

16   Muhammad Zaheer Abbas, "Practical Implications of 'Vaccine Nationalism': A Short-Sighted and Risky Approach in Response to COVID-19," *South Centre,* Research Paper no. 124 (2020): https://www.econstor.eu/bitstream/10419/232250/1/south-centre-rp-124.pdf.

thousands of volunteers.[17] By 2021, China had five different vaccines at phase three clinical trials from major Chinese companies, including CanSino, Sinopharm, Sinovac, and Anhui Zhifei Longcom.[18] China's COVID-19 vaccine assistance campaign took off in July 2020 following the completion of Sinovac's Coronovac vaccine trials in Brazil.[19] Both China and Brazil declared the early trials a success, even though the success rate hovered around 50 percent, which, though acceptable by then WHO standards, would eventually be criticized by many nations and organizations in the global community.[20] By November 2020, Beijing had agreements with dozens of low- and middle-income countries around the world for its vaccine allocations. In early 2021, Beijing committed millions of free doses to nearly 70 countries in Africa, Latin America, and the Middle East, as well as to its regional neighbors in Central and Southeast Asia. It also committed to selling millions of doses in an additional 28 countries.[21]

By the end of 2021, China delivered over 2 billion vaccine doses to more than 120 countries in mostly bilateral state-to-state exchanges.[22] The Chinese government has also worked directly with heads of state from over thirty countries, inviting them to vaccine handover ceremonies and encouraging them to be publicly vaccinated. In 2021, China was handily the leading vaccine donor to low-income countries worldwide. Map 3 shows China's vaccine distributions worldwide. Table 12 list the top ten recipients of China's vaccine donations.

---

17   Cohen, "China's Vaccine."

18   Dechun Zhang and Ahmed Bux Jamali, "China's 'Weaponized' Vaccine: Intertwining Between International and Domestic Politics," *East Asia* (2022): 1–18.

19   Angus Liu, "China's Sinovac Plots Pivotal COVID-19 Vaccine Trial in Brazil After Positive Phase 2," *FiercePharma,* June 15, 2020, https://www.fiercepharma.com/vaccines/china-s -sinovac-says-covid-19-vaccine-shows-early-positive-results-phase-2.

20   Stephanie Nebehay and Kate Kelland, "Sinopharm, Sinovac COVID-19 Vaccine Data Show Efficacy: WHO," *Reuters,* March 31, 2021, https://www.reuters.com/article/us-health -coronavirus-who-china-vaccines/sinopharm-sinovac-covid-19-vaccine-data-show -efficacy-who-idUSKBN2BN1K8; Hart, Robert, "China's Sinovac Vaccine Under Scrutiny As Covid Soars in Highly Vaccinated Countries," *Forbes,* June 17, 2021, https://www .forbes.com/sites/roberthart/2021/06/17/chinas-sinovac-vaccine-under-scrutiny-as -covid-soars-in-highly-vaccinated-countries/?sh=1077f231444b.

21   Seow Ting Lee, "Vaccine Diplomacy: Nation Branding And China's COVID-19 Soft Power Play," *Place Branding and Public Diplomacy* (2021): 1–15.

22   Luo Zhaohui, "China's Foreign Aid and International Development Cooperation in a COVID-19 Pandemic World," *China Int'l Stud.* 92 (2022): 25, http://en.cidca.gov.cn/2022 -06/14/c_770501.htm.

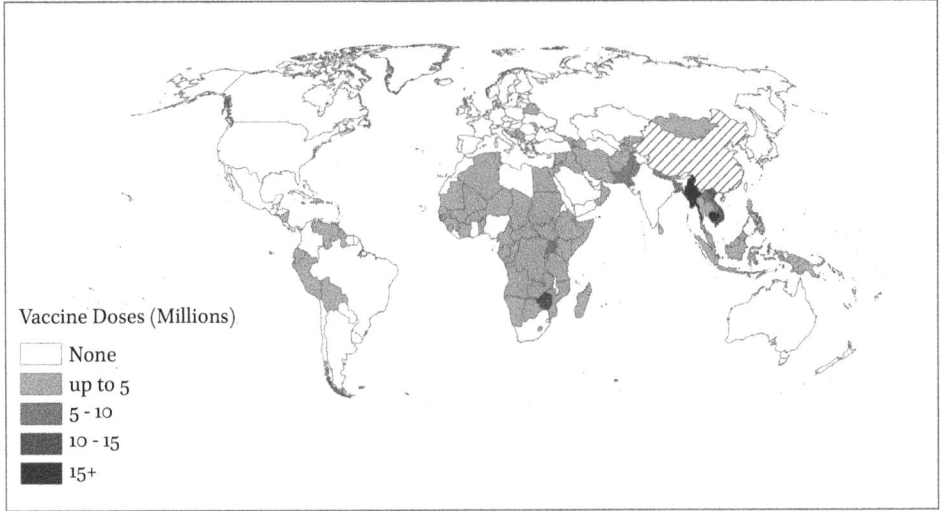

MAP 3   China's vaccine distributions

TABLE 12   The top 10 recipients of Chinese vaccines

Country	Doses (millions)
Cambodia	31,403,000
Zimbabwe	11,900,000
Myanmar	11,500,000
Vietnam	10,800,000
Bangladesh	7,600,000
Nepal	7,400,000
Laos	7,302,000
Pakistan	6,220,000
Philippines	5,000,000
Afghanistan	4,100,000

Vaccine assistance is an established part of China's strategy to project power across borders and into other political-territorial spaces.[23] China's geopolitical logic premised on state-centrism has influenced its decisions on how it selected vaccine recipients and the volume of vaccines they received,

---

23   The term "political-territorial" appears in: Biljana Vanskosvka, "Geopolitics of Vaccines: War by Other Means?" *Security Dialogue* 12 no. 2 (2021): 41–56.

prioritizing those who could strengthen China's image and power both domestically and globally. As much of the world blamed China for the rapid spread of
COVID-19, China saw COVID-19 aid and vaccine campaigns as an opportunity
to rebuild its image as an "efficient country" who positioned itself as a "global
leader" in health management, alongside a renewed opportunity to promote
its "Health Silk Road" initiative. These Sino-centric views form the conceptual foundation for China's foreign aid decision making, leading it to focus its
humanitarian efforts especially on nations that could promote Chinese investments, mutual trade agreements, development projects, and overall economic
growth.

Though China has refrained from positioning itself within the standard
framework of humanitarian rhetoric and rhetoric of vaccine diplomacy,
it did work to include COVID-19 relief and emergency aid as part of its geostrategic endeavors to reorient the liberal international order around a more
Sino-Centric narrative through the promotion of its state-centric logic of
global development and domestic prosperity. That said, China was deliber-
ate in its decisions regarding COVID-19 vaccines and recipients. Although
significant in the total volume, vaccines were part of the small assistance
initiative, per CIDCA's designation. This is consistent with China's "small yet
smart" approach to its humanitarian aid. These "small" assistance programs,
including vaccine assistance, were directed at countries that would provide
mutual "long term benefits," "[shared] governance experience," and cultural
exchange and human development. Vaccine aid, as part of the small assistance initiative, focused heavily on nations who are parties to CIDCA and BRI.
The CIDCA declared that China is "leading developing countries in Africa and
other regions at fighting the pandemic" through aid programs and vaccine
assistance.[24]

To assess the determinants for China's vaccine allocations, we assume that
decisions concerning aid are made in two stages. During the first "selection"
stage, the donor decides which countries will receive free vaccines. In the second "outcome" stage, decisions are made about the number of vaccines each
recipient country selected in stage one. To reflect this decision-making process,
we conduct analysis in two stages. In the first, "selection" stage, the dependent
variable is a binary "yes/no" measure of whether a country was selected to
receive free vaccines (coded "1" and "0" otherwise). In the second "outcome"
stage, the dependent variable is a count of the total number of vaccine doses
distributed to a recipient country.

---

24   Zhaohui, "China's Foreign."

Our primary expectation is that China's vaccine allocations will follow the logic of its COVID-19 assistance and humanitarian aid, in general. Therefore, our primary independent variables uncover the relationship between vaccine assistance and participation in Chinese development projects. We proxy the latter by coding countries that have signed a memorandum of understanding (MOU) on BRI with China and a development cooperation agreement (DCA) with CIDCA. Other variables (included in the analysis of China's COVID-19 assistance) are the total number of deaths due to COVID-19, the number of hospital beds per thousand population, adherence to the One China policy, the number of alliances with China, distance to Beijing, liberal democracy score, total trade balance (log-transformed), the country's GDP per capita (log-transformed), and the total amount of US aid received by the recipient country (log-transformed). The data spans the period of December 2020, which marks the first month of any global vaccine distribution from any donor nation, through November 2021, encompassing the prime initial donation period for China, as well as for Russia and the US.[25]

Table 13 presents the results of the two models analyzing the selection and outcome stages of Chinese vaccine aid allocations. One of the strongest relationships demonstrated in the analysis is reflected in the recipient country's DCA with CIDCA. Countries, which signed development cooperation agreements with CIDCA prior to the pandemic were more likely to be selected as recipients of vaccines from Beijing and were also more likely to receive higher volumes of vaccine doses from China. CIDCA has played an active role in overseeing decisions concerning vaccine allocation. While China has provided aid to countries, which haven't signed a DCA with CIDCA, those agreements increase avenues for broader strategic engagement of China with the recipient states.[26] Tanzania and Zambia, for example, partners in the Chinese-built Tanzania-Zambia railway to the Karakoram Highway, worked closely with the CIDCA to secure 1.57 and 1.7 million doses of Sinopharm and Sinovac respectively.[27] Tanzanian health minister expressed appreciation, specifically for

---

25   As will be explained later in the chapter, the US continued to grow its vaccine campaign into 2022, but as 2021 was the most competitive year in terms of donations among China, Russia, and the US, data including all of 2021 can provide strong insights into both individual and comparative motivations behind vaccine assistance.

26   Leah Lynch, Sharon Anderson, and Tianyu Zhu, "China's Foreign Aid: A Primer for Recipient Countries, Donors, and Aid Providers," *Center for Global Development*, July 9, 2020, https://www.cgdev.org/publication/chinas-foreign-aid-primer-recipient-countries-donors-and-aid-providers.

27   UNICEF, "COVID-19 Vaccine Market Dashboard," accessed June 29, 2022, https://www.unicef.org/supply/covid-19-vaccine-market-dashboard; All Africa, "Tanzania Receives

TABLE 13   Determinants of China's vaccine distributions

	(1) Vaccine binary	(2) Number of vaccines
CIDCA	1.812*	3.738*
	(0.868)	(1.863)
BRI	0.570	-0.145
	(0.668)	(1.345)
Recognition of Taiwan	-1.417**	-2.893
	(0.460)	(1.830)
Hospital Beds	-0.377*	-0.261
	(0.155)	(0.196)
Liberal Democracy	-4.682***	-23.41***
	(1.413)	(2.751)
Membership in Alliances	0.269	1.678
	(0.402)	(1.193)
Distance to Capital	0.0000539	0.000393***
	(0.0000683)	(0.0000953)
COVID-19 Deaths	0.000599	0.00252***
	(0.000339)	(0.000656)
Trade Balance	-0.0917*	-0.0348
	(0.0426)	(0.0617)
US COVID-19 Aid	0.0849	0.384***
	(0.0476)	(0.0725)
GDP (per capita)	-0.0523	0.615*
	(0.355)	(0.293)
Constant	2.890	9.071*
	(3.238)	(4.064)
lnalpha		2.995***
		(0.147)
N	142	142
pseudo R-squared	0.398	0.023
chi2	38.81	165.7

Note: Robust errors in parentheses

* $p < 0.05$, ** $p < 0.01$, *** $p < 0.001$

the timeliness of Chinese donations, especially as countries like Tanzania, Burundi, and Chad were among the "last in line" to receive consideration for US and COVAX vaccines.[28] The top 10 recipients of Chinese vaccine were all partners of CIDCA.

One of the first vaccine distribution and production contracts China signed was with BRI and CIDCA partner United Arab Emirates (UAE). China developed a working relationship with the UAE in terms of testing its virus vaccines, which was especially fruitful because the UAE, with its workforce coming from 125 different countries, allowed them the capability to test on individuals with myriad genetic backgrounds and health histories.[29] In this partnership, the UAE not only agreed to be recipients of the Sinopharm vaccine but also moved to host production and distribution of the vaccine as well. It was an implicit understanding that given UAE wealth and influence in MENA, they would serve as a "regional hub" of China's vaccine campaign and promote them throughout the Middle East.[30] This partnership received much publicity through CIDCA news press, highlighting the important role that UAE would play geopolitically as part of the community for the "shared future of mankind." This strategic partnership would not only revolve around economy, trade, and finance but also the promotion of Chinese culture through establishing schools and language centers.[31]

The UAE relationship with China was upgraded to the "highest level" by President Xi Jinping during a visit to Abu Dhabi in 2018.[32] At the start of the pandemic in 2019, the UAE was China's second-largest trading partner at more than $55.9 billion in trade. This is more than double the amount of trade that China had done with the US in the same year.[33] It became clear that China

Additional 800,000 Sinopharm Vaccine Doses From China," *All Africa*, January 26, 2022. https://allafrica.com/stories/202201270435.html.

28   Krista Larson, "Vaccine Deserts: Some Countries Have No COVID-19 Jabs At All," *AP*, May 9, 2021, https://apnews.com/article/africa-coronavirus-vaccine-coronavirus-pandemic -business-government-and-politics-2d5eab50c1ef8bd63b1a48331f4c3025.

29   Cohen, "China's Vaccine."

30   Zhang and Jamali, "China's 'Weaponized' Vaccine."; Westall, Sylvia, Adveith Nair, and Farah Elbahrawy, "China Picks UAE to Make Millions of Vaccines, Boosting Gulf Ties," *Bloomberg*, March 29, 2021, https://www.bloomberg.com/news/articles/2021-03-28/julphar -signs-deal-with-abu-dhabi-firm-to-produce-sinopharm-shot#xj4y7vzkg.

31   CIDCA, "Abu Dhabi Crown Prince Sheikh Mohammed bin Zayed Al Nahyan of the UAE Meets with Wang Yi," accessed July 1, 2022, http://subsites.chinadaily.com.cn/cidca /2021-03/31/c_607824.htm.

32   Lee, "Vaccine Diplomacy."

33   Lee, "Vaccine Diplomacy."

trusted the UAE not only for bilateral cooperation but also to promote Chinese interests through its ties to its MENA neighbors.

In Africa, Morocco, another country party to CIDCA, was among the first to accept Chinese foreign minister Wang Yi in the summer of 2020, and his promise that Chinese vaccines would be a "global public good." In December of 2020, Morocco "kicked off" a mass vaccination plan relying on the Chinese Sinopharm vaccine, hoping to vaccinate 25 million of its people.[34] By summer 2021, Morocco was slated to be the next production center of the Sinopharm vaccine and would continue to receive vaccine support from China through the end of the year. Following this assistance was "one of the first 'if not the first diplomatic' activity of 2022,"[35] in which Morocco signed an agreement on the joint implementation plan for the BRI. It was during this signing that Moroccan Foreign Minister Nasser Bourita reemphasized the long-standing partnership between Morocco and China, referencing a history of development projects connecting the two countries. The vice-chairman of China's National Development and Reform Commission stated that the BRI "carries a spirit of peace and cooperation."[36] Morocco stands as one of the top 10 countries to receive Chinese vaccines (in total deliveries).

Following our expectations, states that do not recognize the One China policy received statistically significantly fewer vaccine doses than those countries that support One China. Nations with diplomatic relations with Taiwan have a reduced odds of 0.24 to 1 of being selected to receive China vaccine assistance. That support for One China policy is directly linked to the selection stage of Chinese vaccine aid is somewhat unsurprising when considering arguments that Chinese Foreign Policy scholars make on the direct intentionality of China to keep Taiwan and its allies from acquiring vaccine assistance.[37] Though China claimed to administer vaccine assistance with "no political conditions attached,"[38] critics of Chinese policy argue that China tied its vaccine

---

34   VOA, "Morocco to Kick Off Mass Vaccination Plan with Chinese Drug," VOA, December 8, 2020, https://www.voanews.com/a/covid-19-pandemic_morocco-kick-mass-vaccination-plan-chinese-drug/6199310.html.

35   Safaa Kasraoui, "Morocco, China Sign Agreement on Joint Implementation Plan for Belt and Road Initiative," Morocco World News, January 5, 2022, https://www.moroccoworldnews.com/2022/01/346356/morocco-china-agree-on-morocco-china-belt-and-road-initiative.

36   Kasraoui, "Morocco, China."

37   Daouda Cissé, "China and Taiwan: The 'One-China' Policy and the Controversy of 'Vaccine Diplomacy,'" University of Nottingham, June 14, 2021, https://taiwaninsight.org/2021/06/14/china-and-taiwan-the-one-china-policy-and-the-controversy-of-vaccine-diplomacy/.

38   Embassy of the People's Republic of China in Solomon Islands, "Foreign Ministry Spokesperson Zhao Lijian's Regular Press Conference on July 29, 2021," Accessed June 16, 2022, https://www.fmprc.gov.cn/ce/cesb/eng/fyrth_17/t1896083.htm.

assistance campaign with "strings attached" to its One China policy.[39] China neglected to provide early vaccine assistance to countries like Paraguay and Honduras, which both maintain diplomatic relations with Taiwan, despite an active vaccine assistance campaign in many other Latin American nations. While support for One China policy is statistically linked to the selection of *who* receives Chinese vaccine aid, there was not enough evidence to tie to a probabilistic estimate of the number of vaccines distributed in the outcome stage.

In terms of great power competition, the expectation that China would compete with the US in terms of humanitarian assistance within the same nations is upheld by the results. The more aid a state received from the US, the more likely they were to receive vaccine assistance from China (selection stage). The magnitude of the increase in odds of vaccine assistance in relation to total US aid is small in the selection stage but is statistically significant ($p \leq 0.1$). There is even more confidence in the evidence at the outcome stage; for every log-transformed million USD that a country received in aid, the number of doses they are likely to receive increases by a unit of 1.5 times. This relationship is highlighted by China's vaccine distributions in places like Egypt, which is a top recipient of US aid and received over 25 million Chinese vaccine doses, and Colombia, another top recipient of US aid, who accepted millions of Sinovac doses beginning as early as February 2021, long before the US was able to provide Colombia with vaccine assistance.[40] China's strategy in targeting these countries was a "carefully executed and carefully thought out strategy" in an attempt to compete in the vaccine race with the US.[41]

Finally, and consistent with expectations established from the results of the COVID-19 aid analysis, China is more likely to distribute vaccine doses in countries with extreme needs as assessed in terms of the number of deaths due to COVID-19. Chinese officials regularly maintained a posture of providing vaccine assistance in countries that "need it most."[42] Chinese news media reported that Chinese vaccine assistance would prioritize addressing the vaccine gap and maintaining a "continuous flow of vaccines to developing

---

39   Cissé, "China and Taiwan."

40   Huaxia, "Colombia Receives New Supply of Sinovac COVID-19 Vaccines," *Xinhua*, October 26, 2021, http://www.news.cn/english/2021-10/26/c_1310270883.htm; Oliver Griffin, "Colombia Reaches COVID-19 Vaccine Agreements with Moderna, Sinovac," *Reuters*, January 30, 2021, https://www.reuters.com/business/healthcare-pharmaceuticals/colombia-reaches-covid-19-vaccine-agreements-with-moderna-sinovac-2021-01-30/.

41   Cohen, "China's Vaccine."

42   Huaxia, "Interview: China Holds Health Security Commitment as Global Vaccine Supplier, Says Scholar." *Xinhua*, September 9, 2021, http://www.news.cn/english/2021-09/23/c_1310204873.htm.

countries."[43] Uruguay was among the early recipients of Sinovac vaccines, which also had one of the highest COVID-19 death rates at the time.[44] The first vaccine distributions came in early Spring 2021, and while the Chinese Public Health Ministry reported that Sinovac had lowered the COVID-19 death toll by nearly 95 percent,[45] independent studies were not able to confirm a significant relationship with lower mortality rates.[46]

3   Russia's COVID-19 Vaccine Assistance

Russia's decisions on vaccine distribution closely followed its broader beliefs about the role of humanitarian aid in solidifying its position as a global leader and great power nation. This political and sociological stance has made humanitarianism an inextricable part of its foreign policy priorities. This was evidenced in Russia's quick reaction to the global pandemic and its early attempts to propel itself to the leadership in vaccine production and distribution. Russia's great power identity has created a specific, spatialized geo-imagery of the global order in terms of power configurations and leadership images projected into the international space. Vaccine assistance has been another mechanism, through which Russia attempted to gain geopolitical leverage over other nations, while also promoting its soft-power status and "strong moral character."

In August 2020, the Russian vaccine Sputnik V was the first COVID-19 vaccine to be registered in the world, with Belarus, Argentina, Bolivia, Serbia, and Algeria among the first to use Sputnik V on their populations.[47] In order to

---

43   Huaxia, "Interview: China Holds."

44   Jessica Li, "Covid-19 Vaccination in Uruguay," *The Borgen Project*, July 16, 2021, https://borgen project.org/covid-19-vaccination-in-uruguay/.

45   This claim was also reported by some "propagandized" Latin American media sources. Huaxia, "Figures & Facts: Chinese COVID-19 Vaccines Proved Safe and Effective Across World," *Xinhua*, July 13, 2021, http://www.xinhuanet.com/english/2021-07/13/c_1310057969 .htm; Huaxia, "Sinovac Vaccine Cuts COVID-19 Deaths Among Uruguayan Adults by 95 pct: Study," *Xinhua*, June 10, 2021. http://www.xinhuanet.com/english/2021-06/10/c_13100 00287.htm;

46   Jiangmei Liu, Lan Zhang, Yaqiong Yan, Yuchang Zhou, Peng Yin, Jinlei Qi, Lijun Wang et al., "Excess Mortality in Wuhan City and Other Parts of China During the Three Months of the Covid-19 Outbreak: Findings From Nationwide Mortality Registries," *bmj* 372 (2021): https://www.bmj.com/content/372/bmj.n415.

47   Kristyna Foltynova, "Sputnik V: The Story Of Russia's Controversial COVID19 Vaccine," *Radio Free Europe/Radio Liberty*, March 4, 2021, https://www.rferl.org/a/sputnik-v-vaccine /31133608.html; Natasha Turak, "Russia's Sputnik Vaccine Gets its First Approval in the

move to market quickly, Russia based the Sputnik V vaccine in technology utilized in its 2015 Ebola vaccine GamEvac-Combi, rather than new mRNA methods that were being developed in the West. Upon Sputnik V's release, the Kremlin declared the vaccine to be "safe and effective," touting a 92 percent protection rate against COVID-19.[48] Chief Executive Officer Kirill Dmitriev confirmed that immediately following the new vaccine's registration, Russia received requests for over one billion doses of Sputnik V.[49] In November 2021, the Kremlin announced that Sputnik V was authorized in 70 countries.[50]

Italy was one of the first countries and one of the only EU members to consider using the Sputnik V vaccine. Prime Minister Mario Draghi worked with Russia on a collaborative deal with the Italian Gamaleya Institute to refine and test Sputnik V. Subsequently, Italian-Swiss pharmaceutical company Adienne Pharma reportedly committed to producing 10,000 doses of the vaccine. The company later denied that such a decision was ever made blaming Russia for using misinformation for promoting its image in Europe.[51]

Adienne Pharma's renege on its commitment to producing Sputnik V came alongside increasing uncertainty about the vaccine itself. Doubts began to surface about the vaccine's safety and efficacy both from domestic and international audiences. Russia's President Vladimir Putin, himself, hesitated to take the vaccine, waiting several months before being inoculated.[52] At home, the Russian population was hesitant to get the vaccine for several reasons, including a lack of transparency regarding scientific and safety data and low levels of trust in the government.[53] Russia had low vaccination rates at home with only 36 percent of the population vaccinated by November 2021, and generous

---

EU, Greenlight From UAE Amid Ongoing Trials," *CNBC*, January 21, 2021, https://www .cnbc.com/2021/01/21/russias-sputnik-vaccine-gets-its-first-approval-in-the-eu-uae.html; TASS, "Factbox: How Countries Approved Sputnik V Anti-Coronavirus Vaccine," *TASS*, August 10, 2021, https://tass.com/world/1324643.

48   Serena Giusti, and Eleonora Tafuro Ambrosetti, "Making the Best Out of a Crisis: Russia's Health Diplomacy during COVID-19," *Social Sciences* 11, no. 2 (2022): 53.

49   Talha Khan Burki, "The Russian Vaccine for COVID-19," *The Lancet Respiratory Medicine* 8, no. 11 (2020): e85–e86.

50   Reuters, "First Session of the G20 Summit," October 30, 2021, https://www.reuters.com /world/africa/libya-launches-covid-19-vaccination-drive-after-delays-2021-04-10/.

51   Jonathan Smith, "Europe Shuns Russian Covid-19 Vaccines as Ukraine War Continues," *Labiotech*, April 1, 2022, https://www.labiotech.eu/trends-news/sputnik-v-russia-europe/; Giusti & Ambrosetti, "Making the Best."

52   Paul Stronski, "What Went Wrong With Russia's Sputnik V Vaccine Rollout?" *Carnegie Endowment for International Peace*, November 15, 2021, https://carnegieendowment .org/2021/11/15/what-went-wrong-with-russia-s-sputnik-v-vaccine-rollout-pub-85783.

53   Sarah Rainsford, "Why Many in Russia Are Reluctant to Have Sputnik Vaccine," *BBC News*, March 3, 2021, https://www.bbc.com/news/world-europe-56250456.

estimates suggest that as of May 2022 vaccination rates were just over 50 percent of the total Russian population.[54] As a likely result, Russia has nearly the highest number of COVID-19-related deaths in Europe, and ranks in the top quartile globally.[55]

Similar concerns with the Russian vaccine were seen abroad. The European Medicines Agency (EMA) did not approve Sputnik V, which led Europeans to "shun" the vaccine.[56] In Brazil, despite a deal brokered between the Russian and Brazilian governments to import the vaccine, its health regulatory agency Anvisa elected to not authorize the import of Sputnik V due to safety concerns that made the vaccine potentially "dangerous" to its recipients.[57] Even though the Gamaleya Institute, still working to produce Sputnik V, fought back that Anvisa's claims were unfounded and "have no scientific grounds,"[58] it would still take time for Anvisa to reverse its decision and allow limited imports, to the tune of only 1 percent of Brazil's original order of 67 million doses.[59] By October 2021, Brazilian health authorities would reject the vaccine entirely.[60]

Despite the many issues with its vaccines, Putin was able to alleviate some of the criticisms through a conserted state-controlled media campaign. Following Russia's historical legacy of projecting a strong central government both domestically and into the global arena, Putin worked diligently to shift blame regarding vaccine concerns and inefficiencies to weaker regional institutions.[61]

---

54   Reuters, "Reuters Covid-19 Tracker: Russia," accessed May 11, 2022, https://graphics
      .reuters.com/world-coronavirus-tracker-and-maps/countries-and-territories/russia/;
      Statista, "Number of COVID-19 vaccine doses administered in Europe as of June 14, 2022,
      by country," accessed May 11, 2022, https://www.statista.com/statistics/1196071/covid-19
      -vaccination-rate-in-europe-by-country/.

55   Reuters, "Reuters Covid-19."

56   Giusti and Ambrosetti, "Making the Best."

57   Sofia Moutinho, and Meredith Wadman, "Is Russia's COVID-19 Vaccine Safe? Brazil's Veto
      of Sputnik V Sparks Lawsuit Threat and Confusion," *Science*, April 30 2021, https://www
      .science.org/content/article/russias-covid-19-vaccine-safe-brazils-veto-sputnik-v-sparks
      -lawsuit-threat-and.

58   Sputnik V, "Sputnik V Statement on Brazilian Health Regulator Anvisa's Decision To Post-
      pone Sputnik V Authorization in Brazil," accessed May 11, 2022, https://sputnikvaccine
      .com/newsroom/pressreleases/sputnik-v-statement-on-brazilian-health-regulator-anvisa
      -s-decision-to-postpone-authorization/.

59   Moutinho and Wadman, "Is Russia's."

60   Manuela Andreoni, and Bryan Pietsch, "Brazil's Health Authority Rejects Importing
      Russia's Sputnik V Vaccine," *New York Times*, October 8, 2021, https://www.nytimes
      .com/2021/04/26/world/covid-vaccine-brazil-russia-sputnik.html.

61   Chaisty, Paul, Christopher J. Gerry, and Stephen Whitefield, "The Buck Stops Elsewhere:
      Authoritarian Resilience and the Politics of Responsibility for COVID-19 in Russia,"
      Post-Soviet Affairs 38, no. 5 (2022): 366–385.

By delegating responsibility to regional actors, Putin was able to maintain an image of strong central leadership while continuing to project its commitment to great power responsibility.

In all of 2021, Russia committed to sending more than 1 billion doses of Sputnik V globally. However, by October 2021, Russia had only sent about 4.8 percent of its promise of a billion doses.[62] Most of the Sputnik doses distributed, much like Russia's COVID-19 assistance, went to countries of the former Soviet Union, Africa, Southeast Asia, and the Middle East. Despite major promises to distribute vaccines, Russia followed through on very few of these commitments. Russia not only failed to deliver on most of its committed Sputnik donations but also only engaged in a few vaccine sales contracts. Map 4 shows the recipients of Russia's vaccine donations. Table 14 lists the top recipients of Sputnik V donations by volume.

Similar to the analysis of China's vaccine allocations, we examine Russia's decisions on vaccine assistance in two stages. The selection stage is tested via logistic regression with a binary dependent variable indicating whether or not a state received vaccine assistance from Russia. The outcome stage is tested using a negative binomial regression on a dependent variable, which is the count of vaccine doses received.

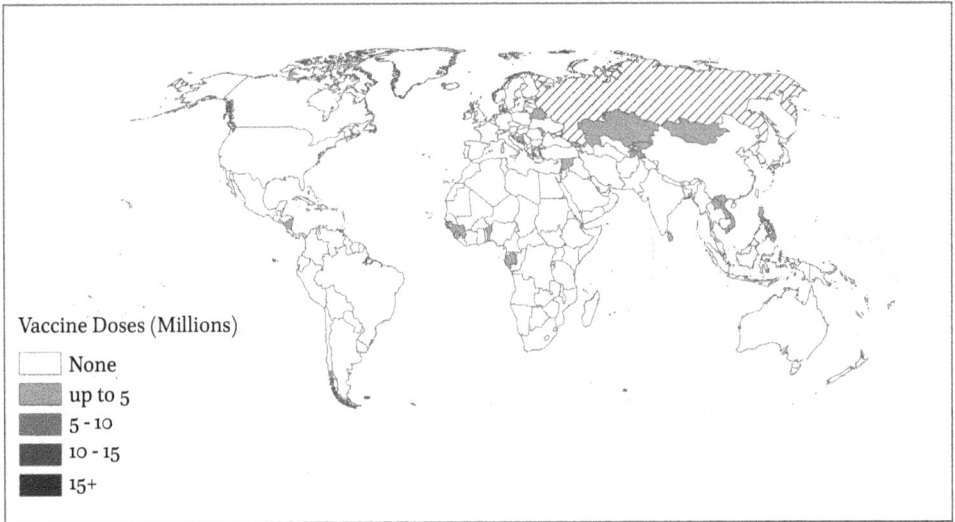

MAP 4   Russia's vaccine distributions

62   Georgi Kantchev, "Russia Struggles to Meet Demand for Its COVID-19 Vaccine," *The Wall-street Journal*, May 14, 2021. https://www.wsj.com/articles/russia-struggles-to-meet-demand-for-its-covid-19-vaccine-11620993601.

TABLE 14   The top 10 recipients of Russian vaccines

Country	Doses (millions)
Kyrgyzstan	700,000
Mongolia	300,000
Sri Lanka	300,000
Belarus	250,000
Syria	250,000
Moldova	210,000
Kazakhstan	150,000
Vietnam	102,000
Benin	100,000
Djibouti	100,000

We maintain the same independent variables in the vaccine assistance models as were included in the COVID-19 aid models. These include total deaths due to COVID-19, trade balance (log-transformed), UN Resolution 74/17 regarding Crimea, membership in an alliance with Russia, measure of liberal democracy, arms transfers, population and GDP (log-transformed). Finally, we include a new variable which measures the total amount of development assistance (log-transformed) from the US as reported by the OECD. The results of the analysis are presented in Table 15.

Because there were so few countries which received Russian vaccines, the number of non-zero observations in both the logistic and negative binomial regressions is high. This may explain why there were higher levels of insignificant coefficients in the logistic regression model than we saw in the earlier COVID-19 aid analysis. That said, there was a strong association between those countries that were selected to receive vaccines and their votes on UN Resolution 74/17. This measure is used as a proxy for political affinity and is consistent with our expectations. Recall, that this resolution is an ordinal measure denoting whether a country voted to condemn Russia's militarization of Crimea in 2019. This resolution saw several countries voting in Russia's favor or abstaining from the vote altogether, such as Bosnia and Herzegovina, Moldova, and Macedonia, as well as Middle Eastern nations such as Algeria, Iran, and Iraq, all of whom were selected to receive Russia's vaccines. In fact, in the outcome model, the negative binomial analysis demonstrates that states who voted in line with Russia on this resolution received vaccine doses at an increased amount of

TABLE 15 Determinants of Russia's vaccine distributions

	(1) Vaccine binary	(2) Number of vaccines
COVID-19 Deaths	0.0023	0.0229**
	(0.00207)	(0.00787)
Trade Balance	-0.0704	-0.435***
	(0.0506)	(0.124)
UN Resolution 74/17	0.959*	2.884***
	(0.374)	(0.590)
Population	-0.741*	-7.584***
	(0.336)	(2.301)
Distance to Capital	-0.0000139	-0.000113
	(0.000149)	(0.000180)
Liberal Democracy	-3.968**	-58.84***
	(1.223)	(7.395)
Membership in Alliances	1.220	6.114**
	(0.879)	(1.880)
GDP	0.394*	6.132**
	(0.191)	(2.048)
Development Aid	-0.0283	-0.888*
	(0.104)	(0.405)
US Development Aid	0.0851	0.734***
	(0.172)	(0.165)
Arms Transfers	-0.0000223	-0.00305***
	(0.000190)	(0.000736)
Constant	4.434	71.94***
	(4.059)	(16.96)
lnalpha		4.295***
		(0.246)
N	153	153
pseudo R-squared	0.260	0.036
chi2	35.82	147.2

Note: Robust errors in parentheses

$* p < 0.05, ** p < 0.01, *** p < 0.001$

17.9 times. Bolivia was one such country that continually displayed political allyship toward Russia, so when the time came to call upon Russia for vaccine assistance, the Kremlin responded with a promise of 5.2 million doses, enough doses to provide nearly 45 percent of the Bolivian population with one shot, or enough to fully vaccinate over 22 percent of its people.[63] Additionally, Russia welcomed orders from Egypt and Iran for 25 and 60 million doses respectively, both of which abstained from the vote, and Russia committed to delivering, even though it ultimately failed to meet these demands.[64]

We can also say with a level of confidence that authoritarian states were more likely to receive vaccine assistance from Russia than were liberal democracies. This result holds both in the outcome and selection stages at a substantially large magnitude. Democratic states have 0.018 chance of receiving Russian vaccine assistance, and the rate at which democratic states receive vaccine doses is substantively almost zero. This preference toward authoritarian states (and authoritarian counterparts' receptiveness to Russia's offers of humanitarian assistance) can be traced to certain characteristics of authoritarian regimes.[65] Autocratic governments are concerned with the prospects of obtaining benefits (or sustaining costs) for a small group of the government insiders rather than broader swaths of population. The lack of accountability to the public is one of the hallmarks of authoritarian regimes. Since the autocratic incentive structure is based on the distribution of private benefits and reduction of private costs to the regime insiders, both the autocratic donor and the autocratic recipient can benefit from the lack of accountability to their respective populations. From the autocratic donor's perspective, it is easier to manipulate the autocratic recipient's decisions – with the transfer of COVID-19 aid and vaccines Russia can bet on the recipient states' "pay back" in ways beneficial to Moscow. From the autocratic recipient's standpoint, it is easier to get private benefits from the aid provided by the autocratic donor.

63   Aislinn Laing and Cassandra Garrison, "Amid Scramble for COVID-19 Vaccine, Latin America Turns to Russia," *Reuters*, March 1, 2021, https://www.reuters.com/business /healthcare-pharmaceuticals/amid-scramble-covid-19-vaccine-latin-america-turns-russia -2021-03-01/.

64   Statista, "Number of Doses of the COVID-19 Vaccine Sputnik V Ordered from Russia or Agreed to Be Produced Abroad as of January 2022, by Country," *Statista*, accessed June 20, 2022, https://www.statista.com/statistics/1123927/sputnik-v-exports-from-russia-by -country/.

65   Julia Bader, Jörn Grävingholt, and Antje Kästner, "Would Autocracies Promote Autocracy? A Political Economy Perspective on Regime-Type Export in Regional Neighbourhoods," *Contemporary Politics* 16, no. 1 (2010): 81–100.

In the outcome stage, it becomes clear that there are several additional determinants beyond political affinity and regime type for how many vaccine doses a country will receive. First, Russia appears to stick to its commitments to provide need-based vaccine assistance: the death rates due to COVID-19 is a significant predictor of increased numbers of vaccine doses delivered to the COVID-19 afflicted countries by Russia. For example, Moscow prioritized its nearby neighbors of Macedonia and Bosnia and Herzegovina, whose populations were reeling from the effects of COVID-19. Macedonia was in the top 10 countries for highest deaths per capita due to COVID-19, and Russia accepted their order of 200,000 Sputnik V doses, enough to vaccinate 10 percent of its population. This was one of the few promises for vaccine assistance on which Russia was able to make good. Additionally, Bosnia and Herzegovina was ranked third in the world for highest death rates per capita due to COVID-19, and Russia came to its aid when they requested enough doses to vaccinate 10 percent of its population.[66]

Countries that have alliances with Russia, when selected, receive more vaccine doses. Many of these countries, such as Uzbekistan, Belarus, Kazakhstan, and Turkmenistan, represent members of either the Collective Security Treaty Organization (CSTO) or Shanghai Cooperation Organization (SCO) and serve as a reliable proxy for Russia's intent to deliver vaccines to nations in close geographic proximity and former members of the Soviet Union. Additionally, those who engage in military arms sales with Russia receive higher levels of vaccine assistance. Though the coefficient is small, it statistically links arms transfers to vaccine aid. The effects of maintaining alliances and arms transfers with Russia on being selected as a Sputnik V recipient are readily apparent in Russia's relations with Algeria and Libya.

Algeria, a close Russian ally with arms sales agreements, received its first 50,000 doses of Sputnik in February 2021, and shortly after began negotiations with Russia to launch local production of Sputnik V by Fall. Pharmaceutical Industry Minister Lofti Benbahmed stated that Sputnik V would help Algeria "meet the vaccine challenge" and share the responsibility of vaccinating all African nations.[67] Meanwhile, President Abdelmadjid Tebboune considered Russia to be a "brotherly country", committing Algeria to remain a "major

---

66   Statista, "Number of Doses."

67   Reuters Staff, "Algeria to Start Russia's Sputnik V Vaccine Production in September," *Reuters*, April 7, 2021, https://www.reuters.com/article/us-algeria-russia-vaccine/algeria -to-start-russias-sputnik-v-vaccine-production-in-september-idUSKBN2BU3HG.

purchaser of Russian weaponry," and one of Russia's top three trade partners in Africa.[68] In May 2022, this relationship culminated in new bilateral treaties involving trade and economic cooperation. Russian President, Vladimir Putin, and Russian Foreign Minister, Sergey Lavrov, also underlined plans for joint military and technical cooperation with Algeria in addition to acknowledging their humanitarian concerns with the health situation in the country.[69] With the announcement of this treaty, U.S. Secretary of State Anthony Blinken urged Algeria to "reconsider ties with Russia,"[70] in hopes of "rejuvenating"[71] US–Algerian ties and standing against Russian aggression in Ukraine.[72]

By April 2021, more than 100,000 doses of Sputnik V were delivered to Tripoli, Libya, which had historically been a close ally with the Soviet Union and currently serves as host to Russian state-affiliated PMC Wagner Group.[73] Within days of the shipment, Libyan Prime Minister Abdulhamid Dbeibeh was publicly inoculated on live television, calling it a "blessed day."[74] In 2020, Russian foreign policy shifted to make relations with Libya a priority, in what Russia considered to be a "zero-sum struggle" of "strategic positioning" with the West, resulting in an increase of public support for Russian PMCs and a speculated increase in the stationing of Russian military aircraft and arms transfers in Libya.[75] In the early months of the pandemic and the months

68   Matthew Lee, "Blinken Urges Algeria to Reconsider Ties with Russia," *PBS*, March 30, 2022, https://www.pbs.org/newshour/politics/blinken-urges-algeria-to-reconsider-ties-with-russia; TASS, "Russia, Algeria Plan to Sign Document Confirming New Quality of Relations — Lavrov," *TASS*, May 10, 2022, https://tass.com/russia/1448953.

69   TASS, "Russia, Algeria."; AP Staff, "Russia's FM Lavrov Meets Algeria Leader to Deepen Thick Ties," *Associated Press*, May 10, 2022, https://apnews.com/article/russia-ukraine-europe-africa-algiers-algeria-7d91687c656ab73fa427145fee3f9b48.

70   Lee, "Blinken Urges."; TASS, "Russia, Algeria."

71   Julian Pecquet, "US/Africa: Secretary of State Blinken Woos Algeria and Morocco for Help with Russia," The Africa Report, March 30, 2022, https://www.theafricareport.com/188429/us-africa-secretary-of-state-blinken-woos-algeria-and-morocco-for-help-with-russia/.

72   Lee, "Blinken Urges."; TASS, "Russia, Algeria."

73   Al Jazeera, "'First Drop of Rain': Libya Receives Russia's Sputnik Vaccine," *Al Jazeera*, April 4, 2021, https://www.aljazeera.com/news/2021/4/4/first-drop-of-rain-libya-receives-covid-vaccine-delivery.

74   Angus McDowall, "Libya Launches COVID-19 Vaccination Drive After Delays," *Reuters*, April 10, 2021, https://www.reuters.com/world/africa/libya-launches-covid-19-vaccination-drive-after-delays-2021-04-10/.

75   Anna Borshchevskaya, "Russia's Growing Interests in Libya," *The Washington Institute for Near East Policy*, January 24, 2020, https://www.washingtoninstitute.org/policy-analysis/russias-growing-interests-libya; Michelle Nichols, "Russia Steps Up Support for Private Military Contractor in Libya: U.N. Report," *Reuters*, September 2, 2020, https://www.reuters.com/article/us-libya-security-un/russia-steps-up-support-for-private-military-contractor-in-libya-u-n-report-idUSKBN25T37G; The Moscow Times, "U.S. Says Photos

preceding it, Russia sent hundreds of private military personnel to al-Jufrah Air Base in Waddan. US intelligence community suspected the purpose of this joint military operation was to train Libyan forces and snipers in drone jamming and air defense precision capable of shooting down US drones.[76] In 2022, though, many Russian fighters have gone to Ukraine. Still, Libya continues housing Russian paramilitary and mercenary forces, in what may very well be a "perennial and permanent…footprint in Libya."[77] In addition, Putin was vocal about peace talks and reuniting the east and west in Libya, as a likely way to boost Russian image in the nation, "especially absent a greater U.S. role."[78] The *New York Times* once called Russia's campaign in Libya's Second Civil war a win of a "geopolitical prize" for Russia over a "muddled" administration in the US.[79] Through all of this, Libya continued to order doses of Sputnik V, even when COVAX and Western vaccines such as AstraZeneca became available. President Putin implied that the Sputnik V deal was merely another show of the "rich experience of mutually beneficial cooperation" between Russia and Libya.[80] In a gesture of promoting Russian goodwill, Putin also offered good wishes to the Libyan people at the start of Ramadan in 2021.[81]

We also tested a variable, which measured the total amount of development assistance for each recipient country from the US as reported by the OECD. This is an important variable that serves as a proxy for capturing the geopolitical competition between Russia and the US. As expected, Russian vaccine assistance followed US development assistance in that higher amounts of vaccine doses were sent to countries that had received a greater amount of US development assistance. The data show that most top recipients of US

Show Russian Arms Supplies to Libya Rebels," accessed July 1, 2022, https://www.themoscow times.com/2020/07/24/us-says-photos-show-russian-arms-supplies-to-libya-rebels -a70976.

76   In fact, it is believed that either the Russian PMCs or Haftar Loyalists were successful in shooting down a US drone using Russian air defense systems. Borshchevskaya, "Russia's Growing."

77   Giorgio Cafiero and Emily Milliken, "Russians Unlikely to Leave Libya, Despite Ukraine War," *Al Jazeera*, April 15, 2022, https://www.aljazeera.com/news/2022/4/15/russians -unlikely-leave-libya-despite-ukraine-war.

78   Borshchevskaya, "Russia's Growing."

79   David Kirkpatrick, "The White House Blessed a War in Libya, but Russia Won It," *The New York Times* 4 (2020): 14, https://www.nytimes.com/2020/04/14/world/middleeast/libya -russia-john-bolton.html.

80   President of Russia, "Telephone Conversation with Prime Minister of National Unity Government of Libya Abdul Hamid Dbeibeh," *The Kremlin,* April 15, 2021, http:// en.kremlin.ru/events/president/news/65375.

81   President of Russia, "Telephone Conversation."

development assistance were in the Middle East and African nations, as well as Afghanistan. In 2021 alone, the US sent more than \$35.5 billion in development aid to recipient nations, while Russia trailed, providing just over \$1 billion.[82] Ethiopia has consistently been one of the top recipients of US development aid, but did not negotiate the distribution of vaccines from the US until late summer 2021.[83] Meanwhile, Russia had an initial conversation with Ethiopian Ambassador to Russia Alemayehu Tenegu in December 2020, and began planning doses with Ethiopia for Sputnik V in Spring 2021.[84]

For decades, Russia has sought to position itself ahead of the West in the race for influence and leverage in the global arena. Much of Russia's push to move Sputnik V so quickly to market was rooted in their efforts to compete with the US and Europe. As a result, the Russian approach to vaccine diplomacy has been highly geopolitical, strategic, and has led to more competition than cooperation.[85] In addition, Russia responded to the calls of low- and middle-income countries when they were "shut out" by the US and the West.[86]

Russia's relationship with Mexico surrounding COVID-19 vaccine campaigns is an example of Russia's direct competition for influence in Latin America with the US. In January 2021, Mexican President López Obrador appealed to President Biden directly for vaccine assistance. The administration denied

---

82   This figure is estimated from the 2019 amount as reported by the OECD. In 2019, Russia provided development assistance in the amount of \$1.2 billion. Because of Russia's fullscale war in Ukraine, more recent data regarding Russia's aid have been removed from the OECD website; OECD, "Development Resource Flows," accessed June 22, 2022, https://www.oecd-ilibrary.org/development/total-official-and-private-flows/indicator/english_52c1b6b4-en.

83   Ethiopia did receive a commitment from COVAX for several million doses of AstraZeneca, and later Pfizer, in February 2021, but these donations cannot be traced directly back to the US, and still occurred after Russia's initial conversation with Ethiopian ambassadors which took place in December 2020; GAVI, "US-Donated Vaccine Deliveries to Africa Set to Begin, With First Deliveries Planned to Burkina Faso, Djibouti, and Ethiopia," July 16, 2021, https://www.gavi.org/news/media-room/us-donated-vaccine-deliveries-africa-set-begin-first-deliveries-planned; UNICEF, "1.4 Million Doses of COVID-19 Vaccine Arrive in Afghanistan Through COVAX Global Dose-Sharing Mechanism," July 9, 2021, https://www.unicef.org/press-releases/14-million-doses-covid-19-vaccine-arrive-afghanistan-through-covax-global-dose.

84   Ethiopian Monitor, "Ethiopia, Russia Set to Ink Deal on Sputnik V Supplies," *Ethiopian Monitor*, May 2, 2021, https://ethiopianmonitor.com/2021/05/02/ethiopia-russia-set-to-ink-deal-on-sputnik-v-supplies/.

85   Giusti and Ambrosetti, "Making the Best."

86   Ian Hills, "Russia and China's Vaccine Diplomacy: Not Quite the Geopolitical Slam Dunk," *Australian Institute of International Affairs*, September 14, 2021, https://www.internationalaffairs.org.au/australianoutlook/russia-and-chinas-vaccine-diplomacy-not-quite-the-geopolitical-slam-dunk/.

this request citing issues with vaccine acquisition and distribution at home, forcing Obrador to turn elsewhere. Three days later, on January 25, Obrador called Putin and sealed a deal for 24 million doses of Sputnik V, among a few other smaller deals with China and COVAX. As a result of this deal, as well as the deals with Argentina, Brazil, and Guatemala among others, Russia sought to position itself to be a leader in COVID-19 vaccine campaigns in Latin America over the US and in direct competition with China.

However, the number of Sputnik V doses Russia ultimately delivered fell well short of the 24 million promised. By May 2021, Mexico had only received 1.9 million doses, forcing Foreign Minister Marceo Ebrard to visit Moscow to find a solution.[87] While there was no immediate solution to the production delays that could be resolved in Moscow, Ebrard arranged a deal for Mexican pharmaceutical company Birmex to locally perform the finishing operations for the Sputnik V vaccine.[88] Though the first round of Birmex's Sputnik V vaccines was released in July 2021, a formalized agreement was not reached until October 2021, by which time Mexico had largely shifted vaccine production toward China's CanSino and the British AstraZeneca vaccines.[89] Ebrard announced in late April 2022, that the bottling of Sputnik by Birmex would begin in a few days, but whether or not this process has actually begun is still unconfirmed as of June 2022.[90]

Similarly, in competition with Europe, Russia has worked to build its image and secure vaccine deals with Italy, the Czech Republic, Slovakia, Hungary, and Belarus. After the deal with the Italian Gamaleya Institute, Russia received a request in early 2021 from the Czech Republic for Sputnik V vaccines as Prague continued to wait for European vaccines that seemingly were not coming in the near future. In fact, the Czech Republic "blamed" the EU's slow vaccine production for the high number of COVID-19 infections and deaths; one of the worst tolls in the EU.[91] President Milos Zeman wrote that there was no shame in reaching

87   Paul Stronski, "In Mexico, the Window on Russia's Vaccine Diplomacy is Closing?" *Carnegie Endowment for International Peace,* April 28, 2022, https://carnegieendowment .org/2022/04/28/in-mexico-window-on-russia-s-vaccine-diplomacy-is-closing-pub-87013.

88   This included bottling and filling, though it did not include the actual production of the vaccine contents itself. Stronski, "In Mexico."

89   Stronski, "In Mexico."

90   Polina Ivanova, "Mexico Plays Down Sputnik Vaccine Delays After Domestic Production Deal," April 28, 2021, https://www.reuters.com/business/healthcare-pharmaceuticals/mexico -agrees-domestic-production-russias-sputnik-v-vaccine-2021-04-28/.

91   Al Jazeera, "Czech Republic Turns to Russian Vaccine Amid Soaring COVID cases," *Al Jazeera,* February 28, 2021, https://www.aljazeera.com/news/2021/2/28/czech-places -order-for-russias-sputnik-amid-covid-soaring-cases.

out to President Putin because vaccines "have no ideology."[92] The Czech Republic went through several foreign and health ministers throughout the COVID-19 pandemic, and several of them, including Foreign Minister Tomás Petříčk, were fired specifically because of their opposition to the Sputnik V vaccine.[93]

In another example of geopolitical competition, Slovakia initially purchased 200,000 doses of Sputnik V even though its national drug agency, SUKL, had not yet approved the vaccine. In January 2021, "many Slovaks" reported to Euronews that they would be "happy to take" the Sputnik V vaccine, citing trust in Russia and wariness about the side effects of the British AstraZeneca.[94] In the early days of the Russian vaccine campaign, several Slovakian politicians continued to vocally support the Kremlin's campaign against NATO enlargement in 2020 and 2021.[95] The approval of Russia and its leaders were not just restricted to select Slovakian political officials. A public opinion poll of Slovaks in 2020 showed that approval ratings for Putin were up to 55 percent, and 53 percent of those surveyed simultaneously feared that the "U.S. threatened their [Slovak] identity and values."[96] Putin sought to maintain a strong relationship with Slovakia based on "neighborliness and mutual respect" alongside a shared "closeness" of their peoples.[97] As the months followed and the pandemic raged on, Slovakia, no longer able to wait for European vaccines, requested more than 2 million doses,[98] and began inoculating its population with Sputnik V in May 2021 without the authorization of the SUKL.[99]

---

92   Al Jazeera, "Czech Republic." This quote also referenced the request for Chinese Sino-pharm vaccines.

93   Siegfried Mortkowitz, "Czech Government Fires Anti-Sputnik Vaccine Foreign Minister," *Politico*, April 12, 2022, https://www.politico.eu/article/czech-republic-foreign-minister-tomas-petricek-anti-sputnik-coronavirus-vaccine/.

94   Daniel Bellamy and Pleschberger, Johnanes, "Slovaks Divided Over Russia's Sputnik V Vaccine after Quality Concerns," *Euronews*, May 1, 2021, https://www.euronews.com/2021/05/01/slovaks-divided-over-russia-s-sputnik-v-vaccine-after-quality-concerns; The news source stated that 15 percent of those surveyed also reported that they preferred Sputnik to AstraZeneca. While not a majority, this figure was three times those preferring Sputnik V in other European states.

95   David Hutt, "Vladimir Putin Used to be Popular in Slovakia. Then He Invaded Ukraine," *Euronews*, March 29, 2022, https://www.euronews.com/my-europe/2022/03/29/vladimir-putin-used-to-be-popular-in-slovakia-then-he-invaded-ukraine.

96   Hutt, "Vladimir Putin."

97   TASS, "Russia Ready to Revive Cooperation with Slovakia in Case of Interest, says Putin," *TASS*, December 1, 2021, https://tass.com/politics/1369329.

98   This was a closed door deal between RDIF and Matovic, and it would later come under scrutiny.

99   This was largely due to missing data and concerns that existing clinical trials were fake. Al Jazeera, "Czech Republic."

4   US COVID-19 Vaccine Assistance

Though slow to start, the US has dedicated itself to being a leader in the global COVID-19 vaccine campaign. However, once its vaccine campaign was up and running, it was influenced by a distinct American geopolitical logic that grounds humanitarian assistance in moral commitments to humanity, alongside the balancing of geostrategic and geoeconomic priorities. Over time, US vaccine aid became tied to global markets, economic exchanges, and development assistance, falling in line with historical patterns of foreign aid based on neoliberal concepts of free markets and a broader liberal international order.[100] US reasoning regarding COVID-19 assistance, including its vaccine campaign, has been conceptualized as one that emphasizes the morality in preserving the dignity of human life and the "moral economy," which provides access to subsistence and can provide opportunities for post-crisis rebuilding and long term stability.[101]

The US has worked both bilaterally and through multilateral institutions to distribute its vaccines in allies and partners, as well as in places where the populations have been most affected by the novel coronavirus. Though not part of its initial vaccine allocations' campaign, the US eventually committed to donate directly from its own supply of vaccines, ramp up vaccine production with the intent to distribute abroad, and help expand low-income countries' capacity to produce vaccines at home. In 2021 alone, the US delivered 350 million vaccine doses to more than 100 countries offering nearly $20 billion in vaccine assistance. Map 5 shows bilateral donations of US vaccines. The top recipients of US vaccine donations, which include Bangladesh, Mexico, and Pakistan, are presented in Table 16.

In June 2021, when the US began its global vaccine assistance campaign in full force, President Biden made a statement committing 6 million doses in bilateral donations, prioritizing "those in crisis, and other partners and neighbors."[102]

---

100   Michael Barnett, "Covid-19 and the Sacrificial International Order," *International Organization* 74, no. S1 (2020): E128–E147.

101   Barnett, "Covid-19."

102   Joseph R Biden, "Statement by President Joe Biden on Global Vaccine Distribution," *The White House Briefing Room,* June 3, 2021, https://www.whitehouse.gov/briefing-room /statements-releases/2021/06/03/statement-by-president-joe-biden-on-global-vaccine -distribution/; The White House, "Fact Sheet: Biden-Harris Administration Unveils Strategy for Global Vaccine Sharing, Announcing Allocation Plan for the First 25 million Doses to be Shared Globally," *The White House Briefing Room,* June 3, 2021, https://www .whitehouse.gov/briefing-room/statements-releases/2021/06/03/fact-sheet-biden-harris -administration-unveils-strategy-for-global-vaccine-sharing-announcing-allocation -plan-for-the-first-25-million-doses-to-be-shared-globally/.

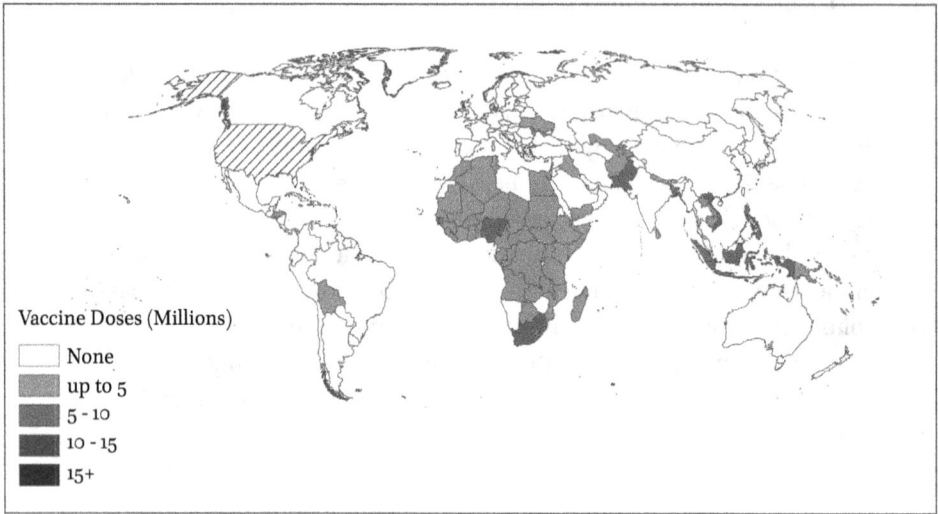

MAP 5   US vaccine distributions

TABLE 16   The top 10 bilateral recipients of American vaccines

Country	Doses (millions)
Bangladesh	20,779,810
Mexico	10,410,900
Pakistan	10,200,060
Indonesia	9,500,260
Guatemala	8,500,000
Colombia	7,008,000
Philippines	6,408,910
Nigeria	6,184,480
Vietnam	6,000,120
South Africa	5,660,460

"Immediate neighbor"[103] Mexico has been one of the top 3 global recipients of US bilateral vaccine donations. Early in its vaccine assistance campaign, the US delivered nearly 3 million doses of AstraZeneca and promised 1.35 million

---

103   The White House, "Fact Sheet: Biden-Harris."

doses of Johnson & Johnson to Mexico in a bilateral agreement meant to "help reopen [Mexico's] northern border," which President Obrador said would "benefit societies of both countries."[104] Roberto Velasco of Mexico's Foreign Ministry said that this cooperation for their vaccine campaign "symbolizes the excellent relationship" with the US, and the "invaluable" support, specifically from US Vice President Kamala Harris.[105]

In Africa, Nigeria and South Africa were the top recipients of American vaccine assistance. In July 2021, South Africa was among the first nations in Africa to receive US vaccines, receiving the largest bilateral donation at the time at 5.7 million doses.[106] Additionally, the US committed to deliver bilateral donations to dozens of African countries such as Burkina Faso, Djibouti, Senegal, Gambia, and US strategic ally, Ethiopia.[107] However, despite the success of vaccine delivery to South Africa, the US campaign to vaccinate the whole of Africa was met with many challenges, including lack of medical personnel to administer doses and lack of infrastructure to store vaccines, like the US-made Pfizer, which requires deep freeze storage. For many African nations, the vaccines did not arrive on schedule and were inconsistent in volume, without explanation other than production delays and concerns about recipient country's capacity to store and administer vaccines.[108]

Though the US engaged in some bilateral vaccine assistance commitments, most US vaccine dose donations were administered via COVAX, following the longstanding trend of its humanitarian assistance being administered through multilateral mechanisms. This could ensure that vaccine efforts would not be sacrificed to the geopolitical and geoeconomic priorities of a broader foreign

---

104   Government of Mexico, "1.35 Million Doses of the Johnson & Johnson Vaccine Arrive Following Bilateral Agreement With US," June 15, 2021, https://www.gob.mx/sre/prensa /bilateral-agreement-with-us-leads-to-the-arrival-of-1-35-million-doses-of-the-johnson -johnson-vaccine; Tamara Keith, "Biden Takes First Jab At Vaccine Diplomacy, Sharing Doses With Mexico, Canada," NPR, March 19, 2021, https://www.npr.org/2021/03/19/979279426 /biden-takes-first-jab-at-vaccine-diplomacy-sharing-doses-with-mexico-canada.

105   Government of Mexico, "1.35 Million Doses."

106   U.S. Mission to South Africa, "United States Donates 5.7 Million COVID-19 Doses to South Africa," U.S. Embassy & Consulates in South Africa, July 28, 2021, https://za.usembassy.gov /united-states-donates-5-7-million-covid-19-doses-to-south-africa/.

107   Gayle E Smith, "Digital Press Briefing on the U.S. Donations of COVID-19 Vaccines to the African Union," U.S. Department of State, July 21, 2021. https://www.state.gov/digital-press -briefing-on-the-u-s-donations-of-covid-19-vaccines-to-the-african-union/.

108   Jason Beubien, "What U.S. Vaccine Donations Mean for Sierra Leone and Africa," NPR, June 12, 2021, https://www.npr.org/2021/06/12/1005937103/what-u-s-vaccine-donations-mean-for -sierra-leone-and-africa%206-1-22; Bengali, Shashank, "African Health Experts Hail Biden's Vaccine Pledge, but Call for More Transparency," The New York Times, September 23, 2021, https://www.nytimes.com/2021/09/23/world/vaccine-covid-africa.html.

policy agenda. The Biden administration announced that it would work through COVAX purposefully in order to "ensure that the vaccines are delivered in a way that is equitable" and committed to refrain from using "our vaccines to secure favors from other countries."[109] The US supported the 2021 COVAX goal of distributing more than 2 billion doses worldwide and committed to supplying vaccine doses and billions of dollars in financial support.[110] The US was the largest vaccine donor to COVAX, donating more then 300 million vaccines in 2021.[111]

In 2022, the US shifted its vaccine assistance priorities to better reflect its earlier COVID-19 assistance efforts to focus even more heavily on need-based distributions, with a commitment to distribute 1 billion doses globally.[112] In February 2022, the US donated 400 million doses to COVAX with the understanding that more recent shipments would go to places like Pakistan and Bangladesh, which were experiencing a surge in Omicron cases, poor medical infrastructure and testing, as well as tracing capabilities, and very low vaccination rates.[113] Additionally, concerns arose in these countries about COVID-19 spread due to increased mobility and travels and gatherings for the upcoming Eid al-Fitr later in the spring.[114] By mid-2022, the US had sent both bilaterally and via COVAX over 61 million doses to Pakistan and over 64 million to Bangladesh.[115]

109   The White House, "Remarks by President Biden on the COVID-19 Response and the Vaccination Program," *The White House Briefing Room,* May 17, 2021, https://www.whitehouse.gov/briefing-room/speeches-remarks/2021/05/17/remarks-by-president-biden-on-the-covid-19-response-and-the-vaccination-program-4/.

110   The White House, "Fact Sheet: President Biden to Take Action on Global Health through Support of COVAX and Calling for Health Security Financing," *The White House Briefing Room,* February 18, 2021, https://www.whitehouse.gov/briefing-room/statements-releases/2021/02/18/fact-sheet-president-biden-to-take-action-on-global-health-through-support-of-covax-and-calling-for-health-security-financing/.

111   Antoine De Bengy Puyvallée, and Storeng, Katerini Tagmatarchi, "COVAX, Vaccine Donations and the Politics of Global Vaccine Inequity," *Globalization and Health* 18, no. 26 (2022): https://globalizationandhealth.biomedcentral.com/articles/10.1186/s12992-022-00801-z.

112   The White House, "Global COVID-19 Summit: Ending the Pandemic and Building Back Better," *The White House Briefing Room,* September 24, 2021, https://www.whitehouse.gov/briefing-room/statements-releases/2021/09/24/global-covid-19-summit-ending-the-pandemic-and-building-back-better/.

113   UNICEF, "Bangladesh's COVID-19 Vaccination Rate Has Soared in a Year," May 31, 2022, https://www.unicef.org/stories/bangladesh-covid-19-vaccination-rate-has-soared.

114   Soucheray, Stephanie. "US Donates 400 Million COVID-19 Vaccine Doses to COVAX." *CIDRAP,* January 26, 2022. https://www.cidrap.umn.edu/news-perspective/2022/01/us-donates-400-million-covid-19-vaccine-doses-covax; IHME, "COVID-19 Results Briefing." *Institute for Health Metric and Evaluation,* January 21, 2022. https://www.healthdata.org/sites/default/files/files/165_briefing_Pakistan_4.pdf.

115   KFF. "U.S. International COVID-19 Vaccine Donations Tracker – Updated as of July 1." Accessed June 6, 2022. https://www.kff.org/coronavirus-covid-19/issue-brief/u-s-international-covid-19-vaccine-donations-tracker/#recipient-country.

President Biden has maintained a steadfast position that the US would be a global leader in COVID-19 vaccine distributions. Throughout 2022, the US continued to donate COVID-19 vaccine doses, especially to low-income nations such as Libya, Maldives, Kenya, Yemen, its neighbors in the Caribbean, among many others. As of summer 2022, the US had shipped over 575 million doses globally since the beginning of the pandemic, and was making progress toward accomplishing its vaccine assistance goal of 1 billion doses worldwide both bilaterally and through COVAX.[116] Repeating the statements by the US government officials that "US vaccine donations come with no political strings attached,"[117] President Biden avowed that "The United States [would] be the world's arsenal of vaccines in our shared fight against the virus..." and would continue to do all it can "to build a world that is safer and more secure against the threat of disease."[118] A publicly announced US plan for determining recipients of vaccine assistance called for the prioritization of vaccinations of vulnerable populations and making more doses available to neighbors and those "in need" on a "per capita basis."[119]

Despite American discursive commitments to equitable vaccine distribution and general moral rectitude in response to the pandemic, like COVID-19 humanitarian efforts before, American vaccine assistance has been marred in political barriers reflecting geostrategic and geoeconomic concerns. Both the US and COVAX have been criticized by small and low income nations of prioritizing wealthy Western nations, such as Britain and Canada, at the expense of deliveries to places like Africa and Southeast Asia.[120] Additionally, countries such as Mexico have commented that bilateral donations from the

---

116 The White House, "Global COVID-19 Summit."; Joseph R Biden, "Remarks by President Biden at the Global COVID-19 Summit," *The White House Briefing Room,* May 12, 2022, https://www.whitehouse.gov/briefing-room/speeches-remarks/2022/05/12/remarks-by -president-biden-at-the-global-covid-19-summit/.

117 US Embassy & Consulates in Italy, "U.S. COVID-19 Vaccine Donations Spanned the Globe in 2021," January 3, 2022, https://it.usembassy.gov/u-s-covid-19-vaccine-donations -spanned-the-globe-in-2021/.

118 Share America, "U.S. Sends COVID-19 Vaccines Worldwide [December 2021]," *Share America,* December 23, 2021, https://share.america.gov/us-sends-covid-19-vaccines-worldwide -december-2021/.

119 The White House, "Fact Sheet: Biden-Harris."

120 Though the US was one of the few wealthy nations to not take any vaccines from COVAX, it did make a substantial donations to Canada. The US also continued to provide financial support to COVAX, despite the fact that other wealthy European nations were dipping into COVAX vaccine reserves; UNICEF, "COVID-19."; Maria Cheng, and Lori Hinnant, "Rich Nations Dip into COVAX Supply While Poor Waits for Shots," *The Associated Press,* August 14, 2021, https://apnews.com/article/joe-biden-middle-east-africa-europe-coronavirus -pandemic-5e57879c6cb22d96b942cbc973b9296c.

US have come with "strings attached,"[121] while others have criticized the lack of transparency in the US decision making regarding recipients of its vaccine assistance.[122] Notwithstanding criticisms and challenges faced along the way, the US remains the leading donor of vaccines, far surpassing the volumes of donations from any other wealthy or vaccine producing nation. It appears that the US has quietly responded to these criticism in 2022 as it has seemingly embraced a global vaccine campaign that is based on the humanitarian principles of need, impartiality to political and economic agendas, and shifting global discourse toward a more human-centered logic regarding vaccine assistance. To better understand the decision-making process regarding US vaccine assistance, we aim to statistically analyze the distribution of US vaccine donations in reference to characteristics of recipient nations. This ultimately tests the level of follow-through that the US has made on its commitments regarding which nations will receive vaccines based on which criteria.

We conceptualize vaccine assistance decision-making for the US in the same two-step process of "selection" and "outcome." As in the models on Chinese and Russian vaccine assistance, the models on US vaccine assistance follow the same measure of dependent variables. Again, we perform independent analysis across the two stages. The selection stage uses a logistic regression with a binary dependent variable to indicate whether or not a country received vaccines from the US, while the outcome stage is a negative binomial count model where the dependent variable is the total number of vaccine doses received. We maintain the independent variables in the vaccine assistance models as were used in the COVID-19 assistance models. These variables include: total deaths per million, the total amount of US development assistance, total aid received from China (geopolitical competition), political proximity measured by voting alignment in the UN General Assembly and membership in a joint alliance, geographic proximity, GDP per capita, total trade balance, and regime type. The results of the analysis are presented in Table 17.

---

121 The terms of these loans, which coincided with a similar arrangement with Canada, were not released; Al Jazeera, "US to 'Loan' COVID-19 Vaccines to Canada and Mexico," *Al Jazeera,* March 18, 2021, https://www.aljazeera.com/news/2021/3/18/the-us-to-loan-covid-19-vaccines-to-canada-and-mexico.

122 Erin Banco, "'It's a Sore Spot': Why Officials are Raising Questions about Biden's Vaccine Donations," *Politico,* December 8, 2021, https://www.politico.com/news/2021/12/08/biden-administration-officials-questions-vaccine-donations-523922; Rachel Thrasher, "The Global COVID-19 Summit Must Tackle the Vaccine Demand Gap," *Devex,* May 6, 2022, https://www.devex.com/news/opinion-the-global-covid-19-summit-must-tackle-the-vaccine-demand-gap-103121.

TABLE 17   Determinants of US vaccine distributions

	(1) Vaccine binary	(2) Number of vaccines
GDP (per capita)	0.217	0.609***
	(0.124)	(0.127)
Political Affinity	1.392**	1.818***
	(0.450)	(0.499)
Distance to Capital	0.0000130	-0.00000291
	(0.0000717)	(0.0000775)
Liberal Democracy	-1.111	-5.651***
	(1.165)	(1.595)
Membership in Alliance	0.146	1.789*
	(0.469)	(0.702)
US Development Aid	0.294**	0.915***
	(0.0922)	(0.146)
Trade Balance	0.0200	0.0858*
	(0.0354)	(0.0392)
China Development Aid	-0.569	-0.331
	(0.435)	(0.603)
COVID-19 Deaths	0.00149	0.00644
	(0.00198)	(0.00518)
Constant	-11.16***	-13.59***
	(2.986)	(3.672)
lnalpha		3.064***
		(0.150)
N	153	153
pseudo R-squared	0.265	0.018
chi2	37.02	109.3

Note: Robust errors in parentheses
$^* p < 0.05, ^{**}p < 0.01, ^{***}p < 0.001$

Both Presidents Trump and Biden declared a commitment to providing vaccine assistance to US partners and allies, and this is statistically demonstrated in the analysis in terms of alliances. In fact, after stating in September 2020 that the US would not participate in global vaccine efforts, the Trump administration changed course and laid out a plan to share COVID-19 vaccines that subsequently placed political allies such as Taiwan and Israel, ahead of poorer states with greater need.[123] Even President Biden's initial announce-ment stated that the US would prioritize regional neighbors, allies, alongside those in need.[124] After making this declaration, the US sent millions of doses to close political allies such as Canada and Egypt, and still neglected poorer nations in Africa and Southeast Asia until much later in 2021 and 2022. This political allyship is also reflected in the mirroring of UN voting records, as those who vote with the US were more likely to receive vaccines and higher amounts of vaccine doses.

With the release of President Trump's vaccine plan in early 2021, it was also clear that wealthy nations would be prioritized (p-value $\leq$ 0.1). Rich nations like Canada and South Korea were high on the list of priority vaccine recipi-ents. US media source *Politico* directly asked an official involved in developing this vaccine plan if "there were concerns about deprioritizing poorer nations" and the official responded, "not really."[125] The change in presidential admin-istration did not appear to initially shift vaccine assistance priorities because one year into the Biden administration, the US was still among the rich coun-tries being criticized for "monopolizing" and hoarding COVID-19 vaccines.[126]

In contrast to earlier findings in the China analysis, which showed that China's vaccine distributions closely followed US aid, the US does not appear to be chasing Chinese aid distributions in its vaccines-related decisions. The continent of Africa received more Chinese aid than any other region, and nations such as Egypt and Ethiopia have received millions more doses (donations and sales) from China than from the US (bilaterally).[127] This suggests that the US has sought to prioritize recipients on its own terms rather than in consideration of geopolitical competition with China. These findings may also be impacted by the fact that the US has

123   Sinéad Baker, "Secret Trump-Era Vaccine Plan Prioritized Rich Allies like Taiwan and Israel Above Poor Nations Which Needed Them More," *Insider*, January 28, 2022, https://www.businessinsider.com/trump-era-vaccine-sharing-plan-rich-allies-before-needy-nations-2022-1; Elliot Hannon, "The Trump Administration Refuses to Participate in Global Coronavirus Vaccine Effort," *Slate*, September 2, 2020, https://slate.com/news-and-politics/2020/09/trump-refuses-who-covax-global-coronavirus-vaccine-effort-gavi.html.

124   Biden, "Statement by."

125   Baker, "Secret Trump."; Banco, "Trump Plan."

126   Umair Irfan, "Why Are Rich Countries Still Monopolizing Covid-19 Vaccines?" *Vox*, November 9, 2021, https://www.vox.com/22759707/covid-19-vaccine-gap-covax-rich-poor-countries-boosters; Owens, Caitlin, "The Global Coronavirus Vaccine Gap," *Axios*, Octo-ber 20, 2021, https://www.axios.com/2021/10/20/coronavirus-vaccines-world-biden-mod erna.

127   Bridge, "China COVID-19."

designated hundreds of millions of doses through COVAX, possibly abating potential public diplomacy gains that might result from bilateral donations.

It is also clear that US vaccine assistance follows its development assistance programs. Washington's decisions about vaccine assistance appear to be tied to their considerations about foreign and development aid. In 2021, for example, the US committed $63.75 million to Jordan's COVID-19 Response System for equitable access to COVID-19 vaccines. The US is Jordan's single largest provider of bilateral foreign assistance contributing more than $300 million in aid to Jordan in 2021. Since July 2021, the US has bilaterally donated 500,000 vaccine doses to Jordan and committed to purchase an additional million doses from US Pfizer.[128]

President Biden's Administration has intended to shift gears on US vaccine assistance policies in 2022 and directly focus on need-based vaccine assistance above all else. The results using data through 2021 show that vaccine donations initially might not have been dependent on a country's need considering its total COVID-19 deaths. This speaks to some of the criticisms directed at the US concerning its early propensity to prioritize its neighbors and wealthy European nations. However, more recently, the US has directed its bilateral attention as well as COVAX designations to countries like Madagascar and Haiti, which have low vaccinations rates, poor medical infrastructure, and cumulatively high levels of COVID-19 cases and deaths. It is still to be seen whether or not this pivot in its vaccine assistance campaign will allow the US to have a clear and significant designation of its vaccine donations based on recipient need.

---

128 US Department of State, "Jordan: Fact Sheet," Accessed June 29, 2022, https://www .state.gov/countries-areas/jordan/; Reuters, "Jordan Secures 3 Million Doses of COVID-19 Vaccine - Prime Minister," *Reuters,* January 3, 2021, https://www.reuters.com/article /uk-health-coronavirus-jordan-vaccine-idUKKBN2980J4.

Conclusion

The humanitarian system continues facing an unprecedented set of challenges. While the COVID-19 pandemic entered the endemic stage with seasonal peaks of various intensity in different countries, COVID continues posing a serious health risk fueled by the new coronavirus variants, slow roll-out of vaccinations in many developing countries, and impaired health infrastructure. And COVID-19 is not the only health risk that the international community must confront. Climate change, increased international travel, and a growing population, especially in the developing countries, raise the likelihood of a new pandemic within the next decade.[1] Weeks after the WHO ended the COVID-19 global health emergency, its director-general Dr. Tedros Adhanom Ghebreyesus called for vigilance and continued preparation for a pandemic that is yet to come. The future pandemic is likely to be caused by a more formidable virus that will evade the type of immunity conferred through the exposure to pathogen through a vaccine.[2] Many viruses that carry deadly tropical diseases cannot be stopped by the current generation of vaccines that have been used in fighting polio, measles, and novel coronavirus. To develop new technologies capable of inducing unordinary protective immunity and scale up the production of most expensive and complex vaccines will require far higher levels of investments in health research and vaccine development, enhanced international cooperation with medical scientists around the world, and innovative low-cost manufacturing.[3]

Although, the COVID-19 health crisis served as impetus for international collaboration in vaccine development, it also shuttered national economies and contributed to reductions in funding for health research. COVID devasted peoples' livelihoods and weakened already unequitable scientific foundations of countries' health infrastructure, thus deepening structural inequalities and reversing gains in health and food security, and education. Russia's war

---

1   Eleanor Pringle, "Disease Forecasters are Convinced There's a 27% Chance of Another COVID-like Pandemic Within 10 Years – but Experts Believe There's a Silver Bullet," *Fortune*, April 18, 2023, https://fortune.com/well/2023/04/18/disease-forecasters-predict-new-covid-like-pandemic-within-10-years/.

2   Aliza Chasan, "Prepare for Next Pandemic, Future Pathogens with 'Even Deadlier Potential' than COVID, WHO Chief Warns," CBS News, May 23, 2023, https://www.cbsnews.com/news/next-pandemic-threat-pathogen-deadlier-than-covid-world-health-organization/.

3   Peter J. Hotez, "Vaccines as Instruments of Foreign Policy: The New Vaccines for Tropic Infectious Diseases May Have Unanticipated Uses Beyond Fighting Diseases," EMBO Rep. 2, no. 10 (October 2001): 862–868.

in Ukraine has further exacerbated the global food, energy, and climate crises already strained by COVID-19. Humanitarian organizations find their resources outmatched by the gravity and complexity of intertwined emergencies that have already displaced more than one percent of the world's population,[4] and pushed millions into famine and poverty. The practitioners of humanitarian aid warn of another humanitarian disaster on a global scale unless state donors, international humanitarian agencies, and non-state humanitarian organizations address the multiple gaps in disaster response architecture, emergency workforce, and leadership that is necessary for investing in sustainable solutions and early warning in humanitarian disasters, and galvanizing collaborative response to humanitarian crises. Many of these measures depend on the consistent and growing levels of funding and skillful diplomacy in support of the humanitarian system reform.

What motivates states to supply humanitarian aid? Is there a difference in the motives of the so-called traditional donors, like the United States, and the "emerging" donors, like China and Russia? How do alternative approaches to emergency relief assistance affect the future of the global humanitarian regime? By focusing on China's, Russia's, and US' decisions about COVID-19 aid, including distributions of COVID-19 vaccines, this book sought to contribute to the vast literature on humanitarian aid that deals with donors' determinants of aid allocations. In doing so, it probed the donors' divergent geopolitical logics for humanitarian assistance informed by their distinctive visions of the world, their place in global politics, and state identity, as well as their histories of accumulated experiences with foreign assistance. The book draws on the theoretical insights of the critical geopolitics perspective, which maintains that states' foreign policy decisions and behaviors are bound up with their geopolitical knowledge and understandings that play out through the complex web of language in interaction and competition with alternative geopolitical conceptions of the world. We use this framework to explore different traditions and contexts that informed Chinese, Russian, and American conceptual mappings of aid that we line up with specific hypotheses about their COVID-19 aid allocations tested on the original dataset of the coronavirus assistance. The book deploys critical geopolitics as a lens of analysis, rather than a phenomenological perspective on knowledge acquisition. Such a pragmatic application of the critical approach allowed us to systematically examine the discursive,

---

4   United Nations Office for the Coordination of Humanitarian Affairs, "UN and Partners Release Record Humanitarian Response Plan as COVID-19 Wreaks Havoc," OCHA, December 1, 2020. https://iran.un.org/en/103126-un-and-partners-release-record-humanitarian-response-plan-covid-19-wreaks-havoc.

context-specific, and power- and interest-laden geopolitical logics that inform states' decision-making in the foreign policy and humanitarian realms.

1   Overview of Findings

In this book we argued that states' motivations for humanitarian assistance are both complex and evolving, and, therefore, irreducible to the popular "need-based" versus "interest-based" explanations for aid. Our point of departure is that states' motivations for humanitarian aid are shaped by their geopolitical knowledge, i.e., ideas, concepts, and knowledge about the state and the world. This geopolitical imagery is always subjective – reflecting specific historical, cultural, and international contexts, values, and previously conceived national interests. Although this imagery exists in the form of ideas, it is highly impactful in that is instills specific meanings in what donors prioritize in their aid decisions and define the ethical frameworks within which these decisions are made. Furthermore, the book showed how states' motives for humanitarian assistance are affected by shifting global power relations and accompanying this shift contestation between the dominant and alternative approaches to humanitarian aid. This competition, in turn, prompts states react to humanitarian crises in ways that reproduce the many limitations of the dominant humanitarian system and the geopolitical (neoliberal) logic enfolding it.

In the 21st century, the US has championed all other donors in terms of the total volume of humanitarian assistance. Washington has also led the humanitarian response to COVID-19 based on the dollar amount of the coronavirus aid and vaccine contributions. In 2020 alone, the US government obligated $908 million in COVID-19 aid, although limitations on the PPE procurement, restrictions on funding for the WHO, and a new inter-agency process put in place for determining the coronavirus aid allocations contributed to delays in the delivery of humanitarian aid.[5] Similarly, the US has been the single largest donor of COVID-19 vaccines contributing 41 percent of vaccine doses to COVAX, a global vaccine-sharing hub, in 2021.[6]

---

5   United States General Accounting Office, "Foreign Disaster Assistance: AID Has Been Responsive but Improvements Can Be Made," Washington, DC, United States General Accounting Office (GAO), 1992, https://www.gao.gov/assets/nsiad-93-21.pdf.

6   UNICEF's COVID-19 vaccine market dashboard. Available from: https://www.unicef.org/supply/covid-19-vaccine-market-dashboard. See also Antonie De Bengy Puyvallée and Katerini Tagmatarchi Storeng. "COVAX, Vaccine Donations and the Politics of Global Vaccine Inequity," *Globalization and Health,* March 5, 2022, https://globalizationandhealth.biomedcentral.com/articles/10.1186/s12992-022-00801-z.

According to the US government, the moral imperative of alleviating individual suffering due to disasters and crises has long served as an ethical foundation for the US humanitarian aid. This universalizing logic envisioning the world as common humanity transcending state-centric conceptions of the global affairs and appealing to a shared responsibility toward fellow humans in need has been at odds with the geostrategic and geoeconomic logics permeating the practices of development and security aid giving by the US. In the post-WWII context, for example, when the US sharply increased its foreign aid, it habitually exploited the humanitarian rhetoric for advancing its geopolitical interests of containing the spread of communism in the ideologically divided atmosphere of the Cold War. At the same time, aid was enfolded into a geoeconomic vision of development that imposed a neoliberal template of national industrialization and modernization centered on capitalist growth. The geoeconomic and geostrategic narratives have always been intimately connected with development projects regarded as the bulwark against security threats to the US.[7] Yet, even at the height of the Cold War, the Office of the US Foreign Disaster Assistance (OFDA) in charge of Washington's humanitarian initiatives followed steadfastly the humanitarian principles of neutrality, impartiality, and need.[8] The institutional design for American disaster response that afforded the OFDA a degree of political and financial independence allowed it to deliver aid promptly to the communities in need, unhindered by politics or red tape of the US government.

Following the breakup of the Soviet Union, the United States, a superpower with unraveled economic and military capabilities, assumed responsibilities for maintaining global order rooted in liberal ideas, principles, and institutions. This new era was marked by the heightened interdependence of capitalist economies and increased American military presence around the world. The global war on terror provided a renewed impetus for the articulation of geoeconomic and geopolitical logics of assistance leading the US government to a conclusion that certain domestic conditions, such as poverty and authoritarianism, were responsible for terrorism and violent conflict. This framing of the interconnected security and economic challenges calling for development assistance has been constitutive of the political rationality of neoliberalism because the sources of state weakness have been found in countries' inability or unwillingness to integrate themselves into the flows and institutions of neoliberal globalization. The geopolitical insecurities resulting from state

---

7 Jamey Essex, *Development, Security and Aid: Geopolitics and Geoeconomics at the U.S. Agency for International Development* (Athens, GA: The University of Georgia Press, 2013).

8 United States General Accounting Office, "Foreign Disaster Assistance", p. 5.

weakness were also conceived in both geopolitical and geoeconomic terms as threats associated with terrorism and destabilization as well as threats to continued capitalist accumulation.[9]

US humanitarian discourse and action have become part and parcel of the US-led liberal global governance.[10] US interventions in disasters and crises have been driven not only by humanitarian concerns but also fears of state failure and the national security consequences of persistent underdevelopment in the affected countries.[11] US humanitarian initiatives deployed in the complex emergencies have expanded beyond their immediate remit to provide means to maintain contact with the warring parties, to mitigate tensions over Washington's policies, or provide support to allies. Consequently, the disaster relief aid has become an integral part of US strategy to transform conflicts, bring the warring parties to a negotiating table, and set the stage for political and economic reforms.[12]

To adapt its humanitarian response to rapidly changing conflict and development dynamics, the US made changes to its humanitarian aid infrastructure that resulted in the dispersal of authority for disaster relief and the loss of some independence in the administration of humanitarian assistance. Another consequence of this bureaucratic change was the institution of close linkages between humanitarian aid and development assistance. Subsequently, when the US was pressed for time to get aid to the affected countries in the wake of the COVID-19 outbreak, a large share of US COVID-19 bilateral assistance was transmitted through the established development assistance channels and relying on the metrics for determining recipients of development aid. Our analysis of US COVID-19 aid allocations showed that Washington's coronavirus assistance closely trailed the patterns of development aid allocations established before COVID-19. This trend continued in vaccine allocations, which were significantly higher in volume for states that received development assistance from the US. Washington's development assistance has always been conditioned on the recipient countries' good governance metrics and their relations with the US. US humanitarian aid, too, has become tethered to these same considerations. We found that the US government provided higher levels

---

9   Essex, *Development, Security and Aid.*

10   Daniel Laqua, "Inside the Humanitarian Cloud: Causes and Motivations to Help Friends and Strangers," *Journal of Modern European History* 12, no. 2 (2014): 175–185.

11   Essex, *Development, Security and Aid.*

12   Rhoda Margesson, "International Crises and Disasters: US Humanitarian Assistance Response Mechanisms," Library of Congress, Washington D.C.: Congressional Research Service, 2015.

of COVID-19 aid and vaccine assistance to its democratic allies and those countries supporting US foreign policy in the UN.

China has not acceded to the principles of neutrality, need, and impartiality
of humanitarian assistance espoused by the Western donors but has advanced
its own concepts and approaches to disaster relief. Beijing's humanitarian aid
has been informed by the ideas of state as a chief moral agent and final authority for foreign aid. The state-centric position on humanitarian assistance has
spun off the principles of respect for state-sovereignty and political non-
interference in aid administration. The ethical weight that China has attached
to the state and state sovereignty has had significant practical implications for
its decisions about humanitarian aid. First, the state has been the major actor
in the Chinese system of emergency relief. Beijing has prioritized bi-lateral,
state-to-state disaster relief allocations requested and accepted by the recipient state. The second major characteristic of Chinese aid is that it eschews
political (but not economic) conditionality and delivers aid under conditions
of host state consent.

China's geopolitical logic embraces two additional beliefs. First, there is an
idea of the unity of thinking about its domestic and global contexts as well as
its internal politics and foreign policy. Second, there is a principled view that
foreign policy must be subordinate to the domestic politics' priorities, most
notably, economic development and peace. According to the first idea, development paradigms that the consecutive Chinese governments have applied
at home now serve as the blueprints for China's approaches abroad. Domestically, disaster relief has been used to increase capacity for economic development of the affected communities and reduce the risk of public unrest.
Similarly, internationally, humanitarian assistance has been deployed with
the view of promoting international development and contributing to global
piece. Yet, according to the second idea, investments in the global development and peace are critical foundations for the economic growth at home.
Reversely, China's own stability and growth are believed to be essential for
global development and peace. In short, China's own development and foreign
aid are believed to be able to create a "win-win" situation for co-prosperity and
peace beneficial to China, and its humanitarian aid is inextricably linked to
Beijing's development aid.

Our analysis of China's COVID-19 aid showed that Beijing's coronavirus assistance has followed the pattern of mostly bi-lateral (state-to-state)
in-kind assistance involving the transfer of Chinese medical supplies and
equipment and the dispatch of Chinese doctors and other medical personnel. Bilateral agreements were also the primary means through which China
provided vaccine assistance to recipient nations. We also found that China's

coronavirus aid and vaccine disbursements trailed its development assistance, which, in China's conception, involve the bundles of aid, investments, and trade. China's bilateral partnership in the BRI and CIDCA determined the sites of the COVID-19 allocations. Consistent with the principles of political non-conditionality, political regime had no bearing on China's decisions about COVID-19 assistance. However, the countries' support for China's politics and foreign policy, as reflected in their position on "One-China" policy and the human rights issues in Xinjiang also colored China's decisions on the allocations of coronavirus aid and the selection of vaccine recipients.

Russia resurged in the global development and humanitarian fields in the 2000s following the foreign aid hiatus of the 1990s. Like China, Russia has premised its humanitarian activities on a belief about the state as the primary moral agent. Yet, if China's aid policies have been influenced by the principle of South-South cooperation and linked to China's global status through contributions to development, Russia's views on humanitarian aid have been anchored in its self-image of great power and concerns with defending its great power position. According to the Russian government, great power status has bestowed on Russia special rights and responsibilities to play a bigger role in shaping regional and global security processes. Implicit in this geopolitical logic is a kind of moral argument maintaining that Russia's great power aspirations, involving claims to its "near abroad," are different from actions of other global actors, such as the US, because they are aimed at restoring parity in international relations by building a multi-polar international system in place of an "unjust" international order led by the US.

Between 2005 and 2014, Moscow showed interest in integrating into the dominant humanitarian regime and thought to portray itself as a responsible power and a constructive player in global politics capable of providing humanitarian aid to people in need. Moscow has also used aid to project and defend its great power interests and ambitions. This juxtaposition of identity-based and pragmatic considerations in humanitarian aid allocations have characterized Russia's approach to aid. Following Russia's illegal annexations of Crimea in 2014 and the imposition of Western sanctions that ensued, Moscow's integration into international humanitarian agencies was brought to a halt. Subsequently, bi-lateral and state-to-state channels of aid allocation became more prominent in Russia's foreign policy, and the Kremlin began overtly deploying humanitarian aid in support of its foreign policy priorities, such as countering American influence in the Eurasian region. Humanitarian aid has often been accompanied by the anti-Western and anti-American narratives contrasting the principles of sovereignty and security with the value-based conditionality imposed by the West.

Russia's COVID-19 assistance has followed the identified trends. While some of Russia's coronavirus assistance was tied to the humanitarian objectives – Moscow's decisions about coronavirus aid and vaccine allocations were correlated with the recipient countries' deaths rates due to COVID-19 - it was also an integral part of Moscow's strategy for projecting power on the global stage and supporting diverse political objectives. Countries in Russia's proximity (many of which are also members of alliances with Moscow) as well as those supporting Russia's foreign policy orientation were more likely to secure more COVID-19 aid and Sputnik vaccines. In the Soviet tradition of "aid for votes," Russia used aid to reward countries, which expressed support to its foreign policy priorities by siding with Moscow on the United Nations' roll call votes. Furthermore, to subvert the liberal foundations of the global order spearheaded by the US, Moscow prioritized countries governed by non-democratic governments in its COVID-19 aid and vaccine allocations.

Looking at states' motives through a lens of principled considerations (need, impartiality, and neutrality) versus interests conceals important differences in the underlying logics that inform donors' approaches to aid. Both traditional (US) and emergent (China and Russia) donors have been motivated by humanitarian concerns, but they have also deployed humanitarian aid to influence recipient governments in ways that benefited their interests. Washington, Beijing, and Moscow have rationalized these interventions in different ways. The US government has placed faith in democratic governance and market economy believed to be essential for development, security, and disaster prevention and response. It, therefore, has channeled more assistance to the countries with good economic policies, potential for economic growth, and a promise of political reforms. Beijing has justified its humanitarian aid interventions by emphasizing political neutrality, a state-led development model, and "win-win" cooperation with the recipient countries. By investing in global development and contributing humanitarian aid to countries experiencing disasters, Beijing has seen important benefits of such assistance for economic growth and stability at home. Russia's views on humanitarian aid have been shaped by ways it has perceived its great power identity and threats to its regional and international status.

These marked differences in the logics of humanitarian assistance have been reflected in the channels of administration of the disaster relief aid. Beijing and Moscow have preferred bi-lateral state-to-state transfers of assistance, while Washington has provided aid to a variety of state and non-state actors as well as international organizations. The US has been a more transparent donor in reporting the levels of assistance, recipients, and programs. China has shunned development and humanitarian assistance reporting tools established by the OECD and UN. Russia had reported limited data on its development and humanitarian assistance at the country-level until its full-scale invasion of Ukraine in February 2022 that resulted in Moscow's international isolation. Both China and Russia are yet to fully institutionalize their foreign aid bureaucracy and approbate the vocabulary consistent with the foreign aid concepts of the traditional donors.[13]

The book has also illuminated how donors' perspectives on humanitarian assistance are influenced by the dominant global order consisting of the sets of rules, norms, practices, and institutions assisting in regulating states' interactions among themselves and with other actors of global politics. As discussed at length in this book, the dominant humanitarian regime, which the traditional donors are part of, has been imbedded in a liberal international order based in the principles of individual freedoms, democracy, multilateralism, and free economic exchange, among other things. The preeminence of the liberal international order and humanitarian regime imbedded in it has been linked to the economic and military dominance of international system by the United States.

In the 21st century, the gap between American and Chinese national power has narrowed driven by external factors and domestic political and economic decisions. Emboldened by its economic weight and increasing political influence, Beijing has begun to assertively propagate its own vision for the global order dubbed the "community of common destiny for mankind." China's ambitious and multifaceted Belt and Road Initiative, known as the "Chinese Marshall Plan,"[14] has become the principle means for instituting a new global order conducive to Beijing's interests. Already embracing nearly every aspect of China's engagement abroad – from investments and trade to digitization and image production – the BRI now includes a humanitarian and health cooperation component. Rooted in a set of different foundational ideas, China's humanitarian aid has been tied to its development assistance bundled in the packages of "aid-investments-trade." According to Beijing, this approach allows the Chinese government to leverage donor-recipient synergy for mutual benefit. The perceived economic conditionality of China's humanitarian aid has caused ire in the development community as these practices run counter to both the neoliberal global geopolitical ecology of trade and investments as

---

13   Salvador Santino F. Regilme, Jr. and Obert Hodzi, "Comparing US and Chinese Foreign Aid in the Era of Rising Powers," *The International Spectator* 56, no. 2 (2021): 114–131.

14   Lily Kuo and Niko Kommenda, "What is China's Belt and Road Initiative?" *The Guardian*, July 3, 2018, https://www.theguardian.com/cities/ng-interactive/2018/jul/30/what-china -belt-road-initiative-silk-road-explainer.

well as the decades of efforts by the traditional donors to untie humanitarian aid from economic interchanges.[15]

For the United States, China's effort to influence, change, or bypass the established humanitarian regime and development system poses a threat to the liberal international order and to Washington's global power buttressing it. Conversely, China views the US as the biggest impediment to its national rejuvenation and a potential threat to the ruling Communist regime. If China's involvement in the global humanitarian system has entailed efforts to alter it by offering an alternative vision to the global order, Russia's humanitarian aid practices have sought to change the aid landscape by tarnishing the foundational ideas and practices of the Western donors. Moscow has spread the narrative of the dominant humanitarian regime being a Western undertaking established for promoting interests of the Western donors. By discrediting Western humanitarian efforts, Russia has tried to sap legitimacy from claims about the universality and impartiality of international humanitarian aid with detrimental consequences for international humanitarian system.

All in all, the contest over the ideas and approaches to humanitarian aid has diluted humanitarian imperatives in both traditional and emerging donors' aid allocations: China, Russia, and the US have taken to emergency relief as an additional tool to counter each other's influence in international affairs. When the Trump administration in the US stumbled in its responses to the spreading pandemic, the Chinese government of Xi Jinping quickly asserted itself as a role model in pandemic control and a leader in COVID-19 assistance to countries wrestling with the health crisis. The worry about China's claims to global remit has prompted the US government to launch its own COVID-19 assistance campaign to counter what was assessed as the growing influence of Beijing. At the time of a dire need for global cooperation and leadership in battling COVID-19, the governments of China, Russia, and the US allowed mutual recriminations and concerns with countering each other's influence to overshadow humanitarian considerations. When geopolitics percolates into decisions about humanitarian aid, the outcome is that the time-honored norm of alleviating human suffering regardless of location, ethnicity, politics, or relations with other countries loses its legitimacy and original purpose.

---

15   Uwe Weissenbach, *The EU, China and Africa: Working for Functional Cooperation?* (New York: Routledge, 2011), p. 251; Ashley Kim Stewart and Xing Li, "Beyond Debating the Differences: China's Aid and Trade in Africa," in *China-Africa Relations in an Era of Great Transformations*, edited by Li Xing and Abdulkadir Osman Farah (Ashgate, 2013), pp. 23–48.

2   **Ways Forward**

In 2009, then editor-in-chief of *Foreign Policy* magazine, Moisés Naím, called out China in the harshest terms as a "roque donor" "underwriting a world that is more corrupt, chaotic, and authoritarian" and posing a "threat to healthy, sustainable development" by progressively increasing the vulnerability of affected populations and decreasing their resilience to disasters and crises.[16] Since 2009, many more observers and practitioners of humanitarian aid have accepted a view of China as a "roque creditor," while others have deepened suspicions of Beijing as a 21st century neo-colonial power plundering resources from developing countries and cementing their dependence on China.[17] The latter sentiment has been amplified by the widespread perception of China as the greatest security threat to the US. To rally its allies' and partners' support in containing China, the US government has warned of the reversal of many hard-earned gains in the fight with corruption, respect for human rights, and democratic policies among the harrowing consequences of an alternative global order championed by Beijing.

    Concerns about China's opportunistic assistance and Russia's deployment of aid for geopolitical benefits are justified as are the misgivings about Beijing's attempt to build a global order in its image. These criticisms, however, neglect to recognize internal contradictions and negative externalities of the dominant humanitarian regime constitutive of the neoliberal ideas and practices that make up the framework of the global order spearheaded by Washington. First, despite the universalizing narrative of shared moral responsibility for others in need, humanitarian action and reasoning takes place in a geopolitical context where nation-states and their geoeconomic and geopolitical interests continue playing a decisive role in defining spaces that call for intervention. These territorial conceptions of states are inherently at odds with the transboundary processes of and thinking about emergencies, pandemics, or environmental crises. Second, the dominant universalizing geopolitical logic of humanitarian regime is not universal but reflective of the distribution of power capabilities within the international system. It bespeaks geopolitical thinking of powerful states and serves their political interests. As discussed throughout the book, the current humanitarian regime has been imbedded in the dominant global order and supporting this order power relations where

---

16   Moisés Naím, "Rogue Aid," Foreign Policy, October, 15, 2009, https://foreignpolicy.com /2009/10/15/rogue-aid/.

17   Marcu Power and Giles Mohan, "Towards a Critical Geopolitics of China's Engagement with African Development," *Geopolitics* 15, no. 3 (2010): 462–495.

the US holds military, economic, and normative preponderance. In the post-Cold War era, the US has infused its humanitarian reasoning with neoliberal geopolitics, in which decisions about aid allocations have been mediated by an extensive repertoire of neoliberal ideas and practices interlinked with geoeconomic and geopoliotical concerns. The translation of this logic into humanitarian and development practices has led to inconsistent results that, at times, exacerbated vulnerabilities and inequalities of the affected countries instead of reducing or mitigating them.[18]

Still, competition for global dominance, including in approaches and perspectives on humanitarian assistance, does more harm than good to the international and national humanitarian efforts. Cooperation among states is a prerequisite for instituting changes to the global humanitarian regime, and for stemming and potentially reversing the tide of conflict-induced humanitarian disasters and health and environmental crises. As articulated by the G7 foreign ministers during their meeting in May 2022, to successfully cope with future humanitarian disasters requires a "paradigm shift toward more efficient, effective and forward-looking humanitarian assistance" to "prevent or reduce acute humanitarian impacts before they fully unfold."[19] Collaboration among donors is needed to build these kinds of early warning systems.[20] Such collaboration has been paralyzed by the current tensions between the US and China, and Russia's aggressive invasion and war in Ukraine.

While the space may be closed for pragmatic cooperation with Moscow until its war in Ukraine is brought to a halt, a moment may arrive in the future when the current or new government in the Kremlin will be willing to break the cycle of international isolation. At the height of the Cold War confrontation, the United States and Soviet Union not only managed their complex relationship but also found extraordinary opportunities to collaborate in the production and distribution of life-saving vaccines, in addition to maintaining open channels in sports, literature, the arts, and other humanitarian affairs.[21]

---

18   Essex, *Development, Security and Aid.*
19   The Climate Center, "G7 Ministers Commit to 'As Anticipatory a Humanitarian System as Possible,'" May 17, 2022, https://www.climatecentre.org/8409/g7-foreign-ministers-commit -to-making-humanitarian-system-as-anticipatory-as-possible/.
20   The Climate Center, "UN: In 5 Years, Everyone on Earth Must be Protected by Early Warning for Extreme Weather, Climate Change." March 23, 2022, https://www.climatecentre .org/8111/un-within-5-years-everyone-on-earth-must-be-protected-by-early-warningfor -increasingly-extreme-weather-and-climate-change/.
21   Peter J. Hotez, "Russian-United States Vaccine Science Diplomacy: Preserving the Legacy," *PLOS Neglected Tropical Diseases* 11, no. 5 (2017): e0005320, https://journals.plos.org /plosntds/article%3Fid%3D10.1371/journal.pntd.0005320.

And, while it is difficult to anticipate the levels of humanitarian assistance by China in the post-COVID-19 world, its recent statements to the UN and to the broader global community unequivocally demonstrate the critical role that Beijing has been prepared to assume in global health security and disaster relief assistance.[22]

There are, certainly, formidable obstacles to US–China collaboration in the humanitarian realm, not least because of the fundamentally different philosophies and geopolitical logics surrounding their humanitarian action. Still, some small but practical steps can be taken on the premise that collaboration in the critically important areas of humanitarian regime is in the interests of Beijing, Washington, and all recipients and donors of assistance. Importantly, the possibility for such collaboration is supported by strong historical precedents. The Cold War rivals – the United States and Soviet Union – managed to launch and sustain unprecedented collaboration on health activities. The virus strains for an oral polio vaccine were developed by an American virologist and medical scientist Albert Sabin, who shared his findings (with the approval of the American and Soviet governments) with the Russian counterparts. The joint Soviet-American research laid foundations for the Global Polio Eradication Initiative that was carried out under the auspices of the WHO.[23] This initiative that delivered life-saving vaccines to the distant corners of the world endured through the most violent conflicts of the era, including the Nigerian civil war of 1967–70, the Indo-Pakistan war of 1971 (over the independence of Bangladesh), and the conflicts in the Horn of Africa in the 1970s. The Cold War competition begot "the single most successful instance of superpower collaboration in Cold War history" setting important precedent for scientific collaboration for vaccine development.[24]

China and the US also have a history of collaborative public health activities.[25] In recent times, the two countries have conducted joint research and

22   Ministry of Foreign Affairs of the People's Republic of China, "Position Paper on China's Cooperation with the United Nations," October 22, 2021, https://www.fmprc.gov.cn/mfa _eng/wjdt_665385/wjzcs/202110/t20211022_9609380.html.

23   Peter J. Hotez and K.M. Venkat Narayan, "Restoring Vaccine Diplomacy," *JAMA* 325, no. 23 (June 2021): 2337–2338, https://pubmed.ncbi.nlm.nih.gov/34047758/.

24   Erez Manela, "A Pox on Your Narrative: Writing Disease Control into Cold War History," *Diplomatic History* 34, no.2 (April 2010), pp. 299–323.

25   Yanzhong Huang and Scott Kennedy, "Advancing U.S.-China Health Security Cooperation in an Era of Strategic Competition, A Report of the CSIS Commission on Strengthening America's Health Security," December 2021, https://csis-website-prod.s3.amazonaws .com/s3fs-public/publication/211201_Kennedy_USChina_HealthSecurityCooperation .pdf?2CC5_x4F2jIhaOgwo8mvqpPKkztE7RFG.

shared epidemiological data during the 2009 swine flu pandemic and the 2013 Avian influenza outbreak and collaborated on the sidelines of the 2014 Ebola epidemic in West Africa. These joint efforts assisted in increasing the effectiveness of the disaster relief and played an important role in saving lives and scarce resources. The US thought leaders and the American public surveyed in 2020 believed that Washington and Beijing should pursue cooperation on some transnational issues that fall under the purview of US interests.[26] Humanitarian assistance is one of those issues.[27]

First, rather than trying to compel Beijing to adhere to norms and principles of the Western-dominated international humanitarian system (it is highly unrealistic that Beijing would be willing to fully integrate into the Western humanitarian regime due to the specificities of China's humanitarian aid), the US and other traditional donors should strengthen their commitments to multilateral aid agencies and take steps to coordinate with China in less sensitive areas for more effective and non-duplicative provision of assistance. The food and health security sectors and preparation for future natural disasters are among those possible areas for collaboration with Beijing.[28]

China has a good working relationship with the World Food Programme (WFP) and a strong presence in many countries in Africa, the Middle East, and East Asia threatened by food insecurity. In 2021, China signed several agreements with the WFP to provide food assistance to vulnerable populations in several African countries for alleviating food insecurity exacerbated by the socio-economic effects of the COVID-19 pandemic.[29] The US and other traditional donors should encourage Beijing to continue playing its role of a "responsible great power" by scaling up its funding and food contributions through the WFP. This strategy can be applied to Russia as well, which, until

26   Center for Strategic and International Studies, "Mapping the Future of U.S.-China Policy: Views of U.S. Thought Leaders, the U.S. Public, and U.S. Allies and Partners," 2020, https://chinasurvey.csis.org.

27   Ina Friesen and Leon Janauschek, "EU-China Engagement in Humanitarian Aid: Different Approaches, Shared Interests?" Briefing Paper, no. 11. *Deutsches Institut für Entwicklungspolitik* (*DIE*), Bonn, 2021, https://www.econstor.eu/bitstream/10419/242619/1/1770452745.pdf.

28   Kurtzer, Jacob, "China's Humanitarian Aid: Cooperation Amid Competition," Center for Strategic and International Studies, 2020, https://www.csis.org/analysis/chinas-humanitarian-aid-cooperation-amidst-competition.

29   China International Development Cooperation Agency, "China Signs Food Assistance Agreement with WFP," July 30, 2021. http://en.cidca.gov.cn/2021-07/30/c_647644.htm; World Food Programme, "China Supports WFP's Lifesaving Assistance to Vulnerable People in Four African Countries," March 19, 2021, https://www.wfp.org/news/china-supports-wfps-lifesaving-assistance-vulnerable-people-four-african-countries.

its invasion of Ukraine, was one of the largest donors to the WFP in the Central Asian republics.[30] The advocacy for greater contributions to the WFP can be combined with a political dialogue on the ways to streamline coordination and develop cooperation on food security assistance.[31]

Second, China can be encouraged to boost its contributions to health security through increased financial and in-kind contributions to COVAX, an innovative vaccine sharing platform jointly led by the WHO, the UN Children's Fund, Gavi, and the Coalition for Epidemic Preparedness Innovations,[32] and the Access to COVID-19 Tools (ACT) Accelerator, which is a global collaboration platform to expedite the development, production, and equitable access to COVID-19 tests, treatments, and vaccines.[33] True vaccine diplomacy requires that countries with vaccine stocks and greater resources for maintaining them make contributions to COVAX. However, even if the US and its European partners share their unused vaccine stocks with COVAX, the global demands for vaccines will not be met. China and other non-traditional donors can be incentivized to fill the gaps by sharing the stocks of their own licensed vaccines or by supporting the production and distribution of other vaccines in circulation. The direct and immediate benefit from China's increased involvement in multilateral humanitarian initiatives lies in the infusion of resources, which may grow in the future if Beijing's economic growth continues. But there are other specific areas of health security where multilateral cooperation with China or bilateral cooperation between Washington and Beijing may be facilitated. There is a gaping hole in the COVAX global vaccine- and therapeutics-sharing scheme that delays global efforts to control and mitigate the spread of new coronavirus variants to bring an end to the pandemic. It is in China's and America's interest to scale up global supply and administration of vaccinations. The US government can back the sharing of mRNA vaccine technologies with China or support the licensing of mRNA vaccines developed in China for mass-production and distribution to developing countries. Beijing can be invited for a dialogue over the intellectual property rights in live-saving medicines at the World Trade Organization. The two countries can revamp their cooperation in joint

---

30   World Food Programme, "Russian Federation Helps World Food Programme to Support
        Poorer Families in Kyrgyzstan," July 1, 2021, https://www.wfp.org/news/russian-federation
        -helps-world-food-programme-support-poor-families-kyrgyzstan; World Food Programme,
        "Russia Contributes US$2 Million to School Feeding in Tajikistan," January 21, 2022,
        https://www.wfp.org/news/russia-contributes-us-2-million-school-feeding-tajikistan.
31   Friesen and Leon Janauschek, "EU-China Engagement in Humanitarian Aid."
32   Hotez and Narayan, "Restoring Vaccine Diplomacy."
33   More information about ACT is available here: https://www.who.int/initiatives/act
        -accelerator/about.

research and academic exchanges in infectious diseases, the sharing of biological samples and data and methods of biosurveillance. The scientists from the US and China can lead the Track-2 discussions involving members of the epistemic communities from other countries over the new norms, regulations, and approaches to global biosecurity governance and shared countermeasures to biosafety accidents and bioterrorist attacks.[34]

Third, there is much untapped potential for collaboration with China over building an infrastructure for early warning, disaster risk reduction, and preparedness and response to humanitarian emergencies, which is one of the core priorities acknowledged by the state donors and international humanitarian agencies. Over its long history of coping with natural disasters at home and through its involvement in disaster relief missions abroad, China has built significant expertise in responding to environmental crises. Beijing's International Search and Rescue Team is one of the best urban search and rescue teams in the world. It received the highest external classification for rescue forces in 2019 from the UN.[35] Notably, China's disaster management approach is tailored for responses in developing countries' settings.[36] One of the important innovations that USAID has introduced in its operations during the pandemic was the "Over the Horizon" strategic approach, which was designed to look beyond the immediate effects of the health crisis to identify longer-term impacts, such as pressures on economy and political stability that can give rise to new crises.[37] In light of the donors' interest in anticipatory humanitarian action, knowledge exchange in disaster risk preparedness and reduction has the potential to open the door for future cooperation. At the minimum, knowledge sharing in this area can inform the approaches for facilitating the creation of the early warning systems and other infrastructure for humanitarian crisis management.

Certainly, the opacity of China's funding schemes that predates the COVID-19 pandemic is one of the chief obstacles to closer engagement with Beijing in the humanitarian realm. Even the recipient countries often lack proper information on how much and what types of assistance they are receiving from

34   Huang and Kennedy, "Advancing U.S.-China Health Security Cooperation in an Era of Strategic Competition."

35   Du Zhuoran and Zhao Jing, "China Becomes the First Country in Asia to Have Two UN-Standard Rescue Teams," October 24, 2019, https://news.cgtn.com/news/2019-10-24/China-becomes-the-first-in-Asia-to-have-two-UN-standard-rescue-teams--L2XZ7bfPS8/index.html.

36   Friesen and Leon Janauschek, "EU-China Engagement in Humanitarian Aid."

37   USAID, "Over the Horizon: Snapshot," October 27, 2020, https://2017-2020.usaid.gov/work-usaid/resources-for-partners/preparing-world-altered-covid-19/snapshot.

Beijing. The establishment of China's first independent aid agency – the China International Development Cooperation Administration (CIDCA) – in 2018 was intended to reform Beijing's aid management, to improve coordination among the various government agencies, and strengthen the impact of Chinese assistance. Years later, China's aid system remains fragmented, especially at the implementation level, and difficult to navigate.[38] Yet, it is clear that foreign aid will be prioritized as a tool of China's foreign policy and economic interests. Traditional donors, including the US, could engage with the Chinese authorities in streamlining its aid infrastructure and improving the effectiveness of China's foreign aid, the two goals that are shared by Beijing.

3   Lessons for the Traditional Donors

The current humanitarian regime wouldn't survive without the steadfast leadership of dedicated and capable state donors engaging with multilateral humanitarian agencies, serving as role models in response to calls for resource pooling, galvanizing the international community to coordinate their responses to humanitarian crises, and championing the reform of humanitarian system to make it more anticipatory of future disasters. The US has been a critical actor in the humanitarian realm despite the retrenchment from its leadership role and animosity toward multilateral institutions of the Trump administration. The US government has sustained its many commitments to humanitarian aid, whose levels are unlikely to be matched by any other donor, including China, in the near future. Yet, as the COVID-19 pandemic has taught us, financial resource pooling is not enough for a successful and coordinated global response to a humanitarian crisis. Humanitarian aid contributions alone do not suffice to maintain and improve on the integrity of the humanitarian regime.

The global response mechanisms to COVID-19 have been hampered not only by the dearth of health funding, but also the misalignment of national policies, political blame gaming, inconsistent and ambiguous messaging, downplaying narratives, and a deluge of misinformation. These more intangible aspects of the global response, which are often tacked under the rubric of global health diplomacy, involve the necessity to build public trust in science and

---

38   Leah Lynch, Sharon Andersen, and Tianyu Zhu, "China's Foreign Aid: A Primer for Recipient Countries, Donors, and Aid Providers," Center for Global Development, July 9, 2020, https://www.cgdev.org/publication/chinas-foreign-aid-primer-recipient-countries -donors-and-aid-providers.

government institutions, grounding policymaking in scientific expertise, and delivering scientific knowledge and explanations of policies to society in comprehensive, accessible, and consistent ways.[39] A successful global health diplomacy requires leadership shored up by not only material power, but also soft power capabilities to shape the preferences of others through attraction and appeal.[40] Soft power is produced and maintained by the strength of a country's values (when a country lives up to them at home and abroad) and legitimacy of its foreign policies.[41] Relationships with other countries – alliances and partnerships – is another soft power currency that enhances its ability to lead and forge international collaboration.

International views of the US had plummeted long before the onset of the pandemic. The global perception of Washington further faltered following its handling of the coronavirus crisis at home and public responses to the pandemic abroad.[42] As one of the critics of the Trump administration's response to COVID-19 put it, "during COVID, the act of turning the other way – of asking other nations to support America with protective equipment, with diagnostic supplies, with key necessary tools, and then of pulling out of the World Health Organization" has blemished Washington's reputation as the global leader.[43] President Trump's promotion of misguided treatments for the infection and support for counterparts in other countries, who, in a likeminded fashion, ignored the science in developing policies to manage health crises in their own countries, had sown mistrust in approaches and recommendations by the global health authorities seeking to coordinate states' responses to COVID-19. With the health crisis now in the vaccine phase and the Biden administration following through on American commitments to work with

39   Mohammed AlKhaldi, Nigel James, Vijay Kumar Chattu, Sara Ahmed, Hamza Meghari, Kirsty Kaiser, Carel IJsselmuiden, and Marcel Tanner, "Rethinking and Strengthening the Global Health Diplomacy through Triangulated Nexus Between Policy Makers, Scientists and the Community in Light of COVID-19 Global Crisis," *Global Health Research and Policy* 6, no. 12 (2021), p. 12; Sanaz Taghizade, Vijay Kumar Chattu, Ebrahim Jaafaripooyan and Sebastian Kevany, "COVID-19 Pandemic as an Excellent Opportunity for Global Health Diplomacy." *Frontier in Public Health* 9 (July 2021):1–9, https://www.ncbi.nlm.nih.gov/pmc/articles/PMC8310918/pdf/fpubh-09-655021.pdf.

40   Joseph Nye, *Bound to Lead: The Changing Nature of American Power* (Basic Book, 1990).

41   Joseph Nye, *The Future of Power* (New York: Public Affairs, 2011), p. 84.

42   Michael Dimock and John Gramlich, "How America Changed During Donald Trump's Presidency," Pew Research Center, January 29, 2021, https://www.pewresearch.org/2021/01/29/how-america-changed-during-donald-trumps-presidency/.

43   David Gelles, "When Disaster Hits Home for a Global Aid Organization," *New York Times*, January 8, 2021, https://www.nytimes.com/2021/01/08/business/raj-shah-rockefeller-foundation-corner-office.html.

other countries on vaccine distribution, including through the WHO, the global views of the US have rebounded, but still vary considerably across the publics surveyed. Concerns over the prospects of another foreign policy turn toward "America first" and isolationism continue loom large as are the lagging perception that the US mainly looks after its own national interests in global affairs.[44] Both Russia and China have been quick to exploit Washington's foreign policy missteps and to amplify concerns with its nationalist and protectionist measures. The COVID-19 responses have served as a reminder that soft power and reputation are painstakingly difficult to build, and easy to wreck with detrimental consequences for international cooperation.

The analysis of the COVID-19 assistance has revealed two additional challenges to the US ability to respond promptly to countries in need and champion international cooperation in areas that extend beyond the COVID-19 assistance. While the USAID's Office of US Foreign Disaster Assistance (OFDA) had autonomy, flexibility, and capacity to be agile and independent in its responses to humanitarian crises, the funding immediately available to the OFDA was small relative to the volume and intensity of the flash points of complex emergencies and disasters around the globe. Considerably larger funding for humanitarian response is budgeted and appropriated through a cumbersome and lengthy federal budgeting process, which may delay the allocation and spending of the approved funds and resources for years. This places the US at disadvantage vis-à-vis China, which is unburdened by the same lengthy bureaucratic processes and the vicissitudes of domestic politics. Beijing, therefore, is capable of responding faster to global and country-specific humanitarian needs than the US.

And, as we discussed in chapter on US COVID-19 aid, the authority for American foreign assistance has been spread across several government agencies and accounts funded by the Congress. The later has become increasingly involved in shaping the character and destinations of the US foreign aid by providing direction or attaching constraints on how American public resources could be spent. Since US humanitarian assistance has been coordinated with development assistance, these constraints have reduced flexibility in meeting the recipients' humanitarian needs. Learning from its history of humanitarian assistance, the US government – USAID, State Department and Congress – should work together to grant more independence and flexibility

---

44   Richard Wike, Jacob Poushter, Laura Silvr, Janell Fetterolf and Mara Mordecai, "America's
        Image Abroad Rebounds With Transition from Trump to Biden," Pew Research Center,
        June 10, 2021, https://www.pewresearch.org/global/2021/06/10/americas-image-abroad
        -rebounds-with-transition-from-trump-to-biden/.

in humanitarian aid decisions to the Bureau for Humanitarian Assistance (BHA), which subsumed the OFDA and Food for Peace (FPP) offices in 2020. The USAID/BHA professionals should be entrusted with decisions on how to respond quickly to emergencies around the world in ways that promote US interests and without compromising transparency and accountability in assistance. In addition, the US government should reform the highly bureaucratized and lengthy process for awarding assistance grants and contracts and ensure greater participation of the range of stakeholders from the affected countries in the process of aid allocations.[45]

The branding of humanitarian aid has been another controversial topic among traditional donors. On the one hand, by seeking to build donor's image and win hearts and minds in the recipient countries, the branding of aid violates the principles of neutrality of humanitarian aid. It may also be dangerous when used in conflict settings where the aid recipients and implementing partners may become the targets of violence due to their collaboration with donors recognized in aid signage. On the other hand, removing clear and simple markings of the origins of aid can lead to a distorted image about the major donors of assistance. Beijing has taken advantage of this dilemma by unapologetically promoting the Chinese brand by embracing highly visible projects touted in news headlines and demanding recipients' public attribution of Chinese aid. Finding a reasonable approach to aid designation that leverages donors' interests without politicizing assistance is a big challenge that needs to be addressed. If branding aid in complex emergencies is imprudent, there may be circumstances, like building an early warning infrastructure, where the clearer acknowledgement of donors' contributions could be made.[46] The US government could reconsider its resistance to funding US-branded projects: in the end, investing in the health security infrastructure in a foreign nation and negotiating access to health research and data can be beneficial to the US and the world.[47]

While this book's focus is on state donors of humanitarian aid, modern humanitarianism involves a variety of stakeholders, experts, and enterprises shaping policies, experiences, and outcomes of humanitarian assistance and operating independently or in collaboration with states at the national and international levels. The framework of COVID-19 responses, for example, have

---

45   Jim Richardson, "To Win Friends and Influence People, America Should Learn from the CCP," *Foreign Policy*, July 22, 2021, https://foreignpolicy.com/2021/07/22/china-belt-road-development-projects-usaid-state-department-foreign-aid-assistance-budget/.

46   Margesson, "International Crises and Disasters."

47   Richardson, "To Win Friends and Influence People, America Should Learn from the CCP."

included state-led efforts to procure and deliver medical assistance to other countries experiencing acute health crises, the efforts of multilateral agencies, such as WHO, and the GAVI alliance to facilitate international collaboration over COVID-19 responses, the sharing of best practices, and medical and scientific information that could shape public health policies. Then, there were manifold private and informal efforts – peer-to-peer scientific collaborations, private foundations-funded health initiatives, public-private partnerships in vaccine production, aid deliveries through sister cities and towns networks – that supplemented the activities of state donors and international organizations. The success of future humanitarian endeavors will be defined by the ability of these diverse actors build horizontal (among the same groups of actors) and virtual (among different groups of actors and levels) synergies and complementarities of their discrete initiatives. For instance, to successfully cope with future pandemics will require the removal or lowering of the barriers for vaccine development and distribution. These barriers are scientific expertise needed to produce antibodies to enable immune system's response to the new virus and invent technologies for scaling up production and distribution of new vaccines. Scientific and medical skills are also necessary for establishing high quality controls in vaccine administration. These barriers are compounded by the lack of manufacturing and storage facilities, and the lack of funding for educating indigenous health professionals' workforce. In addition, the informational medium is critical for the success of health policies. Social media channels get quickly filled with disinformation and misinformation about the sources of a humanitarian disaster or purported dangers of safe vaccines. Conspiracy theories and pseudo-scientific accounts spread doubt about the efficacy of health protocols, jeopardize the effectiveness of vaccination programs, and establish additional hurdles in the certification and licensing of vaccines. Addressing this situation will require collaboration among international organizations, state donors, business entrepreneurs, health and education professionals, and scientists across multiple nations.[48] The current system of global health governance and humanitarian regime privilege state actors, and therefore, needs to be reformed to allow for more diverse alliances and partnership that are necessary to respond to global health crises.[49]

---

48   Hotez and K.M. Venkat Narayan, "Restoring Vaccine Diplomacy."
49   Alan Ingram, "The New Geopolitics of Disease: Between Global Health and Global Security," *Geopolitics* 10:3 (2005): 522–545.

References

Abbas, Muhammad Zaheer. "Practical Implications of 'Vaccine Nationalism': A Short-Sighted and Risky Approach in Response to COVID-19." South Centre Research Paper no. 124 (2020): https://www.econstor.eu/bitstream/10419/232250/1/south-centre-rp-124.pdf.

Agnew, John. "Emerging China and Critical Geopolitics: Between World Politics and Chinese Particularity." *Eurasian Geography and Economics* 51, no. 55 (2010): 569–582.

Al Jazeera. "'First Drop of Rain': Libya Receives Russia's Sputnik Vaccine." *Al Jazeera*, April 4, 2021. https://www.aljazeera.com/news/2021/4/4/first-drop-of-rain-libya-receives-covid-vaccine-delivery.

Al Jazeera. "US to 'Loan' COVID-19 Vaccines to Canada and Mexico." *Al Jazeera*, March 18, 2021. https://www.aljazeera.com/news/2021/3/18/the-us-to-loan-covid-19-vaccines-to-canada-and-mexico.

Al Jazeera. "Czech Republic Turns to Russian Vaccine Amid Soaring COVID Cases." *Al Jazeera*, February 28, 2021. https://www.aljazeera.com/news/2021/2/28/czech-places-order-for-russias-sputnik-amid-covid-soaring-cases.

Alesina, Alberto, and David Dollar. "Who Gives Foreign Aid to Whom and Why?" *Journal of Economic Growth* 5, 1 (2000): 33–63.

AlKhaldi, Mohammed, Nigel James, Vijay Kumar Chattu, Sara Ahmed, Hamza Meghari, Kirsty Kaiser, Carel IJsselmuiden, and Marcel Tanner. "Rethinking and Strengthening the Global Health Diplomacy through Triangulated Nexus Between Policy Makers, Scientists and the Community in Light of COVID-19 Global Crisis." *Global Health Research and Policy* 6, no. 12 (2021). https://doi.org/10.1186/s41256-021-00195-2.

All Africa. "Tanzania Receives Additional 800,000 Sinopharm Vaccine Doses from China." All Africa, January 26, 2022. https://allafrica.com/stories/202201270435.html.

Andreoni, Manuela, and Bryan Pietsch. "Brazil's Health Authority Rejects Importing Russia's Sputnik V Vaccine." *New York Times*, October 8, 2021. https://www.nytimes.com/2021/04/26/world/covid-vaccine-brazil-russia-sputnik.html.

AP Staff, "Russia's FM Lavrov Meets Algeria Leader to Deepen Thick Ties," *Associated Press*, May 10, 2022. https://apnews.com/article/russia-ukraine-europe-africa-algiers-algeria-7d91687c656ab73fa427145fee3f9b48.

Appel, Cameron, Diana Beltekian, Daniel Gavrilov, Charlie Giattino, Joe Hasell, Bobbie Macdonald, Edouard Mathieu, Esteban Ortiz-Ospina, Hannah Ritchie, Lucas Rodés-Guirao, and Max Roser, *Our World in Data*, 2020. https://covid.ourworldindata.org/.

Asmus, Gerda, Andreas Fuchs, and Angelika Müller. "BRICS and Foreign Aid," in *The Political Economy of the BRICS Countries. Vol. 2: BRICS and the Global Economy*, edited by Soo Yeon Kim, 139–177. World Scientific, 2017.

Averre, Derek, and Lance Davies. "Russia, Humanitarian Intervention and the Responsibility to Protect: The Case of Syria." *International Affairs* 91, no. 4 (2015): 813–834.

Bader, Julia, Jörn Grävingholt, and Antje Kästner. "Would Autocracies Promote Autocracy? A Political Economy Perspective on Regime-Type Export in Regional Neighbourhoods," *Contemporary Politics* 16, no. 1 (2010): 81–100.

Bailey, Michael A., Anton Strezhnev, and Erik Voeten. "Estimating Dynamic State Preferences from United Nations Voting Data." *Journal of Conflict Resolution* 61, no. 2 (2017): 430–456.

Baker, Sinéad. "Secret Trump-era Vaccine Plan Prioritized Rich Allies Like Taiwan and Israel Above Poor Nations Which Needed Them More." *Insider*, January 28, 2022. https://www.businessinsider.com/trump-era-vaccine-sharing-plan-rich-allies -before-needy-nations-2022-1.

Baldry, John. "Soviet Relations with Saudi Arabia and The Yemen 1917–1938." *Middle Eastern Studies* 20, no. 1 (1984): 53–80.

Baluyevsky, Yury Nikolayevich. "Theoretical and Methodological Bases for the Military Doctrine of the Russian Federation." *Vestnik of the Academy of Military Sciences*, no. 1 (2007).

Baluyevsky, Yury Nikolayevich. "Regional and Global Threat Assessment; Nature of Future War; Future Force Structure of the Russian Armed Forces." *Vestnik of the Academy of Military Sciences*, no. 1 (2008).

Banco, Erin. "Trump Plan Favored Giving Vaccines to Israel, Taiwan Over Poorer Countries." *Politico*, January 27, 2021. https://www.politico.com/news/2022/01/27 /trump-plan-favored-vaccines-isreal-taiwan-00002893.

Banco, Erin. "'It's a Sore Spot': Why Officials are Raising Questions about Biden's Vaccine Donations." *Politico*, December 8, 2021. https://www.politico.com/news/2021/12/08 /biden-administration-officials-questions-vaccine-donations-523922.

Barnett, Michael. "Evolution Without Progress? Humanitarianism in a World of Hurt." *International Organization* 63, no.4 (2009).

Barnett, Michael. *Empire of Humanity: A History of Humanitarianism*. Ithaca: Cornell University Press, 2011.

Barnett, Michael. "Covid-19 and the Sacrificial International Order." *International Organization* 74, no. S1 (2020): E128–E147.

Barnett, Michael, and Thomas G. Weiss, "Humanitarianism: A Brief History of the Present," in *Humanitarianism in Question*, edited by Michael Barnett and Thomas G. Weiss. Ithaca: Cornell University Press, 2008.

BBC News. "Coronavirus: What Does 'From Russia with Love' Really Mean?" *BBC News*, April 3, 2020. https://www.bbc.com/news/world-europe-52137908.

BBC News. "Ukraine Attention Shows Bias against Black Lives, WHO Chief Says." *BBC News*, April 13, 2022. https://www.bbc.com/news/world-61101732.

Bellamy, Daniel, and Johannes Pleschberger. "Slovaks Divided over Russia's Sputnik V Vaccine after Quality Concerns." *Euronews*, May 1, 2021. https://www.euronews.com/2021/05/01/slovaks-divided-over-russia-s-sputnik-v-vaccine-after-quality-concerns.

Bengali, Shashank. "African Health Experts Hail Biden's Vaccine Pledge, but Call for More Transparency." *The New York Times*, September 23, 2021. https://www.nytimes.com/2021/09/23/world/vaccine-covid-africa.html.

Berthélemy, Jean-Claud. "Bilateral Donors' Interest vs. Recipients' Development Motives in Aid Allocation: Do All Donors Behave the Same?" *Review of Development Economics* 10, no. 2 (2006): 179–194.

Beubien, Jason. "What U.S. Vaccine Donations Mean for Sierra Leone and Africa." NPR, June 12, 2021. https://www.npr.org/2021/06/12/1005937103/what-u-s-vaccine-donations-mean-for-sierra-leone-and-africa%206-1-22.

Biden, Joseph R. "Remarks by President Biden at the Global COVID-19 Summit." The White House Briefing Room, June 3, 2021. https://www.whitehouse.gov/briefing-room/statements-releases/2021/06/03/statement-by-president-joe-biden-on-global-vaccine-distribution/.

Bill & Melinda Gates Foundation. "Bill and Melinda Gates Pledge $10 Billion in Call for Decade of Vaccines," Bill & Melinda Gates Foundation. https://www.gatesfoundation.org/ideas/media-center/press-releases/2010/01/bill-and-melinda-gates-pledge-$10-billion-in-call-for-decade-of-vaccines.

Boffey, Daniel. "Revealed: Italy's Call for Urgent Help was Ignored as Coronavirus Swept Through Europe." *The Guardian*, July 15, 2020. https://www.theguardian.com/world/2020/jul/15/revealed-the-inside-story-of-europes-divided-coronavirus-response.

Borshchevskaya, Anna. "Russia's Growing Interests in Libya." The Washington Institute for Near East Policy, January 24, 2020. https://www.washingtoninstitute.org/policy-analysis/russias-growing-interests-libya.

Boussalis, Constantine and Caryn Peiffer. " Health, Need and Politics: the Determinants of Bilateral HIV/AIDS Assistance." *Journal of Development Studies* 47, no. 12 (2011): 1798–1825.

Brady, Anne-Marie. *Looking North, Looking South: China, Taiwan and the South Pacific (Vol. 26)*. Singapore, Malaysia: World Scientific Pub. Co. Inc., 2010.

Brezhneva, Anna, and Daria Ukhova. *Russia as a Humanitarian Aid Donor*. OXFAM Discussion Paper, July 15, 2013. https://www-cdn.oxfam.org/s3fs-public/file_attachments/dp-russia-humanitarian-donor-150713-en_0.pdf.

Bridge. "China COVID-19 Vaccine Tracker." Accessed June 10, 2022. https://bridgebeijing.com/our-publications/our-publications-1/china-covid-19-vaccines-tracker/.

Bryan, Joe. "War Without End? Miliary Humanitarianism and the Limits of Biopolitical Approaches to Security in Central America and the Caribbean." *Political Geography* 47(2015): 33–42.

Bull, Hedley. *The Anarchical Society,* 3rd edition. Basingstoke: Palgrave, 2002.

Bush, George H.W. "Statement on Signing the FREEDOM Support Act," The American Presidency Project, October 24, 1992, https://www.presidency.ucsb.edu/documents /statement-signing-the-freedom-support-act.

Burki, Talha Khan. "The Russian Vaccine for COVID-19." *The Lancet Respiratory Medicine* 8, no. 11 (2020): e85–e86.

Cafiero, Giorgio, and Emily Milliken. "Russians Unlikely to Leave Libya, Despite Ukraine War." *Al Jazeera,* April 15, 2022. https://www.aljazeera.com/news/2022/4/15/russians -unlikely-leave-libya-despite-ukraine-war.

Center for Security Studies. "Russia's 'Humanitarian Aid', or What the Russian Military Personnel are Doing in Europe." May 5, 2020. https://censs.org/russias-humanitarian -aid-or-what-the-russian-military-personnel-are-doing-in-europe/?lang=en#_edn1.

Center for Strategic and International Studies. "Mapping the Future of U.S.-China Policy: Views of U.S. Thought Leaders, the U.S. Public, and U.S. Allies and Partners." 2020. https://chinasurvey.csis.org, accessed 3 December 2022.

Chadwick, Vince. "Germany to Push China, Gulf States on Humanitarian Assistance." *DEVEX,* September 7, 2020. https://www.devex.com/news/germany-to-push-china -gulf-states-on-humanitarian-assistance-98034.

Chaisty, Paul, Christopher J. Gerry, and Stephen Whitefield. "The Buck Stops Elsewhere: Authoritarian Resilience and the Politics of Responsibility for COVID-19 in Russia." *Post-Soviet Affairs* 38, no. 5 (2022): 366–385.

Chasan, Aliza. "Prepare for Next Pandemic, Future Pathogens with 'Even Deadlier Potential' than COVID, WHO Chief Warns," *CBS News,* May 23, 2023, https://www.cbsnews .com/news/next-pandemic-threat-pathogen-deadlier-than-covid-world-health -organization/.

Chen, Stella. "Community of Common Destiny for Mankind," *China Media Project.* August 25, 2021. https://chinamediaproject.org/the_ccp_dictionary/community-of -common-destiny-for-mankind/.

Chen, Wei A. "COVID-19 and China's Changing Soft Power in Italy." *Chinese Political Science Review* (2021): 1–21.

Chenchen Zhang. "Right-wing Populism with Chinese Characteristics? Identity, Otherness and Global Imaginaries in Debating World Politics Online." *European Journal of International Relations* 26, no. 1 (2020): 88–115.

Cheng, Maria, and Lori Hinnant. "Rich Nations Dip into COVAX Supply while Poor Wait for Shots." *AP,* August 14, 2021. https://apnews.com/article/joe-biden-middle-east -africa-europe-coronavirus-pandemic-5e57879c6cb22d96b942cbc973b9296c.

China International Development Cooperation Agency. "China Signs Food Assistance Agreement with WFP," July 30, 2021. http://en.cidca.gov.cn/2021-07/30/c_647644.htm.

China Power. "Is China's Covid-19 Diplomacy Succeeding?" 2021. https://chinapower
.csis.org/china-covid-medical-vaccine-diplomacy/.

Choo, Jaewoo. "Ideas Matter: China's Peaceful Rise." *Asia Europe Journal* 7, no. 3 (2009):
389–404.

CIDCA. "Abu Dhabi Crown Prince Sheikh Mohammed bin Zayed Al Nahyan of the
UAE Meets with Wang Yi." 2021. http://kw.china-embassy.gov.cn/eng/zgxw/202010
/t20201013_1573098.htm.

Cissé, Daouda. "China and Taiwan: The 'One-China' Policy and the Controversy of
'Vaccine Diplomacy'." *University of Nottingham*, June 14, 2021. https://taiwaninsight
.org/2021/06/14/china-and-taiwan-the-one-china-policy-and-the-controversy-of
-vaccine-diplomacy/.

Cohen, Jon. "China's Vaccine Gambit." *Science*, 370 no. 6552 (2020): 1263–1267.

Collinson, Erin, and Jocilyn Estes. "A Global Pandemic Needs a Global Response: US
Contributions to COVID Relief." Center for Global Development, April 2, 2021.
https://www.cgdev.org/blog/global-pandemic-needs-global-response-us-contribu
tions-covid-relief.

Cooley, Alexander, and Daniel Nexon. *Exit from Hegemony: The Unraveling of the
American Global Order*, Oxford: Oxford University Press, 2020.

Cooper, Orah, and Carol Fogarty. "Soviet Economic and Military Aid to the Less Developed Countries, 1954–78." *Soviet and Eastern European Foreign Trade* 21 (1985):
54–73.

Coppedge, Michael, et al. "V-Dem Codebook v10" Varieties of Democracy (V-Dem)
Project. 2020. https://www.v-dem.net/en/.

Copper, John F. *China's Foreign Aid and Investment Diplomacy. Vol. II: History and Practice in Asia, 1950-Present.* New York, NY: Palgrave Macmillan, 2016.

Curtis, Devon. "Politics and Humanitarian Aid: Debates, Dilemmas and Dissension,"
Report of a conference organized by ODI, POLIS at the University of Leeds and
CAFOD, London. February 1, 2001.

Dalong, Li. "'The Central Kingdom' and 'the Realm Under Heaven' Coming to Mean
the Same: The Process of the Formation of Territory in Ancient China." *Frontiers in
History of China* 3, no. 3 (2008): 323–352.

Dany, Charlotte. *Beyond Principles vs. Politics: Humanitarian Aid in the European Union.*
ARENA Working Paper 11. November 2014. https://www.sv.uio.no/arena/english
/research/publications/arena-working-papers/2014/wp11-14.pdf.

De Bengy Puyvallée, Antonie, and Katerini Tagmatarchi Storeng. "COVAX, Vaccine
Donations and the Politics of Global Vaccine Inequity." *Globalization and Health* 18,
no. 26 (2022): https://globalizationandhealth.biomedcentral.com/articles/10.1186
/s12992-022-00801-z.

De Graaff, Nana, and Bastiaan Van Apeldoorn. "US-China Relations and the Liberal World Order: Contending Elites, Colliding Visions?" *International Affairs* 94, no. 1 (2018): 113–131.

Delgado, Daniel Lemus, Bravo Vergara, and Jose Jesus. "Geopolitics, Real and Imagined Spaces: China and Foreign Policy in the Context of East Asia." *International Journal of China Studies* 8, no. 3 (2017): 397–421.

Development Initiatives. "Global Humanitarian Assistance Report 2019," http://devinit.org/wp-content/uploads/2019/09/GHA-report-2019.pdf.

Dimock, Michael, and John Gramlich. "How America Changed During Donald Trump's Presidency," Pew Research Center, January 29, 2021. https://www.pewresearch.org/2021/01/29/how-america-changed-during-donald-trumps-presidency/.

D'Mello, Bernard. "Soviet Collaboration in Indian Steel Industry, 1954–84." *Economic and Political Weekly* (1988): 473–486.

Dollar, David, and Victoria Levin. "The Increasing Selectivity of Foreign Aid, 1984–2003." *World Development* 34, no. 12 (2006): 2034–2046.

Dreher, Axel, and Andreas Fuchs. "Rogue Aid? The Determinants of China's Aid Allocation," Courant Research Centre Discussion Paper 93, September 6, 2011.

Dreher, Alex, Peter Nennenkamp and Reiner Thiele. "Are 'New' Donors Different? Comparing the Allocation of Bilateral Aid Between non-DAC and DAC Donor Countries." *World Development* 39 (2011): 1950–1968.

Drury, A. Cooper, and Richard Stuart Olson. "Disasters and Political Unrest: An Empirical Investigation." *Journal of Contingencies and Crisis Management* 6 (1998): 153–161.

Drury, A. Cooper, Richard S. Olson and Douglas A. van Belle. "The Politics of Humanitarian Aid: U.S. Foreign Disaster Assistance, 1964–1995." *Journal of Politics* 67, no. 2 (2005): 454–473.

Edwards, R. Randle, Louise Henkin, and Andrew J. Nathan, *Human Rights in Contemporary China*, New York: Columbia University Press, 1986.

Eisensee, Thomas, and David Strömberg. "News Droughts, News Floods, and U.S. Disaster Relief." *Quarterly Journal of Economics* 122, no. 2 (2007): 693–728.

Embassy of the People's Republic of China in Solomon Islands. "Foreign Ministry Spokesperson Zhao Lijian's Regular Press Conference on July 29, 2021," http://se.china-embassy.gov.cn/eng/fyrth/202107/t20210729_9026599.htm.

Embassy of the People's Republic of China in the Republic of Botswana. "China's Shandong Province Donates Anti-Pandemic Materials to Botswana." April 5, 2020. http://bw.china-embassy.gov.cn/eng/sgxw/202005/t20200507_5708942.htm#:~:text=China%27s%20Shandong%20Province%20Donates%20Anti%2DPandemic%20Materials%20to%20Botswana&text=On%207th%20May%202020%2C%20a,the%20Chinese%20Embassy%20in%20Gaborone.

Emmott, Robin, and Andrew Osborn. "Russia Aid to Italy Leaves EU Exposed." Reuters. March 26, 2020. https://www.reuters.com/article/us-health-coronavirus-russia-eu /russian-aid-to-italy-leaves-eu-exposed-idUSKBN21D28K.

Enlai, Zhou. "China's Eight Principles for Economic Aid and Technical Assistance to Other Countries," (1964), http://www.china.org.cn/government/whitepaper/2011-04 /21/content_22411843.htm.

Erickson, John. "'Russia will Not be Trifled with': Geopolitical Facts and Fantasies," *Journal of Strategic Studies* 22 no. 2–3 (1999): 242–268.

Essex, Jamey. *Development, Security and Aid: Geopolitics and Geoeconomics at the U.S. Agency for International Development.* Athens, GA: The University of Georgia Press, 2013.

Ethiopian Monitor. "Ethiopia, Russia Set to Ink Deal on Sputnik V Supplies." 2021. https://ethiopianmonitor.com/2021/05/02/ethiopia-russia-set-to-ink-deal-on -sputnik-v-supplies/.

Eto, Naoko. "China's Propaganda Maneuvers in Response to COVID-19: The Unified Front Work that Contributes to 'the Community of Common Destiny for Mankind' Promotion." *SPF China Observer, No. 31*, May 20, 2020. https://www.spf.org/spf -china-observer/en/document-detail031.html.

Evanega, Sarah, Mark Lynas, Jordan Adams, Karinne Smolenyak, and Cision Global Insights. "Coronavirus Misinformation: Quantifying Sources and Themes in the COVID-19 'Infodemic'." *JMIR Preprints* 19, no. 10 (2020), https://allianceforscience .org/wp-content/uploads/2020/10/Evanega-et-al-Coronavirus-misinformation -submitted_07_23_20.pdf.

Experts for Development. "Russia Allocates $30 million to the Russia-UNDP Trust Fund for Development, Including to Tackling the Pandemic." May 7, 2020. https:// expertsfordevelopment.ru/news/project-news/rossiya-vydelila-30-millionov -dollarov-trastovomu-fondu-rossiya-proon-v-tselyakh-razvitiya-v-tom-chi.html.

Fassin, Didier. "The Predicament of Humanitarianism," *Qui Parle: Critical Humanities and Social Sciences* 22, no. 1 (2013): 33–48.

Fearon, James, and Alexander Wendt. "Rationalism v. Constructivism: A Skeptical View," in *Handbook of International Relations*, edited by Walter Carlsnaes, Thomas Risse, and Beth Simmons, 52–72. Thousand Oaks, CA: Sage Publications, 2002.

Federal Emergency Management Agency. "Prioritization and Allocation of Certain Scarce and Critical Health and Medical Resources for Domestic Use." *Federal Register 44 CFR Part 328*, updated December 31, 2020. https://www.federalregister .gov/documents/2020/12/31/2020-29060/prioritization-and-allocation-of-certain -scarce-and-critical-health-and-medical-resources-for.

Fidler, David P. "Vaccine Nationalism's Politics." *Science* 369, no. 6505 (2020): 749–749.

Fielding, David. "The Dynamics of Humanitarian Aid Decisions." *Oxford Bulletin of Economics and Statistics* 76, no. 4 (2014): 536–564.

Financial Tracking Service. 2020. Russia: Government Donor Snapshot for 2020. https://fts.unocha.org/donors/3006/summary/2020.

Fink, Günther, and Silvia Redaelli. "Determinants of International Emergency Aid - Humanitarian Need Only?" *World Development* 39, no. 5 (2011): 741–757.

Finnegan, Conor. "Despite Calls for Global Cooperation, US and China Fight over Leading Coronavirus Response." *ABC News*. March 31, 2020. https://abcnews.go.com/Politics/calls-global-cooperation-us-china-fight-leading-coronavirus/story?id=69898820.

Fleck, Robert, and Christopher Kilby. "How Do Political Changes Influence US Bilateral Aid Allocations? Evidence From Panel Data." *Review of Development Economics* 10, no. 2 (2006): 210–223.

Flockhart, Trine. "Democracy, Security and the Social Construction of Europe." *Perspectives on European Politics and Society* 2, no. 1 (2001): 27–52.

Foltynova, Kristyna. "Sputnik V: The Story of Russia's Controversial COVID19 Vaccine." *Radio Free Europe*, March 4, 2021. https://www.rferl.org/a/sputnik-v-vaccine/31133608.html.

Fomin, Ivan. "Sixty Shades of Statism: Mapping the Ideological Divergences in Russian Elite Discourse." *Democratizatsiya: The Journal of Post-Soviet Democratization* 30, no. 3 (2022): 305–332.

Fook, Lye Liang. "China's COVID-19 Assistance to Southeast Asia: Uninterrupted Aid amid Global Uncertainties." *Perspective* 58 (June 2020): 1–13.

Fox, James W. and Lex Rieffel. "Strengthening the Millennium Challenge Corportaiton: Better Results are Possible." The Brookings Institution, December 10, 2008. https://www.brookings.edu/research/strengthen-the-millennium-challenge-corporation-better-results-are-possible/.

France24. "European Commission Apologises to Italy for Lack of Help in Coronavirus Crisis." *France24*, March 4, 2020, https://www.france24.com/en/20200403-european-commission-italy-ursula-van-der-leyen-apology-coronavirus-covid19-giuseppe-conte.

Friesen, Ina, and Leon Janauschek. "EU-China Engagement in Humanitarian Aid: Different Approaches, Shared Interests?" Briefing Paper no. 11. Deutsches Institut für Entwicklungspolitik (DIE), Bonn. 2021. https://www.econstor.eu/bitstream/10419/242619/1/1770452745.pdf.

Fuchs, Andreas, and Nils-Hendrik Klann. "Emergency Aid 2.0." Beiträge zur Jahrestagung des Vereins für Socialpolitik (2013).

Fuchs Andreas, Kaplan Lennart, Kis-Katos Krisztina, Schmidt Sebastian S. and Turbanisch Felix. "China Sent Masks, Gloves and Gowns to Many U.S. States. Here's Who Benefited." *Washington Post,* January 29, 2021. https://www.washingtonpost.com

/politics/2021/01/29/china-sent-masks-gloves-gowns-many-us-states-heres-who -benefited/.

Fuchs, Andrea, and Marina Rudyak, "The Motives of China's Foreign Aid," in *Handbook on the International Political Economy of China* (Edward Elgar Publishing, 2019), pp. 391–410.

Fuchs, Andreas, and Krishna Chaitanya Vadlamannati, "The Needy Donor: An Empirical Analysis of India's Aid Motives." *World Development* 44 (2013): 110–128.

Fukuyama, Francis. "The End of History?" *The National Interest*, no. 16 (1989):3–18.

Garwood-Gowers, Andrew. "China's 'Responsible Protection' Concept: Reinterpreting the Responsibility to Protect (R2P) and Military Intervention for Humanitarian Purposes," *Asian Journal of International Law* 6, no. 1 (2016): 89–118.

GAVI. "US-donated Vaccine Deliveries to Africa Set to Begin, with First Deliveries Planned to Burkina Faso, Djibouti, and Ethiopia." July 16, 2021. https://www.gavi .org/news/media-room/us-donated-vaccine-deliveries-africa-set-begin-first -deliveries-planned.

GAVI. "Gavi, the Vaccine Alliance Helps Vaccinate Almost Half the World's Children Against Deadly and Debilitating Infectious Diseases." https://www.gavi.org/our -alliance/about, accessed 3 December 2022.

Gelles, David. "When Disaster Hits Home for a Global Aid Organization." *New York Times*, January 8, 2021. https://www.nytimes.com/2021/01/08/business/raj-shah-rockefeller -foundation-corner-office.html.

Gigitashvili, Givi. "Russia's Covid-19 'Humanitarian Aid' Comes at a Price." *Emerging Europe*. 2020. https://emerging-europe.com/voices/russias-covid-19-humanitarian -aid-comes-at-a-price/.

Giuffrida, Angela. "Italian Former PM Faces Renewed Questions over Covid Aid from Russia." *The Guardian*, March 23, 2022. https://www.theguardian.com/world/2022/mar /23/italian-former-pm-conte-faces-renewed-questions-over-covid-aid-from-russia.

Giusti, Serena, and Eleonora Tafuro Ambrosetti. "Making the Best Out of a Crisis: Russia's Health Diplomacy during COVID-19." *Social Sciences* 11, no. 2 (2022): 53.

Gleditsch, Kristian S., and Michael D. Ward. "Measuring Space: A Minimum-Distance Database and Applications to International Studies." *Journal of Peace Research* 38, no. 6 (2001): 739–758.

Godement, François. *Expanded Ambition, Shrinking Achievements: How China Sees the Global Order* (Policy Brief March 2017). London, UK: European Council on Foreign Relations, 2017, https://ecfr.eu/publication/expanded_ambitions_shrinking _achievements_how_china_sees_the_global_order/.

Goldman, Marshall I. "A Balance Sheet of Soviet Foreign Aid," *Foreign Affairs* 43, no. 2 (1965): 349–360.

Goldstein, Judith, and Robert O. Keohane, *Ideas and Foreign Policy: Beliefs, Institutions, and Political Change.* Ithaca: Cornell University Press, 1993.

Gong, Lina. "Humanitarian Diplomacy as an Instrument for China's Image-Building," *Asian Journal of Comparative Politics* 6, no. 3 (2021): 238–252.

Gong, Lina, "The Belt and Road Initiative: Vehicle for China's Humanitarian Action?" (Policy Report. Nanyang Technological University, Singapore, 2021), https://www.rsis.edu.sg/wp-content/uploads/2021/06/PR210628_The-Belt-and-Road-Initiative-Vehicle-for-China's-Humanitarian-Action_V2.pdf.

Government of Mexico. "1.35 Million Doses of the Johnson & Johnson Vaccine Arrive Following Bilateral Agreement with US." June 15, 2021. https://www.gob.mx/sre/prensa/bilateral-agreement-with-us-leads-to-the-arrival-of-1-35-million-doses-of-the-johnson-johnson-vaccine.

Gowan, Richard. "China's Pragmatic Approach to UN Peacekeeping." The Brookings Institution, September 14, 2020. https://www.brookings.edu/articles/chinas-pragmatic-approach-to-un-peacekeeping/.

Gray, Patty A. "Looking 'The Gift' in the Mouth: Russia as Donor." 2011. https://mural.maynoothuniversity.ie/3028/1/PG_Gift.pdf.

Griffin, Oliver. "Colombia Reaches COVID-19 Vaccine Agreements with Moderna, Sinovac." *Reuters*, January 30, 2021. https://www.reuters.com/business/healthcare-pharmaceuticals/colombia-reaches-covid-19-vaccine-agreements-with-moderna-sinovac-2021-01-30/.

Halperin, Morton H., and James Michel. "Interagency Review of US Government Civilian Humanitarian and Transition Programs." Washington: US Department of State, 2000.

Hannon, Elliot. "The Trump Administration Refuses to Participate in Global Coronavirus Vaccine Effort." *Slate*, September 2, 2020. https://slate.com/news-and-politics/2020/09/trump-refuses-who-covax-global-coronavirus-vaccine-effort-gavi.html.

Hanson, Fergus. *The Dragon Looks South.* Sydney: Lowy Institute for International Policy, 2008.

Hart, Robert. "China's Sinovac Vaccine Under Scrutiny as Covid Soars In Highly Vaccinated Countries." *Forbes*, June 17, 2021. https://www.forbes.com/sites/robert hart/2021/06/17/chinas-sinovac-vaccine-under-scrutiny-as-covid-soars-in-highly-vaccinated-countries/?sh=1077f231444b.

He, W. "China's Aid to Africa: Views on Chinese Aid and Trade in Africa," in *Challenging the Aid Paradigm: Western Currents and Asian Alternatives*, edited by Jens S. Sörensen, 138–65. London: Palgrave Macmillan, 2010.

Heckman, James J. "Sample Selection Bias as a Specification Error." *Econometrica: Journal of the econometric society* (1979): 153–161.

Henderson, John, and Benjamin Reilly. "Dragon in Paradise: China's Rising Star in Oceania." *The National Interest* 72 (2003): 94–105.

Hill, Fiona, and Clifford Gaddy. "Putin and the Uses of History." *The National Interest.* January 4, 2012. https://nationalinterest.org/article/putin-the-uses-history-6276?page=0%2C1.

Hills, Ian. "Russia and China's Vaccine Diplomacy: Not Quite the Geopolitical Slam Dunk." Australian Institute of International Affairs, September 14, 2021. https://www.internationalaffairs.org.au/australianoutlook/russia-and-chinas-vaccine-diplomacy-not-quite-the-geopolitical-slam-dunk/.

Hirono, Miwa. "Three Legacies of Humanitarianism in China," *Disasters* 37 (2013): S202-S220.

Hirono, Miwa. "Exploring the Links between Chinese Foreign Policy and Humanitarian Action," HPG Working Paper. London: Humanitarian Policy Group, 2018.

Hoeffler, Anke, and Verity Outram. "Need, Merit, or Self-Interest - What Determines the Allocation of Aid?" *Review of Development Economics* 15, no. 2 (2011): 237–250.

Hogan, Michael J. *The Marshall Plan: America, Britain, and the Reconstruction of Western Europe, 1947–1952.* Cambridge University Press, 1987.

Hong, Young-sun, *Cold War Germany, the Third World, and the Global Humanitarian Regime,* Cambridge University Press, 2015.

Hotez, Peter J. "Vaccines as Instruments of Foreign Policy: The New Vaccines for Tropic Infectious Diseases May Have Unanticipated Uses Beyond Fighting Diseases," EMBO Rep. 2, no. 10 (October 2001): 862–868.

Hotez, Peter J. "Russian-United States Vaccine Science Diplomacy: Preserving the Legacy," *PLOS Neglected Tropical Diseases* 11, no. 5 (2017): e0005320, https://journals.plos.org/plosntds/article%3Fid%3D10.1371/journal.pntd.0005320.

Hotez, Peter J., and K.M. Venkat Narayan, "Restoring Vaccine Diplomacy," *JAMA* 325, no. 23 (June 2021): 2337–2338, https://pubmed.ncbi.nlm.nih.gov/34047758/.

Hu, Zuliu, and Mohsin S. Khan. "Why Is China Growing So Fast?" *International Monetary Fund,* June 1997. https://www.imf.org/EXTERNAL/PUBS/FT/ISSUES8/INDEX.HTM.

Huang, Yanzhong, and Scott Kennedy. "Advancing U.S.-China Health Security Cooperation in an Era of Strategic Competition, A Report of the CSIS Commission on Strengthening America's Health Security." December 2021. https://csis-website-prod.s3.amazonaws.com/s3fs-public/publication/211201_Kennedy_USChina_HealthSecurityCooperation.pdf?2CC5_x4F2jIhaOgwo8mvqpPKkztE7RFG.

Huang, Yanzhong. "Pursuing Health as Foreign Policy: the Case of China," *Indiana Journal of Global Legal Studies* 17, no. 1 (2010): 105–146.

Huanxin, Zhao. "China Emerges as Major Food Donor." *China Daily,* July 21, 2007. https://www.chinadaily.com.cn/china/2006-07/21/content_645844.htm.

Huaxia. "Sinovac Vaccine Cuts COVID-19 Deaths among Uruguayan Adults by 95 pct: Study." *Xinua,* June 10, 2021. http://www.xinhuanet.com/english/2021-06/10/c_1310000287.htm.

Huaxia. "Figures & Facts: Chinese COVID-19 Vaccines Proved Safe and Effective across World." *Xinua,* July 13, 2021. http://www.xinhuanet.com/english/2021-07/13/c_1310057969.htm.

Huaxia. "Interview: China Holds Health Security Commitment as Global Vaccine Supplier, says Scholar." *Xinua*, September 9, 2021. http://www.news.cn/english/2021-09/23/c_1310204873.htm.

Huaxia. "Colombia Receives New Supply of Sinovac COVID-19 Vaccines." *Xinua*, October 26, 2021. http://www.news.cn/english/2021-10/26/c_1310270883.htm.

Hutt, David. "Vladimir Putin Used to be Popular in Slovakia. Then He Invaded Ukraine." *Euronews*, March 29, 2022. https://www.euronews.com/my-europe/2022/03/29/vladimir-putin-used-to-be-popular-in-slovakia-then-he-invaded-ukraine.

Huwawei. "Fighting COVID-19 with Technology," May 16, 2022. https://activity.huaweicloud.com/intl/en-us/fight-covid-19.html.

Huwawei. "Huawei's Cloud and Artificial Intelligence Solution to Boost SA's COVID-19 Fight," January 18, 2021. https://www.digitalstreetsa.com/huaweis-cloud-and-artificial-intelligence-solution-to-boost-sas-covid-19-fight/.

Hynes, William, and Simon Scott. "The Evolution of Official Development Assistance: Achievements, Criticisms and a Way Forward," OECD Development Co-Operation Working Paper No. 12, OECD Publishing, 2013. http://dx.doi.org/10.1787/5k3v1dv3fo24-en.

IHME. "COVID-19 Results Briefing." Institute for Health Metric and Evaluation. January 21, 2022. https://www.healthdata.org/sites/default/files/files/165_briefing_Pakistan_4.pdf.

Ikenberry, G. John. *Liberal Leviathan: The Origins, Crisis and the Transformation of the American World Order*. Princeton: Princeton University Press, 2012.

Ikenberry, G. John. "The End of Liberal International Order?" *International Affairs* 94, no. 1 (2018): 7–23.

Information Office. "China's Peaceful Development." China's Cabinet, 2011. http://english1.english. gov.cn/official/2011-09/06/content_1941354.htm.

Ingram, Alan. "The New Geopolitics of Disease: Between Global Health and Global Security," *Geopolitics* 10, no. 3 (2005): 522–545.

Ingram, Alan. "HIV/AIDS, Security and the Geopolitics of the US-Nigerian Relations," *Review of International Political Economy* 14, no. 3 (August 2007): 510–534.

Ingram, George. "Making USAID a Premier Development Agency." The Brookings Institution, February 27, 2021. https://www.brookings.edu/research/making-usaid-a-premier-development-agency/.

Irfan, Umair. "Why are Rich Countries Still Monopolizing Covid-19 Vaccines?" *Vox*, November 9, 2021. https://www.vox.com/22759707/covid-19-vaccine-gap-covax-rich-poor-countries-boosters.

Irwin, Julia F. "The Origins of U.S. Foreign Disaster Assistance." *The American Historian*. 2018. https://www.oah.org/tah/issues/2018/february/the-origins-of-u.s-foreign-disaster-assistance/.

Ivanova, Polina. "Mexico Plays Down Sputnik Vaccine Delays after Domestic Production Deal." April 28, 2021. https://www.reuters.com/business/healthcare-pharmaceuticals/mexico-agrees-domestic-production-russias-sputnik-v-vaccine-2021-04-28/.

Jacob, Jabin T. "'To Tell China's Story Well': China's International Messaging during the COVID-19 Pandemic." *China Report* 56, no. 3 (2020): 374–392.

Jayasuriya Sisira, and McCawley Peter. "The Asian Tsunami Aid and Reconstruction After a Disaster." Asian Development Bank Institute and Edward Elgar Publishing, 2004.

Jiangtao, Shi. "China Blames 'Aggressive US Wars' for Humanitarian Disasters around the World as It Hits Back at Criticism of Human Rights Record." *South China Morning Post*, April 9, 2021. https://www.scmp.com/news/china/diplomacy/article/3128982 /china-blames-aggressive-us-wars-humanitarian-disasters-around.

Jiem Yu, and Jon Wallace, "China's Belt and Road Initiative (BRI)," The Chatham House. September 13, 2021. https://www.chathamhouse.org/2021/09/what-chinas-belt-and -road-initiative-bri.

Jintao, Hu. "Build Toward a Harmonious World of Lasting Peace and Common Prosperity." Statement by H.E. Hu Jintao, President of the People's Republic of China. [Translation]. New York, September 15, 2005. https://www.un.org/webcast/summit 2005/statements15/china050915eng.pdf.

Jones, Marian Moser. "The American Red Cross and Local Response to the 1918 Influenza Pandemic: A Four-City Case Study." *Public Health Rep* 125, no. 3 (2010): 92–104.

Kantchev, Georgi. "Russia Struggles to Meet Demand for Its Covid-19 Vaccine," *The Wallstreet Journal*, May 14, 2021. https://www.wsj.com/articles/russia-struggles-to -meet-demand-for-its-covid-19-vaccine-11620993601.

Kasraoui, Safaa. "Morocco, China Sign Agreement on Joint Implementation Plan for Belt and Road Initiative." *Morocco World News*, January 5, 2022. https://www.morocco worldnews.com/2022/01/346356/morocco-china-agree-on-morocco-china-belt -and-road-initiative.

Keith, Tamara. "Biden Takes First Jab at Vaccine Diplomacy, Sharing Doses With Mexico, Canada." *NPR*, March 19, 2021. https://www.npr.org/2021/03/19/979279426 /biden-takes-first-jab-at-vaccine-diplomacy-sharing-doses-with-mexico-canada.

Kevlihan, Rob, Karl DeRouen Jr., and Glen Biglaiser. "Is US Humanitarian Aid Based Primarily on Need or Self-Interest?" *International Studies Quarterly* 58, no. 4 (2014): 839–854.

KFF. "U.S. International COVID-19 Vaccine Donations Tracker – Updated as of July 1." Accessed June 6, 2022. https://www.kff.org/coronavirus-covid-19/issue-brief/u-s -international-covid-19-vaccine-donations-tracker/#recipient-country.

Kirkpatrick, David. "The White House Blessed a War in Libya, but Russia Won It." *The New York Times*. April 14, 2020. https://www.nytimes.com/2020/04/14/world /middleeast/libya-russia-john-bolton.html.

Kiseleva, Yulia. "Russia's Soft Power Discourse: Identity, Status and the Attraction of Power," *Politics* 35, no. 3–4 (2015): 316–329.

Kissinger, Henry, "Does America Need a Foreign Policy? Toward a Diplomacy for the 21st Century," New York: Simon & Schuster, 2001.

Kitano, Naohiro, and Yumiko Miyabayashi. "Estimating China's Foreign Aid 2001–2013, JICA-Research Institute Working Paper: Comparative Study on Development Cooperation Strategies: Focusing on G20." *Emerging Economies*, no. 78 (2014), https://www.jica.go.jp/Resource/jica-ri/publication/workingpaper/jrft3q00000025no-att/JICA-RI_WP_No.78_2014.pdf.

Kosachev, Konstantin. "Rossotrudnichestvo Kak Instrument 'Myagkoi Sily'," [Rossotrudnichestvo as a Tool of "Soft Power"], Bel'giyskaya Federatsiya Russkoyazychnykh Organizatsiy, 2012. https://www.bfro.be/%2oru/k.kosachev.-rossotrudnichestvo-kak-instrument-mjagkoj-sily.html?cmp_id=108&news_id=5334.

Kosachev, Konstantin. "Rossotrudnichestvo: Pervye Itogi Deyatelnosti i Perspektivy Razvitiya," [Rossotrudnichestvo: Initial Outcomes and Perspectives for Future Development], *Mezhdunarodnaya Zhizn'*, 2012. https://interaffairs.ru/author.php?n=arpg&pg=691.

Kotilainen, Noora. "Resilience of the Humanitarian Narrative in US Foreign Policy," in *Contestations of Liberal Order*, edited by Marko Lehti, Henna-Riika Pennanen, and Jukka Jouhki, pp. 233–261. Palgrave Macmillan, 2020.

Kragelund, Peter. "The Return of Non-DAC Donors to Africa: New Prospects for African Development." *Development Policy Review* 26, no. 5 (2008): 555–584.

Kuo, Lily, and Niko Kommenda. "What is China's Belt and Road Initiative?" *The Guardian*, July 3, 2018. https://www.theguardian.com/cities/ng-interactive/2018/jul/30/what-china-belt-road-initiative-silk-road-explainer.

Kuus, M. "Critical Geopolitics," in *The International Studies Encyclopedia, Vol. II*, edited by R. Denemark, 863–670. Oxford: Blackwell, 2010.

Kurtzer, Jacob. "China's Humanitarian Aid: Cooperation Amid Competition," Center for Strategic and International Studies, 2020, https://www.csis.org/analysis/chinas-humanitarian-aid-cooperation-amidst-competition.

Laing, Aislinn, and Cassandra Garrison. "Amid Scramble for COVID-19 Vaccine, Latin America Turns to Russia." *Reuters*, 2021. https://www.reuters.com/business/healthcare-pharmaceuticals/amid-scramble-covid-19-vaccine-latin-america-turns-russia-2021-03-01/.

Lakoff, Andrew, "Two Regimes of Global Health," *Humanity: An International Journal of Human Rights, Humanitarianism, and Development*, 1, no. 1 (2010): 59–79.

Lambart, Rachel, Carisa Shah, and Josh Wiener. "The Distribution of COVID-19 Vaccines: A Geopolitical and Strategic Analysis of Southeast Asia." *UPENN* (Spring 2021). https://global.upenn.edu/sites/default/files/perry-world-house/Vaccines.pdf.

Lampton, David M. Selina Ho, and Cheng-Chwee Kuik. *Rivers of Iron: Railroads and Chinese Power in Southeast Asia*. Berkley, CA: University of California Press, 2020.

Laqua, Daniel. "Inside the Humanitarian Cloud: Causes and Motivations to Help Friends and Strangers." *Journal of Modern European History* 12, no. 2 (2014): 175–185.

Larson, Krista. "Vaccine Deserts: Some Countries Have no COVID-19 Jabs at All." *AP*, May 9, 2021. https://apnews.com/article/africa-coronavirus-vaccine-coronavirus-pandemic-business-government-and-politics-2d5eab50c1ef8bd63b1a48331f4c3025.

Lavrov, Sergey. "Intervyu Ministra Inostrannykh Del Rossii Gazete 'Kommersant'," [Interview of the Minister of Foreign Affairs to Russian Newspaper "Kommersant], October 3, 2012, https://www.mid.ru/en/press_service/minister_speeches/1631545/?lang=ru.

Lawson, Marian L., and Emily M. Morgenstern. "Foreign Assistance: An Introduction to US Programs and Policy." Congressional Research Service Report 40213, 2020. https://crsreports.congress.gov/product/pdf/R/R40213.

Lee, Matthew. "Blinken Urges Algeria to Reconsider Ties with Russia." *PBS*, March 2022. https://www.pbs.org/newshour/politics/blinken-urges-algeria-to-reconsider-ties-with-russia.

Lee, Seow Ting. "Vaccine Diplomacy: Nation Branding and China's COVID-19 Soft Power Play." *Place Branding and Public Diplomacy* (2021): 1–15.

Leeds, Brett Ashley, Jeffrey M. Ritter, Sara McLaughlin Mitchell, and Andrew G. Long. "Alliance Treaty Obligations and Provisions, 1815–1944." *International Interactions* 28 (2002): 237–260. http://www.atopdata.org/data.html.

Lemos, A., and D. Ribeiro. "Taking Ownership or Just Changing Owners?" in *African Perspectives on China in Africa*, edited by F. Manji and S. Marks. Oxford, UK: Pambazuka Press, 2007.

Li, Jessica. "Covid-19 Vaccination in Uruguay." The Borgen Project, July 16, 2021. https://borgenproject.org/covid-19-vaccination-in-uruguay/.

Lin, Justin Yifu, and Yan Wang. *Going Beyond Aid: Development Cooperation for Structural Transformation*. Cambridge: Cambridge University Press, 2017.

Lin, Peng. "China's Evolving Humanitarian Diplomacy: Evidence from China's Disaster-Related Aid to Nepal," *Asian Journal of Comparative Politics* 6, no. 3 (2021): 221–237.

Lippman, Daniel, and Nahal Toosi. "Trump Administration Weighs Accusing China of 'Genocide' Over Uighurs." *Politico*, August 15, 2020. https://www.politico.com/news/2020/08/25/trump-administration-china-genocide-uighurs-401581.

Liu, Angus. "China's Sinovac Plots Pivotal COVID-19 Vaccine Trial in Brazil after Positive Phase 2." *FiercePharma*. June 15, 2020. https://www.fiercepharma.com/vaccines/china-s-sinovac-says-covid-19-vaccine-shows-early-positive-results-phase-2.

Liu, Jiangmei, Lan Zhang, Yaqiong Yan, Yuchang Zhou, Peng Yin, Jinlei Qi, Lijun Wang et al. "Excess Mortality in Wuhan City and Other Parts of China During the Three Months of the Covid-19 Outbreak: Findings from Nationwide Mortality Registries." 2021. https://www.bmj.com/content/372/bmj.n415.

Lo, Bobo. *Russia and the New World Disorder*. Washington, D.C.: The Brookings Institution Press, 2015.

Lum, Thomas, and Bruce Vaughn. "The Southwest Pacific: US Interests and China's Growing Influence." Library of Congress Washington, D.C.: Congressional Research Service, 2007.

Lüthi, Lorenz M. *The Sino-Soviet Split: Cold War in the Communist World.* Princeton University Press, 2008.

Lynch, Leah, Sharon Andersen, and Tianyu Zhu. "China's Foreign Aid: A Primer for Recipient Countries, Donors, and Aid Providers." Center for Global Development, July 9, 2020. https://www.cgdev.org/publication/chinas-foreign-aid-primer -recipient-countries-donors-and-aid-providers.

Manela, Erez. "A Pox on Your Narrative: Writing Disease Control into Cold War History," *Diplomatic History* 34, no. 2 (April 2010): 299–323.

Margesson, Rhoda. "International Crises and Disasters: US Humanitarian Assistance Response Mechanisms." Library of Congress, Washington D.C.: Congressional Research Service, 2015.

Mawdsley, Emma. "The Millennium Challenge Account: Neo-Liberalism, Poverty and Security." *Review of International Political Economy* 14 (2007): 487–509.

McClintock, Bruce, Jeffrey W. Hornung, and Katherine Costello. *Russia's Global Interests and Actions: Growing Reach to Match Rejuvenated Capabilities.* Santa Monica, CA: RAND Corporation, 2021. https://www.rand.org/pubs/perspectives/PE327.html.

McDowall, Angus. "Libya Launches COVID-19 Vaccination Drive after Delays." *Reuters,* April 10, 2021. https://www.reuters.com/world/africa/libya-launches-covid-19 -vaccination-drive-after-delays-2021-04-10/.

Meredith, Sam. "As Russia and China Seek to Boost Their Global Influence, Analysts Warn Vaccine Diplomacy is Here to Stay." CNBC, February 17, 2021. https://www .cnbc.com/2021/02/17/covid-vaccine-diplomacy-russia-china-seek-to-boost-global -influence.html.

Ministry of Foreign Affairs of the People's Republic of China, "Xi Jinping Delivers Important Speech at UN Sustainable Development Summit, Stressing to Realize Common Development of All Countries from New Starting Point of Post-2015 Development Agenda," 2015, http://lt.china-office.gov.cn/eng/zt/UN/201512/t20151219_2910 425.htm.

Ministry of Foreign Affairs of the People's Republic of China. "Position Paper on China's Cooperation with the United Nations." 2021. October 22, 2021. https://www .fmprc.gov.cn/mfa_eng/wjdt_665385/wjzcs/202110/t20211022_9609380.html.

Ministry of Foreign Affairs of the People's Republic of China. "China and Africa in the New Era: A Partnership of Equals." November, 2021. https://www.fmprc.gov.cn/mfa _eng/wjdt_665385/2649_665393/202111/t20211126_10453904.html.

Ministry of the Foreign Affairs of the People's Republic of China, "Building an Open, Inclusive and Interconnected World for Common Development," Keynote Speech by H.E. Xi Jinping (October 18, 2023). https://www.fmprc.gov.cn/mfa_eng/zxxx _662805/202310/t20231018_11162854.html.

Mol, Rajani, Bawa Singh, Vijay Kumar Chattu, Jaspal Kaur, and Balinder Singh. "India's Health Diplomacy as a Soft Power Tool Towards Africa: Humanitarian and Geopolitical Analysis." *Journal of Asian and African Studies* 57, no. 6 (2021): 1109–1125.

Moore, Thomas. "Saving Friends or Saving Strangers? Critical Humanitarianism and the Geopolitics of International Law." *Review of International Studies* 39, no. 4 (2013): 925–947.

Moreno, Jonathan D., Judit Sándor, and Ulf Schmidt, "The Vaccination Cold War," *Hastings Center Report* 51, no. 5 (September 2021): 2–59, https://onlinelibrary.wiley.com/doi/epdf/10.1002/hast.1282.

Morgenstern, Emily, and Nick M. Brown, "Foreign Assistance: An Introduction to U.S. Programs and Policy," Congressional Research Service, R40213, 2022.

Morris, Scott, Rowan Rockafellow, and Sarah Rose. "Mapping China's Participation in Multilateral Development Institutions and Funds." Center for Global Development, November 28, 2021. https://www.cgdev.org/publication/mapping-chinas-participation-multilateral-development-institutions-and-funds.

Morrison, Wayne M. *China's Economic Rise: History, Trends, Challenges, and Implications for The United States*. Washington, DC: Congressional Research Service, 2019. https://sgp.fas.org/crs/row/RL33534.pdf.

Mortkowitz, Siegfried. "Czech Government Fires Anti-Sputnik Vaccine Foreign Minister." *Politico*, April 12, 2022. https://www.politico.eu/article/czech-republic-foreign-minister-tomas-petricek-anti-sputnik-coronavirus-vaccine/.

Moss, Kellie, Stephanie Oum, and Jennifer Kates, "U.S. Global Funding for COVID-19 by Country and Region." *KFF*, October 23, 2020. https://www.kff.org/global-health-policy/issue-brief/u-s-global-funding-for-covid-19-by-country-and-region/.

Moutinho, Sofia, and Meredith Wadman. "Is Russia's COVID-19 Vaccine Safe? Brazil's Veto of Sputnik V Sparks Lawsuit Threat and Confusion." *Science*, April 30, 2021. https://www.science.org/content/article/russias-covid-19-vaccine-safe-brazils-veto-sputnik-v-sparks-lawsuit-threat-and.

Naganawa, Norihiro. "The Red Sea Becoming Red? The Bolsheviks' Commercial Enterprise in the Hijaz and Yemen, 1924–1938." Unpublished paper (2013), https://www.academia.edu/23791104/The_Red_Sea_Becoming_Red_The_Bolsheviks_Commercial_Enterprise_in_the_Hijaz_and_Yemen_1924_1938.

Naím, Moisès. "Rogue Aid," *Foreign Policy* 159 (2007): 95–96.

National Health Commission of the Republic of China. "China's Gansu Province Donates Medical Supplies to Zimbabwe to Combat COVID-19." June 5, 2020. http://en.nhc.gov.cn/2020-05/07/c_79937.htm.

National Health Commission of the People's Republic of China. "China Committed to Facilitating Equitable Vaccine Distribution Globally." June 24, 2021. http://en.nhc.gov.cn/2021-06/24/c_83960.htm.

Natsios, Andrew S. "The Politics of United States Disaster Response." *Mediterranean Quarterly* 6, no. 2 (Spring 1995):46–59.

Nebehay, Stephanie. "African Countries to Receive First U.S. Donated COVID-19 Vaccines in Days – Gavi." *Reuters*, July 16, 2021. https://www.reuters.com/world/africa/african-countries-receive-first-us-donated-covid-19-vaccines-days-gavi-2021-07-16/.

Nebehay, Stephanie, and Kate Kelland. "Sinopharm, Sinovac COVID-19 Vaccine Data Show Efficacy: WHO." *Reuters,* March 31, 2021. https://www.reuters.com/article/us-health-coronavirus-who-china-vaccines/sinopharm-sinovac-covid-19-vaccine-data-show-efficacy-who-idUSKBN2BN1K8.

Neumayer, Eric. "What Factors Determine the Allocation of Aid by Arab Countries and Multilateral Agencies?" *Journal of Development Studies* 39, no. 4 (2003): 134–147.

Neumayer, Eric. "Is the Allocation of Food Aid Free from Donor Interest Bias?" *The Journal of Development Studies* 41, no. 3 (2005): 394–411.

Nichols, Michelle. "Russia Steps Up Support for Private Military Contractor In Libya: U.N. Report." *Reuters*, September 2, 2020. https://www.reuters.com/article/us-libya-security-un/russia-steps-up-support-for-private-military-contractor-in-libya-u-n-report-idUSKBN25T37G.

Nicita, Alessandro, and Carlos Razo. "China: The Rise of a Trade Titan." *UNCTAD*, April 27, 2001. https://unctad.org/news/china-rise-trade-titan.

Nye, Joseph S. *Bound to Lead: The Changing Nature of American Power.* Basic Book, 1990.

Nye, Joseph S. *The Future of Power.* New York: Public Affairs, 2011.

OCHA. "China, Government of 2018." 2018. https://fts.unocha.org/donors/2976/summary/2018.

OCHA. "China Pledges US$ 100 Million Towards Equitable Access to COVID-19 Vaccines For Lower-Income Countries." August 5, 2021. https://reliefweb.int/report/world/china-pledges-us-100-million-towards-equitable-access-covid-19-vaccines-lower-income.

Odgaard, Liselotte. *China and Co-Existence: Beijing's National Security Strategy for the Twenty-First Century.* Washington, D.C.: Woodrow Wilson Centre Press, 2012.

Odling-Smee, John. "The IMF and Russia in the 1990s. IMF Working Paper, WP/04/155." *IMF*, 2004. https://www.imf.org/external/pubs/ft/wp/2004/wp04155.pdf.

OECD. *The Aid Programme of China.* Paris: OECD Publishing, 1987.

OECD. *Paris Declaration on Aid Effectiveness.* Paris: OECD Publishing, 2005.

OECD. *DAC in Dates: The History of OECD's Development Assistance Committee, 2006 Edition.* 2006. https://www.oecd.org/dac/1896808.pdf.

OECD. *Accra Agenda for Action.* Paris: OECD Publishing, 2008.

OECD. "Better Aid: Managing Aid Practices of DAC Member Countries." 2009. https://www.oecd.org/dac/peer-reviews/35051857.pdf.

OECD. "History of the 0.7% Oda Target." March 2016. https://www.oecd.org/dac/financing-sustainable-development/development-finance-standards/ODA-history-of-the-0-7-target.pdf.

OECD. "United States," in *Development Co-operation Profiles*. Paris: OECD Publishing, 2021.

OECD. "Development Resource Flows." https://www.oecd-ilibrary.org/development/total-official-and-private-flows/indicator/english_52c1b6b4-en, Accessed June 22, 2022.

Office of the U.S. Disaster Assistance. "OFDA Annual Report for Fiscal Year 1995: BHR/OFDA." 1996. https://reliefweb.int/report/world/ofda-annual-report-fiscal-year-1995.

Oliker, Olga, C. Chivvis, Keith Crane, Olesya Tkacheva, and Scott Boston. "Russian Foreign Policy in Historical and Current Context. A Reassessment." Santa Monica, California: RAND Corporation, 2018.

Olsen, Gorm Rye, Nils Carstensen, and Kristian Høyen. "Humanitarian Crises: What Determines the Level of Emergency Assistance? Media Coverage, Donor Interests, and the Aid Business." *Disasters* 27, no. 2 (2003): 109–126.

Olson, Richard Stuart. "The Office of US Foreign Disaster Assistance (OFDA) of the United States Agency for International Development (USAID): A Critical Juncture Analysis, 1964–2003." *Macfadden & Associates* (2005): 1–52.

Omelicheva, Mariya Y. "A 'Good' Samaritan? The Geopolitics of Russia's Covid-19 Assistance," *Canadian Journal of European and Russian Studies* 16, no. 1 (2020): 1–25.

Omelicheva, Mariya Y. "Critical Geopolitics on Russian Foreign Policy: Uncovering the Imagery of Moscow's International Relations." *International Politics* 53 (2016): 708–726.

Ortiz-Ospina, Esteban, Joe Hasell, Bobbie Macdonald, Diana Beltekian, and Max Roser. "Coronavirus Pandemic (COVID-19)." 2020. https://ourworldindata.org/coronavirus.

Osborn, Andrew, and Alexander Marrow. "Russia Examines Ventilator Type Sent to U.S. after Fires Kill Six." *Reuters,* May 12, 2020. https://www.reuters.com/article/us-health-coronavirus-russia-hospital-idCAKBN22O0NW.

Owens, Caitlin. "The Global Coronavirus Vaccine Gap." *Axios*, October 20, 2021. https://www.axios.com/2021/10/20/coronavirus-vaccines-world-biden-moderna.

Pamuk, Humeyra, and David Brunnstrom. "In Parting Shot, Trump Administration Accuses China of 'Genocide' Against Uighurs." *Reuters*, January 19, 2021. https://www.reuters.com/article/us-usa-china-genocide/in-parting-shot-trump-administration-accuses-china-of-genocide-against-uighurs-idUSKBN29O25F.

Paulmann, Jonannes. "The Dilemmas of Humanitarian Aid: Historical Perspectives," in *Dilemmas of Humanitarian Aid in the Twentieth Century*, edited by Jonannes Paulmann. Oxford, Oxford University Press, 2016.

Pecquet, Julian. "US/Africa: Secretary of State Blinken Woos Algeria and Morocco For Help With Russia." The Africa Report, March 30, 2022. https://www.theafricareport.com/188429/us-africa-secretary-of-state-blinken-woos-algeria-and-morocco-for-help-with-russia/.

Pfizer. "Pfizer and BioNTech Announce Collaboration with Brazil's Eurofarma to Manufacture COVID-19 Vaccine Doses for Latin America." 2021. https://www.pfizer.com /news/press-release/press-release-detail/pfizer-and-biontech-announce-collab oration-brazils.

Pforzheimer, Annie. "Pandemic Help to Latin America and the Caribbean: The Roles of USAID and the Department of State." The Wilson Center Latin American Program, March 2021. https://www.wilsoncenter.org/publication/pandemic-help-latin -america-and-caribbean-roles-usaid-and-department-state.

Piccio, Lorenzo. "Konstantin Kosachev: A Change of Course for Russian Foreign Aid." Devex, December 4, 2014. https://www.devex.com/news/konstantin-kosachev-a-change -of-course-for-russian-foreign-aid-85005.

Pifer, Steven. "U.S. Policy on Chechnya." US Department of State Archive. 2002. https://2001-2009.state.gov/p/eur/rls/rm/2002/10034.htm.

Pinna, Alessandra. "International Medical Aid to Italy: Solidarity or Propaganda?" Freedom House, April 20, 2020. https://freedomhouse.org/article/international-medical -aid-italy-solidarity-or-propaganda.

Piper, Kelsey. "A Crucial Federal Program Tracking Dangerous Diseases is Shutting Down," Vox, October 29, 2019. https://www.vox.com/future-perfect/2019/10/29/20936921 /usaid-predict-pandemic-preparedness.

Poggioli, Sylvia. "For Help on Coronavirus, Italy Turns to China, Russia and Cuba." NPR, March 25, 2020. https://www.npr.org/sections/coronavirus-live-updates/2020 /03/25/821345465/for-help-on-coronavirus-italy-turns-to-china-russia-and-cuba.

Power, Marcus, and Mohan, Giles. "Towards a Critical Geopolitics of China's Engagement with African Development," Geopolitics 15, no. 3 (2010): 462–495.

President of Russia. "Telephone Conversation with Prime Minister of National Unity Government of Libya Abdul Hamid Dbeibeh." The Kremlin, Moscow, April 15, 2021. http://en.kremlin.ru/events/president/news/65375.

Primakov, Yevgenii. "Russia's Humanitarian Mission." Pathways to Peace and Security 54, no. 1 Special Issue: Humanitarian Challenges, Humanitarian Support and Human Protection in Armed Conflicts (2018): 182–196.

Pringle, Eleanor. "Disease Forecasters are Convinced There's a 27% Change of Another COVID-like Pandemic Within 10 Years – but Experts Believe There's a Silver Bullet," Fortune, April 18, 2023, https://fortune.com/well/2023/04/18/disease-forecasters -predict-new-covid-like-pandemic-within-10-years/.

Provost, Claire. "The Rebirth of Russian Foreign Aid." The Guardian, May 22, 2011. https://www.theguardian.com/global-development/2011/may/25/russia-foreign -aid-report-influence-imagel.

Putin, Vladimir. "Address by Russian President Vladimir Putin to Visitors to the Official Site of Russia's G8 Presidency in 2006." Official site of Russia's G8 Presidency in 2006, 2006. https://web.archive.org/web/20060214023902/http:/en.g8russia.ru/agenda/.

Putin, Vladimir. "Rossiia na Rubezhe Tysiacheletii." [Russia at the Turn of the Millennium]. *Nezavisimaia Gazeta.* December 30, 1999. http://www.ng.ru/politics/1999 -12-30/4_millenium.html.

Putz, Catherine. "Which Countries Are for or Against China's Xinjiang Policies." *The Diplomat,* June 15, 2019. https://thediplomat.com/2019/07/which-countries-are-for-or -against-chinas-xinjiang-policies/.

Radio Free Europe/Radio Liberty. "Russia Offers to Help Armenia Fight COVID-19 Pandemic." 2020. https://www.azatutyun.am/a/30646563.html.

Rai, Kul B. "Foreign Aid and Voting in the UN General Assembly, 1967—1976." *Journal of Peace Research* 17, no. 3 (1980): 269–277.

Rainsford, Sarah. "Why Many in Russia Are Reluctant to Have Sputnik Vaccine." BBC *News.* March 3, 2021. https://www.bbc.com/news/world-europe-56250456.

Rakhmangulov, Mark. "Establishing International Development Assistance Strategy in Russia," *International Organizations Research Journal* 31, no. 5 (2010): 50–67.

Ralston, Shane J. "American Enlightenment Thought." *Internet Encyclopedia of Philosophy* (2011). https://iep.utm.edu/american-enlightenment-thought/.

Rapp-Hooper, Mira, Michael S. Chase, Matake Kamiya, Shin Kawashima, and Yuichi Hosoya. "Responding to China's Complicated Views on International Order." Carnegie Endowment for International Peace, October 2019. https://carnegieendowment .org/files/ChinaRiskOpportunity-Chinas_Complicated_Views.pdf.

Raschky, Paul A., and Manijeh Schwindt. "On the Channel and Type of Aid: The Case of International Disaster Assistance," *European Journal of Political Economy* 28, no. 1 (2012): 119–131.

Regilme, Jr. Salvador Santino F., and Obert Hodzi. "Comparing US and Chinese Foreign Aid in the Era of Rising Powers," *The International Spectator* 56, no. 2 (2021): 114–131.

Regilme, Jr. Salvador Santino F., and James Parisot. *American Hegemony and the Rise of Emerging Powers.* London: Routledge, 2017.

Relief Web. "OFDA Annual Report for Fiscal Year 1995." 1996. https://reliefweb.int /report/world/ofda-annual-report-fiscal-year-1995.

Reuters. "Reuters Covid-19 Tracker: Russia." *Reuters.* Accessed May 11, 2022. https:// graphics.reuters.com/world-coronavirus-tracker-and-maps/countries-and -territories/russia/.

Reuters. "Mexico Plays Down Sputnik Vaccine Delays after Domestic Production Deal." *Reuters,* April 28, 2021. https://www.reuters.com/business/healthcare-phar maceuticals/mexico-agrees-domestic-production-russias-sputnik-v-vaccine-2021 -04-28/.

Reuters. "Libya Launches COVID-19 Vaccination Drive after Delays." *Reuters.* April 10, 2021. https://www.reuters.com/world/africa/libya-launches-covid-19-vaccination-drive -after-delays-2021-04-10/.

Reuters. "Algeria to Start Russia's Sputnik V Vaccine Production in September." *Reuters,* April 7, 2021. https://www.reuters.com/article/us-algeria-russia-vaccine/algeria-to -start-russias-sputnik-v-vaccine-production-in-september-idUSKBN2BU3HG.

Reuters. "Sinopharm, Sinovac COVID-19 Vaccine Data Show Efficacy: WHO." *Reuters,* March 31, 2021. https://www.reuters.com/article/us-health-coronavirus-who-china -vaccines/sinopharm-sinovac-covid-19-vaccine-data-show-efficacy-who-idUSKBN 2BN1K8.

Reuters. "Jordan Secures 3 Million Doses of COVID-19 Vaccine - Prime Minister." *Reuters,* January 3, 2021. https://www.reuters.com/article/uk-health-coronavirus -jordan-vaccine-idUKKBN2980J4.

Richardson, Jim. "To Win Friends and Influence People, America Should Learn from the CCP." *Foreign Policy,* July 22, 2021. https://foreignpolicy.com/2021/07/22/china -belt-road-development-projects-usaid-state-department-foreign-aid-assistance -budget/.

Robinson, Jonathan. "Five Years of Russian Aid in Syria Proves Moscow is an Unreliable Partner." The Atlantic Council, June 8, 2021. https://www.atlanticcouncil.org/blogs /menasource/five-years-of-russian-aid-in-syria-proves-moscow-is-an-unreliable -partner/.

Rozzelle, Josie. "Whose Suffering Counts? A Discussion Looking at Crisis Cover- age Beyond Ukraine." *The New Humanitarian,* April 8, 2022. https://www.thenew humanitarian.org/opinion/2022/04/08/event-crisis-coverage-beyond-Ukraine.

Rudd, Kevin. "Xi Jinping's Vision for Global Governance." *Foreign Affairs,* 2022. https:// www.foreignaffairs.com/china/world-according-xi-jinping-china-ideologue-kevin -rudd.

Rudolf, Moritz. "China's Health Diplomacy during COVID-19: the Belt and Road Initiative (BRI) in Action." *SWP Comment,* no.9, 2021. https://www.swp-berlin.org/publications /products/comments/2021C09_ChinaHealthDiplomacy.pdf.

Russell, Martin. "Seven Economic Challenges for Russia: Breaking out of Stagnation?" European Parliamentary Research Service. July (2018). https://www.europarl.europa .eu/thinktank/en/document/EPRS_IDA(2018)625138.

Russell, Martin. "At a Glance - Russia's Humanitarian Aid Policy," European Parliamen- tary Research Service, May 2016. https://www.europarl.europa.eu/RegData/etudes /ATAG/2016/582039/EPRS_ATA(2016)582039_EN.pdf.

Russia Today. "'This is NUTS!' Russiagaters See Red over Putin's Planeload of Corona- Aid for Trump, Queue to Look Gift-Horse in Mouth." *Russia Today,* 2020. https:// www.rt.com/usa/484630-russiagaters-russia-us-coronavirus-supplies/.

Salmons, Richard. "Disaster Relief, International Status and Regional Order: A Case Study of Typhoon Haiyan," *Global Change, Peace & Security* 31, no. 3 (2019): 283–301.

Samy, Yiagadeesen. "China's Aid Policies in Africa: Opportunities and Challenges." *The Round Table*, no. 99 (2010): 75–90.

Schindler, Seth, and Jessica DiCarlo, 2022. "Towards a Critical Geopolitics of China – US Rivalry: Pericentricity, Regional Conflicts and Transnational Connections," *Area* 54, no. 4 (2022): 638–645.

Schumaker, Erin. "Timeline: How Coronavirus Got Started." *ABC News*. September 22, 2020. https://abcnews.go.com/Health/timeline-coronavirus-started/story?id =69435165.

Share America. "U.S. Sends COVID-19 Vaccines Worldwide." *Share America*, December, 2021.https://share.america.gov/us-sends-covid-19-vaccines-worldwide-december -2021/.

Sharun, Khan, and Kuldeep Dhama. "COVID-19 Vaccine Diplomacy and Equitable Access to Vaccines Amid Ongoing Pandemic." *Archives of Medical Research* 52, no. 7 (2021): 761–763.

Shimomura, Yasutami, and Wang Ping, "The Evolution of 'Aid, Investment, Trade Synthesis' in China and Japan," in *The Rise of Asian Donors: Japan's Impact on the Evolution of Emerging Donors*, edited by Jin Sato and Yasutami Shimomura (Abington, UK: Routledge, 2012), pp. 114–132.

Shin, Boram. "The East-West Collaboration across the Iron Curtain against Polio Epidemics: Soviet Engagement with Global Health and Poliomyelitis Vaccine Development in 1956–1964," *Journal of Eurasian Studies* 14, no. 1 (2023): 19–29.

Sindle, Erin. "COVID-19 Assistance to Africa: From Russia With Love." *Institute for Defense Analysis Africa Watch* 25 (2021). https://www.jstor.org/stable/pdf/resrep29557 .5.pdf.

Singh, Bawa, Sandeep Singh, Balinder Singh, and Vijay Kumar Chattu. "India's Neighbourhood Vaccine Diplomacy During COVID-19 Pandemic: Humanitarian and Geopolitical Perspectives." *Journal of Asian and African Studies* 58, no. 6 (2023): 1021–1037.

SIPRI. *Arms Transfers Database. SIPRI*, 2022. https://armstrade.sipri.org/armstrade /html/export_values.php.

Six, Clemens. "The Rise of Postcolonial States as Donors: A Challenge to the Development Paradigm?" *Third World Quarterly* 30, no. 6 (2009): 1103–1121.

Smith, Gayle E. "Digital Press Briefing on the U.S. Donations of COVID-19 Vaccines to the African Union." U.S. Department of State, July 21, 2021. https://www.state.gov /digital-press-briefing-on-the-u-s-donations-of-covid-19-vaccines-to-the-african -union.

Smith, Jonathan. "Europe Shuns Russian Covid-19 Vaccines as Ukraine War Continues." *Labiotech*, April 1, 2022. https://www.labiotech.eu/trends-news/sputnik-v-russia -europe/.

Snetkov, Aglaya, and Marc Lanteigne. "'The Loud Dissenter and its Cautious Partner' – Russia, China, Global Governance and Humanitarian Intervention." *International Relations of the Asia-Pacific* 15, no. 1 (2015): 113–146.

Soucheray, Stephanie. "US Donates 400 Million COVID-19 Vaccine Doses to COVAX." *CIDRAP*, January 26, 2022. https://www.cidrap.umn.edu/news-perspective/2022/01 /us-donates-400-million-covid-19-vaccine-doses-covax.

Southerland, Matthew. *The Chinese Military's Role in Overseas Humanitarian Assistance and Disaster Relief: Contributions and Concerns.* US-China Economic and Security Review Commission, 2019.

Sputnik V. "Sputnik V Statement on Brazilian Health Regulator Anvisa's Decision to Postpone Sputnik V Authorization in Brazil." https://sputnikvaccine.com/newsroom /pressreleases/sputnik-v-statement-on-brazilian-health-regulator-anvisa-s -decision-to-postpone-authorization/, April 28, 2021.

Statista. "Number of COVID-19 Vaccine Doses Administered in Europe as of June 14, 2022, by Country." Statista. https://www.statista.com/statistics/1196071/covid-19 -vaccination-rate-in-europe-by-country/, accessed May 11, 2022.

Statista. "Number of Doses of the COVID-19 Vaccine Sputnik V Ordered from Russia or Agreed to be Produced Abroad as of January 2022, by Country." Statista. https:// www.statista.com/statistics/1123927/sputnik-v-exports-from-russia-by-country/, accessed June 20, 2022.

Stewart, Ashley Kim, and Xing Li, "Beyond Debating the Differences: China's Aid and Trade in Africa," in *China-Africa Relations in an Era of Great Transformations*, edited by Li Xing and Abdulkadir Osman Farah (Ashgate, 2013), pp. 23–48.

Stolton, Samuel. "Huawei to 'Scale Down' Supply Of COVID-19 Masks, after Borrell Comments." *EURACTIV*, March 26, 2020. https://www.euractiv.com/section/digital /news/no-more-coronavirus-masks-from-us-huawei-says/.

Stringer, Kevin D. "Pacific Island Microstates: Pawns or Players in Pacific Rim Diplomacy?" *Diplomacy and Statecraft* 17, no. 3 (2006): 547–577.

Strömberg, David. "Natural Disasters, Economic Development, and Humanitarian Aid." *Journal of Economic Perspectives* 21, no. 3 (2007): 199–222.

Stronski, Paul. "In Mexico, the Window on Russia's Vaccine Diplomacy is Closing?" Carnegie Endowment for International Peace, April 28, 2022. https://carnegieen dowment.org/2022/04/28/in-mexico-window-on-russia-s-vaccine-diplomacy-is -closing-pub-87013.

Stronski, Paul. "What Went Wrong With Russia's Sputnik V Vaccine Rollout?" Carnegie Endowment for International Peace, November 15, 2021. https://carnegieen dowment.org/2021/11/15/what-went-wrong-with-russia-s-sputnik-v-vaccine-rollout -pub-85783.

Sun, Yun. "China's Aid to Africa: Monster or Messiah?" The Brookings Institution, February 7, 2014. https://www.brookings.edu/opinions/chinas-aid-to-africa-monster-or -messiah/.

Suzuki, Mao, and Shiming Yang. "Political Economy of Vaccine Diplomacy: Explaining Varying Strategies of China, India, and Russia's COVID-19 Vaccine Diplomacy." *Review of International Political Economy* (2022): 1–26.

Taghizade, Sanaz, Vijay Kumar Chattu, Ebrahim Jaafaripooyan, and Sebastian Kevany, "COVID-19 Pandemic as an Excellent Opportunity for Global Health Diplomacy." *Frontier in Public Health* 9 (July 2021): 1–9, https://www.ncbi.nlm.nih.gov/pmc/articles/PMC8310918/pdf/fpubh-09-655021.pdf.

Taithe, Bertrand. "Reinventing (French) Universalism: Religion, Humanitarianism and the 'French Doctors.'" *Modern & Contemporary France* 12, no. 2 (2004): 147–158.

Tarnoff, Curt. "US Assistance to the Former Soviet Union." Congressional Research Service, 2007. https://sgp.fas.org/crs/row/RL32866.pdf.

TASS. "Russia Ready to Revive Cooperation with Slovakia in Case of Interest, Says Putin." *TASS*, December 1, 2021. https://tass.com/politics/1369329.

TASS. "FACTBOX: How Countries Approved Sputnik V Anti-Coronavirus Vaccine." *TASS*, August 20, 2021. https://tass.com/world/1324643.

TASS. "Russia to Allocate up to $10 million to the UN Development Program by the End of the Year." *TASS*, December 21, 2020. https://n.tass.ru/politika/10313993.

TASS. "Russia, Algeria Plan to Sign Document Confirming New Quality of Relations — Lavrov." May 10, 2020. https://tass.com/russia/1448953.

Teitt, Sarah. "Atrocity or Calamity?" *Cultures of Humanitarianism: Perspectives from the Asia-Pacific Project*, 2013. https://www.nottingham.ac.uk/iaps/documents/project/teitt.pdf.

Telias, Diego, and Francisco Urdínez. "China's Foreign Aid Determinants: Lessons from a Novel Dataset of the Mask Diplomacy During the COVID-19 Pandemic." *Journal of Current Chines Affairs* 51, no. 1 (2021): 108–136.

The Associated Press. "China Report Accuses US of Causing Humanitarian Disasters," *ABC News*, April 9, 2021. https://abcnews.go.com/International/wireStory/china-report-accuses-us-causing-humanitarian-disasters-76965954.

The Climate Center. "G7 Ministers Commit to 'As Anticipatory a Humanitarian System as Possible." May 17, 2022. https://www.climatecentre.org/8409/g7-foreign-ministers-commit-to-making-humanitarian-system-as-anticipatory-as-possible/.

The Climate Center. "UN: In 5 Years, Everyone on Earth Must be Protected by Early Warning for Extreme Weather, Climate Change." March 23, 2022. https://www.climatecentre.org/8111/un-within-5-years-everyone-on-earth-must-be-protected-by-early-warningfor-increasingly-extreme-weather-and-climate-change/.

The Government of the Russian Federation. "Mikhail Mishustin's Meeting with Prime Minister and Chief of Staff of the Presidential Executive Office of Kyrgyzstan Akylbek Japarov." November 22, 2021. http://government.ru/en/news/43876/.

The Government of the Russian Federation. "Decree of the Government of the Russian Federation dated 3 April 2020 No.863-p [in Russian]." Official Internet portal of legal information, 2020. http://publication.pravo.gov.ru/Document/View /0001202004060017.

The Government of the Russian Federation. "Decree of the Government of the Russian Federation dated 28 May 2020 No.1415-p [in Russian]." Official Internet portal of legal information, 2020. http://publication. pravo.gov.ru/Document/View /0001202006010009.

The Government of the Russian Federation. "Decree of the Government of the Russian Federation dated 9 March 2019 No.406-r [in Russian]." Official Internet portal of legal information, 2018. http://publication.pravo.gov.ru/Document/View /0001201803120011.

The Government of the Russian Federation. "Decree of the Government of the Russian Federation of 18 March 2016 N 456-r On the implementation, starting from 2016, of the payment of the annual voluntary contribution of the Russian Federation to the budget of the United Nations Development Program." 2016. https://base.garant .ru/71356744/#friends.

The International Committee of the Red Cross. "The Fundamental Principles of the International Red Cross and Red Crescent Movement." June 11, 2020. https:// www.icrc.org/en/publication/4046-fundamental-principles-international-red -cross-and-red-crescent-movement.

The International Committee of the Red Cross. "Why There Should Be a Humanitarian Dimension to China's Belt and Road Project." ICRC, May 15, 2017. https://www.icrc .org/en/document/humanitarian-dimension-belt-and-road-initiative.

The Kremlin, "First Session of the G20 Summit." October 30, 2021. https://www.reuters .com/world/africa/libya-launches-covid-19-vaccination-drive-after-delays-2021 -04-10/.

The Ministry of Finance of the Russian Federation. "Concept of Russia's Participation in International Development Assistance." 2007. http://www.minfin.ru/common /img/uploaded/library/2007/06/concept_eng.pdf, accessed November 25, 2021.

The Ministry of Finance of the Russian Federation. "Assessing Action and Results Against Development-Related G8 Commitments: The Russian Federation Contri- bution." June 21, 2010. https://minfin.gov.ru/common/gen_html/?id=10050&fld =FILE_MAIN, accessed November 25, 2021.

The Moscow Times. "U.S. Says Photos Show Russian Arms Supplies to Libya Rebels." *The Moscow Times*, July 24, 2020. https://www.themoscowtimes.com/2020/07/24 /us-says-photos-show-russian-arms-supplies-to-libya-rebels-a70976.

The President of the Russian Federation. "Concept of the Russian Federation's State Pol- icy in the Area of International Development Assistance." (Unofficial Translation), approved by Decree No, 259 of the President of the Russian Federation of April 20, 2014. https://www.mid.ru/ru/foreign_policy/official_documents/1584961/?lang=en.

The State Council of the People's Republic of China. "China's Foreign Aid." 2011. http://english.www.gov.cn/archive/white_paper/2014/09/09/content_281474986284620.htm.

The White House. "Global COVID-19 Summit: Ending the Pandemic and Building Back Better." The White House Briefing Room, September 24, 2021. https://www.whitehouse.gov/briefing-room/statements-releases/2021/09/24/global-covid-19-summit-ending-the-pandemic-and-building-back-better/.

The White House. "Statement by President Joe Biden on Global Vaccine Distribution." The White House Briefing Room, June 3, 2021. https://www.whitehouse.gov/briefing-room/statements-releases/2021/06/03/statement-by-president-joe-biden-on-global-vaccine-distribution/.

The White House. "Remarks by President Biden on the COVID-19 Response and the Vaccination Program." The White House Briefing Room, May 17, 2021. https://www.whitehouse.gov/briefing-room/speeches-remarks/2021/05/17/remarks-by-president-biden-on-the-covid-19-response-and-the-vaccination-program-4/.

The White House. "Fact Sheet: Biden-Harris Administration Unveils Strategy for Global Vaccine Sharing, Announcing Allocation Plan for the First 25 Million Doses to be Shared Globally." The White House Briefing Room, February 18, 2021. https://www.whitehouse.gov/briefing-room/statements-releases/2021/06/03/fact-sheet-biden-harris-administration-unveils-strategy-for-global-vaccine-sharing-announcing-allocation-plan-for-the-first-25-million-doses-to-be-shared-globally/.

The White House. "Fact Sheet: President Biden to Take Action on Global Health through Support of COVAX and Calling for Health Security Financing." The White House Briefing Room, February 18, 2021. https://www.whitehouse.gov/briefing-room/statements-releases/2021/02/18/fact-sheet-president-biden-to-take-action-on-global-health-through-support-of-covax-and-calling-for-health-security-financing/.

Thrasher, Rachel. "The Global COVID-19 Summit Must Tackle the Vaccine Demand Gap." *Devex*, May 6, 2022. https://www.devex.com/news/opinion-the-global-covid-19-summit-must-tackle-the-vaccine-demand-gap-103121.

Tobin, Daniel. "How Xi Jinping's 'New Era' Should Have Ended U.S. Debate on Beijing's Ambitions," Testimony before the U.S.-China Economic and Security Review Commission, March 13, 2020. https://www.csis.org/analysis/how-xi-jinpings-new-era-should-have-ended-us-debate-beijings-ambitions.

Trofimov, Yaroslav, Drew Hinshaw, and Kate O'Keeffe. "How China is Taking Over International Organizations, One Vote at a Time." *Wall Street Journal*, September 29, 2020. https://www.wsj.com/articles/how-china-is-taking-over-international-organizations-one-vote-at-a-time-11601397208.

Tsygankov, Andrei P. *Russia's Foreign Policy: Change and Continuity in National Identity*. Rowman & Littlefield, 2013.

Tuathail, Gearóid Ó. "Understanding Critical Geopolitics: Geopolitics and Risk Society", *Journal of Strategic Studies*, 22 No. 2–3 (1999): 107–124.

Tuathail, Gearóid Ó., and Simon Dalby. "Introduction: Rethinking Geopolitics: Towards a Critical Geopolitics," in *Rethinking Geopolitics* edited by Gearoid O Tuathail and Simon Dalby, 1–15. London: Routledge, 1998.

Turak, Natasha. "Russia's Sputnik Vaccine Gets Its First Approval in the EU, Greenlight from UAE Amid Ongoing Trials." *CNBC*, January 21, 2021. https://www.cnbc.com/2021/01/21/russias-sputnik-vaccine-gets-its-first-approval-in-the-eu-uae.html.

UNICEF. "COVID-19 Vaccine Market Dashboard." Accessed March 28 and June 29, 2022. https://www.unicef.org/supply/covid-19-vaccine-market-dashboard.

UNICEF. "Bangladesh's COVID-19 Vaccination Rate has Soared in a Year." May 31, 2022. https://www.unicef.org/stories/bangladesh-covid-19-vaccination-rate-has-soared.

UNICEF. "1.4 million Doses of COVID-19 Vaccine Arrive in Afghanistan through COVAX Global Dose-Sharing Mechanism." July 9, 2021. https://www.unicef.org/press-releases/14-million-doses-covid-19-vaccine-arrive-afghanistan-through-covax-global-dose.

UNICEF. "Immunization." https://www.unicef.org/immunization, accessed June 30, 2022.

United Nations. "Build Towards a Harmonious World of Lasting Peace and Common Prosperity." 2005. https://www.un.org/webcast/summit2005/statements15/china05 0915eng.pdf.

United Nations General Assembly. Resolution A/Res/74/17 "Problem of the Militarization of the Autonomous Republic of Crimea and the City of Sevastopol, Ukraine, as well as Parts of the Black Sea and the Sea of Azov." December 13, 2019. https://documents-dds-ny.un.org/doc/UNDOC/GEN/N19/400/94/PDF/N1940094.pdf?OpenElement.

United Nations General Assembly. Resolution A/RES/46/182 "Strengthening of the Coordination of Humanitarian Emergency Assistance of the United Nations." December 19, 1991. https://documents-dds-ny.un.org/doc/RESOLUTION/GEN/NR0/582/70/IMG/NR058270.pdf?OpenElement.

United Nations News. "Last UN Food Aid Arrives in China as Country Turns from Recipient to Donor." April 8, 2015. https://news.un.org/en/story/2005/04/134232-last-un-food-aid-arrives-china-country-turns-recipient-donor.

United Nations News, "China Emerges as World's Third Largest Food Aid Donor, UN Agency Says," July 20, 2006, https://news.un.org/en/story/2006/07/186362-china-emerges-worlds-third-largest-food-aid-donor-un-agency-says.

United Nations Office for the Coordination of Humanitarian Affairs. "Global Humanitarian Review." OCHA, 2022. https://gho.unocha.org.

United Nations Office for the Coordination of Humanitarian Affairs. "Ukraine: Situation Report." OCHA, 2022. https://reports.unocha.org/en/country/ukraine.

United Nations Office for the Coordination of Humanitarian Affairs. "Global Humanitarian Overview." *OHCA*, 2021. https://www.unocha.org/global-humanitarian-over
view-2021.

United Nations Office for the Coordination of Humanitarian Affairs. "UN and Partners
Release Record Humanitarian Response Plan as COVID-19 Wreaks Havoc." *OCHA*,
December 1, 2020. https://iran.un.org/en/103126-un-and-partners-release-record
-humanitarian-response-plan-covid-19-wreaks-havoc.

United Nations Security Council. "Resolution 2149 (2014), adopted by the Security
Council at its 7153rd meeting, on 10 April 2014." April 2014. https://digitallibrary
.un.org/record/768393?ln=en.

United Nations Statistics Division. *UN COMTRADE. International Trade Statistics*. 2020.
http://comtrade.un.org/.

US Agency for International Development. "FINAL REPORT the office of U.S. Foreign
Disaster Assistance (OFDA) of the United States Agency for International Development (USAID): A Critical Juncture Analysis, 1964–2003." February 21, 2005. https://
www.hsdl.org/?view&did=776900.

U.S. Bureau of the Census. "Statistical Abstract of the United States: 1949." Washington,
D.C. 1949. https://www2.census.gov/library/publications/1949/compendia/statab
/70ed/1949-01.pdf.

US Congress. "American Rescue Plan Act of 2021." 117th Congress, March 11, 2021.
https://www.congress.gov/117/plaws/publ2/PLAW-117publ2.pdf.

US Congress. "An Act to Amend the Internal Revenue Code of 1986 to Repeal the Excise
Tax on High-Cost Employer-Sponsored Health Cverage." Public Law 116–136, 27, 2020.
https://www.congress.gov/116/plaws/publ136/PLAW-116publ136.pdf.

US Congress, "Rules Committee Print 116–68. Text of the House Amendment to the Sen-
ate Amendment to H.R. 144," 2020, https://docs.house.gov/billsthisweek/20201221
/BILLS-116HR133SA-RCP-116-68.pdf.

US Congress. "Coronavirus Preparedness and Response Supplemental Appropriations
Act HR 6074." Public Law 116–123, 6 March 2020, 116 Congress, 2020. https://www
.congress.gov/116/plaws/publ123/PLAW-116publ123.pdf.

US Department of Defense. "DOD Humanitarian Assistance to the Italian Republic
in Response to COVID-19." April 20, 2020. https://www.defense.gov/News/Releases
/Release/Article/2157126/dod-humanitarian-assistance-to-the-italian-republic-in
-response-to-covid-19/.

US Department of State. "Brazil: International Travel Information." Accessed June 1,
2022. https://www.state.gov/countries-areas/brazil/.

US Department of State. "Jordan: Fact Sheet." https://www.state.gov/countries-areas
/jordan/, accessed June 29, 2022.

US Department of State. "Refugee and Humanitarian Assistance." 2021. https://www
.state.gov/policy-issues/refugee-and-humanitarian-assistance/, accessed June 10, 2022.

US Department of State Office of the Historian, "USAID and PL-480, 1961–1969," https://history.state.gov/milestones/1961-1968/pl-480.

US Embassy & Consulates in Italy. "U.S. COVID-19 Vaccine Donations Spanned the Globe in 2021." 2021. https://it.usembassy.gov/u-s-covid-19-vaccine-donations-spanned-the-globe-in-2021/.

US General Accounting Office. "COVID-19: Sustained Government Action is Crucial as Pandemic Enters Its Second Year." Report to Congressional Committees, March 2021. https://www.gao.gov/assets/gao-21-387.pdf.

US General Accounting Office. "Foreign Disaster Assistance: AID Has Been Responsive but Improvements Can Be Made." Washington, DC, United States General Accounting Office (GAO). October 1992. https://www.gao.gov/assets/nsiad-93-21.pdf.

US Government. *The National Security Strategy of the United States of America.* Washington, DC: The White House, 2017.

US Government. *The National Security Strategy of the United States of America.* Washington, DC: The White House, 2010.

US Government. *The National Security Strategy of the United States of America.* Washington, DC: The White House, 2002.

US Government Accountability Office, "COVID 19: Better USAID Documentation and More-Frequent Reporting Could Enhance Monitoring of Humanitarian Efforts," 2022. https://www.gao.gov/assets/gao-22-104431.pdf.

US International Development Finance Corporation. "Annual Management Report Fiscal Year 2021." 2021. https://www.dfc.gov/sites/default/files/media/documents/DFC%20Annual%20Management%20Report%20FY%202021.pdf.

US International Development Finance Corporation. "Who We Are." 2020. https://www.dfc.gov/who-we-are.

US Mission South Africa. "United States Donates 5.7 Million COVID-19 Doses to South Africa." U.S. Embassy & Consulates in South Africa, July 28, 2021. https://za.usembassy.gov/united-states-donates-5-7-million-covid-19-doses-to-south-africa/.

US Subcommittee on the Coronavirus Crisis. "More Effective, More Efficient, More Equitable, Year-End Staff Report: Overseeing an Improving & Ongoing Pandemic Response." 2021. https://coronavirus.house.gov/sites/democrats.coronavirus.house.gov/files/SSCCInterimReportDec2021V1.pdf.

USAID. "Foreign Assistance by Country." https://foreignassistance.gov/cd, accessed June 10, 2022.

USAID. "Operation Policy: The Automated Directives System (ADS)." 2021. https://www.usaid.gov/who-we-are/agency-policy.

USAID. "USAID Humanitarian Assistance Fact Sheet." 2021. https://www.usaid.gov/humanitarian-assistance/documents/bha-101infographicfy2021, accessed June 10, 2022.

USAID. "ADS Chapter 251 International Disaster Assistance." 2020. https://www.usaid.gov/sites/default/files/documents/1866/251.pdf.

USAID, "Over the Horizon: Snapshot," 2020, https://2017-2020.usaid.gov/work-usaid /resources-for-partners/preparing-world-altered-covid-19/snapshot.

USAID. "USAID COVID-19 Activity Update." 2020. https://oig.usaid.gov/sites/default /files/2020-12/COVID-19%20Information%20Brief%202.pdf.

USAID. "USAID's Office of U.S. Foreign Disaster Assistance." 2019. https://2017-2020 .usaid.gov/sites/default/files/documents/1866/OFDA_Fact_Sheet_02-25-2019.pdf.

USAID. *USAID Key Accomplishments.* April 20, 2017. https://www.usaid.gov/reports-and -data/key-accomplishments.

USAID. "Field Operations Guide for Disaster Assessment and Response, Version 4.0." September 2005. https://2012-2017.usaid.gov/sites/default/files/documents/1866 /fog_v4_0.pdf.

USAID. "Blueprint for Development: The Strategic Plan of the Agency for International Development." USAID Document PN – AAS – 485. Washington D.C., 1985.

USAID. "Agency for International Development: Congressional Presentation, Fiscal Year 1983, Main Volume." USAID Document PD – ACE – 292. Washington, D.C., 1982.

USAID. "The Aid Story" (USAID Document PN – ABT – 249). Washington, D.C., 1966.

USAID Office of Inspector General. "Information Brief USAID Covid-19 Activity Update." 2020. https://oig.usaid.gov/sites/default/files/2020-10/COVID-19%20Information %20Brief%2009.21.20.pdf.

van der Veen, Maurits, A. *Ideas, Interests and Foreign Aid.* Cambridge University Press, 2011.

Vanskosvka, Biljana. "Geopolitics of Vaccines: War by Other Means?" *Security Dialogue* 12, no. 2 (2021): 41–56.

Velikaya, Anna A. "The Russian Approach to Public Diplomacy and Humanitarian Cooperation." *Rising Powers Quarterly* 3, no. 3 (2018): 39–61.

VOA. "Morocco to Kick Off Mass Vaccination Plan with Chinese Drug." December 8, 2020. https://www.voanews.com/a/covid-19-pandemic_morocco-kick-mass-vaccination -plan-chinese-drug/6199310.html.

Weissenbach, Uwe. *The EU, China, and Africa: Working for Functional Cooperation?* Routledge, 2011.

Westall, Sylvia, Adveith Nair, and Farah Elbahrawy. "China Picks UAE to Make Millions of Vaccines, Boosting Gulf Ties." *Bloomberg*, March 29, 2021. https://www .bloomberg.com/news/articles/2021-03-28/julphar-signs-deal-with-abu-dhabi -firm-to-produce-sinopharm-shot#xj4y7vzkg.

Whitemire, Alex. "How the 1963 Skopje Earthquake Brought the World a Little Bit Closer." United Macedonian Diaspora, July 25, 2021. https://umdiaspora.org/how-the -1963-skopje-earthquake-brought-the-world-a-little-bit-closer/.

Wike, Richard, Jacob Poushter, Laura Silvr, Janell Fetterolf, and Mara Mordecai. "America's Image Abroad Rebounds with Transition from Trump to Biden." Pew Research Center, June 10, 2021. https://www.pewresearch.org/global/2021/06/10 /americas-image-abroad-rebounds-with-transition-from-trump-to-biden/.

Wisner, B. and J. Adams, *Environmental Health in Emergencies and Disasters: A Practical Guide.* World Health Organization, 2002. https://www.who.int/water_sanitation _health/emergencies/emergencies2002/en/.

Woon, Chih Yuan. "China's Contingencies: Critical Geopolitics, Chinese Exceptionalism and the Uses of History," *Geopolitics* 23, no. 1 (2018): 67–95.

World Bank. *World Development Indicators Database.* 2019.

World Food Programme. "Russia Contributes US$2 Million to School Feeding in Tajikistan." January 21, 2022. https://www.wfp.org/news/russia-contributes-us-2-million -school-feeding-tajikistan.

World Food Programme. "Russian Federation Helps World Food Programme to Support Poorer Families in Kyrgyzstan." July 1, 2021. https://www.wfp.org/news/russian -federation-helps-world-food-programme-support-poor-families-kyrgyzstan.

World Food Programme. "China Supports WFP's Lifesaving Assistance to Vulenrable People in Four African Countries." March 19, 2021. https://www.wfp.org/news/china -supports-wfps-lifesaving-assistance-vulnerable-people-four-african-countries.

World Health Organization. "Africa's COVID-19 Vaccine Uptake Increases by 15%." March 22, 2022. https://www.afro.who.int/news/africas-covid-19-vaccine-uptake-increases -15#:~:text=To%20date%2C%20the%20continent%20has,of%20their%20 population%20fully%20vaccinated, accessed June 2, 2022.

World Health Organization. "Contributors." 2021. http://open.who.int/2020-21/con tributors/contributor?name=China, accessed May 16, 2022.

World Health Organization. "Assessed Contributions Payable by Member States and Associate Members 2020–2021." 2021. https://cdn.who.int/media/docs/default -source/documents/about-us/accountability/assessed-contributions-payable -summary-2020-2021.pdf?sfvrsn=2e62a9c1_3&download=true.

World Health Organization. "172 Countries and Multiple Candidate Vaccines Engaged in COVID-19 Vaccine Global Access Facility." World Health Organization, 2020. https:// www.who.int/news/item/24-08-2020-172-countries-and-multiple-candidate -vaccines-engaged-in-covid-19-vaccine-global-access-facility.

World Health Organization. "Vaccination in Acute Humanitarian Emergencies: A Framework for Decision Making." 2017. https://apps.who.int/iris/bitstream/handle /10665/255575/WHO-IVB-17.03-eng.pdf.

World Health Organization. "Essential Programme on Immunization." https://www.who .int/teams/immunization-vaccines-and-biologicals/essential-programme-on-im munization/implementation/immunization-campaigns, accessed June 30, 2022.

Wu, Haitao. "Statement by Ambassador Wu Haitao at the 71st Session of the UN General Assembly on Agenda Item 69: Strengthening of the Coordination of Humanitarian and Disaster Relief Assistance of the United Nations, Including Special Economic Assistance." December 8, 2016. http://www.china-un.org/eng/chinaandun/economic development/humanitarian/t1422694.htm.

Wye, Roy. "China's Leadership Transition," in *Charting China's Future: Domestic and International Challenges*, edited by D.L. Shambaugh, 22–32. New York, NY: Routledge, 2011.

Xie, John. "In Coronavirus Vaccine Hunt, a Race to Be First." *voa*, May 8, 2020. https://www.voanews.com/a/covid-19-pandemic_coronavirus-vaccine-hunt-race-be-first/6188984.html.

Xinhua Net. "China Provides Anti-Epidemic Assistance to 151 Countries: White Paper." June 24, 2021. http://www.xinhuanet.com/english/2021-06/24/c_1310025458.htm.

Xinhua Net, "Xi Jinping Attended the Central Foreign Affairs Work Conference and Delivered an Important Speech," November 29, 2014. http://www.xinhuanet.com//politics/2014-11/29/c_1113457723.htm.

Xinhua Net. "Cambodia, China's Guangxi Pledge to Broaden Cooperation." June 13, 2013. http://www.chinadaily.com.cn/china/2013-06/13/content_16617734.htm.

Yang, Jian. "China in the South Pacific: Hegemon on the Horizon?" *The Pacific Review* 22, no. 2 (2009): 139–158.

Yang, Lihui, Deming An, and Jessica Anderson Turner. *Handbook of Chinese Mythology*. Abc-clio, 2005.

Ye, Min. *The Belt Road and Beyond: State-Mobilized Globalization in China, 1998–2018.* Cambridge University Press, 2020.

Yermolov, Mikhail O. "Rossiiski Mehanism Mezhdunarodnoi Pomoschi: Nezavershennyi Proekt." *Vestnik Mezhdunarodnyh Organizatsii: Obrazovaniye, Nauka, Novaya Ekonomika* 10, no. 3 (2015): 134–155.

Yi, Xiaoxiong. "Chinese Foreign Policy in Transition: Understanding China's Peaceful Development," *The Journal of East Asian Affairs* (2005): 74–112.

Yu, B. "Xi Jinping: To Promote a More Just and Reasonable Global Governance System." *Xinhuanet*, October 13, 2015. http://www.xinhuanet.com/politics/2015-10/13/c_1116812159.htm.

Yu, Jiantuo, and Evan Due. "Mutual Learning in Development Cooperation: China and the West." *IDS Bulletin* 52, no. 2 (2021): 19–36.

Zaini, Khairulanwar. "China's Vaccine Diplomacy in Southeast Asia - A Mixed Record." Research Institute at ISEAS, June 24, 2021. https://www.iseas.edu.sg/wp-content/uploads/2021/06/ISEAS_Perspective_2021_86.pdf.

Zaitsev, Y.K, Perfil'eva O.V., Rakhmangulov, I.A., and Y.A. Shvets, *Mezhdunarodnye Instituty v Global'noi Arkhitekture Sodeistviia Razvitiiu* [International institutions in the global architecture of development assistance]. *Moscow*: Izdatel'skii dom Gosudarstvennogo Universiteta Vysshei Shkoly Ekonomiki. 2010.

Zhang, Dechun, and Ahmed Bux Jamali. "China's 'Weaponized' Vaccine: Intertwining Between International and Domestic Politics." *East Asia* (2022): 1–18.

Zhang, Denghua. *A Cautious New Approach*. ANU Press, 2020.

Zhang, Denghua. "Positive Disruption? China's Humanitarian Aid." Humanitarian Horizons Practice Paper Series, December 2019. https://www.icvanetwork.org/uploads/2021/09/Positive-Disruption_-Chinas-Humanitarian-Aid-December-2019.pdf.

Zhang, Y., and Huang, Y. "Zhongguo he xifang zai duiwai yuanzhu linian shang de chaiyixing bianxi [Analysis of different aid conceptions between China and the West]." *Contemporary International Relations*, 2 (2012): 41–47.

Zhao, Suiseng. "Rethinking the Chinese World Order: The Imperial Cycle and the Rise of China," *Journal of Contemporary China* 24, no. 96 (2015): 961–982.

Zhaohui, Luo. "China's Foreign Aid and International Development Cooperation in a COVID-19 Pandemic World." *China International Studies* 92 (2022): 25.

Zhongming, Zhu, Lu Linong, Yao Xiaona, Zhang Wangqiang, and Liu Wei. "China's Foreign Aid: A Primer for Recipient Countries, Donors, and Aid Providers." 2020. https://www.cgdev.org/publication/chinas-foreign-aid-primer-recipient-countries-donors-and-aid-providers.

Zhou, H. "Zhongguo yuanwai liushinian de huigu yu zhanwang [Look back and look forward: Sixty years of China's foreign aid]." *Foreign Affair Review*, 5 (2010): 3–11.

Zhou, Yanqiu Rachel. "Vaccine Nationalism: Contested Relationships Between COVID-19 and Globalization." *Globalizations* 19, no. 3 (2022): 450–465.

Zhuoran, Du, and Zhao Jing. "China Becomes the First Country in Asia to Have Two UN-Standard Rescue Teams." October 24, 2019. https://news.cgtn.com/news/2019-10-24/China-becomes-the-first-in-Asia-to-have-two-UN-standard-rescue-teams--L2XZ7bfPS8/index.html.

Ziegler, Charles E. "Conceptualizing Sovereignty in Russian Foreign Policy: Realist and Constructivist Perspectives," *International Politics* 49 (2012): 400–417.

Zimmermann, Felix, and Kimberly Smith. "More Actors, More Money, More Ideas for International Development Cooperation." *Journal of International Development* 23, no. 5 (2011): 722–738.

Index

www.ingramcontent.com/pod-product-compliance
Lightning Source LLC
Chambersburg PA
CBHW050429280326
41932CB00013BA/2040